SERIAL KILLERS

The Growing Menace

JOEL NORRIS

ARROW BOOKS

Arrow Books Limited
20 Vauxhall Bridge Road, London SW1V 2SA

An imprint of the Random Century Group

London Melbourne Sydney Auckland
Johannesburg and agencies throughout
the world

First published in Great Britain by Arrow 1990

3 5 7 9 10 8 6 4 2

© 1988 by Joel Norris and William J. Birnes

The right of Joel Norris to be identified as the author
of this work has been asserted by him in accordance
with the Copyright, Designs and Patents Act, 1988

This book is sold subject to the condition that it shall
not, by way of trade or otherwise, be lent, resold, hired
out, or otherwise circulated without the publisher's
prior consent in any form of binding or cover other
than that in which it is published and without a similar
condition including this condition being imposed on
the subsequent purchaser

Typeset by Deltatype Limited, Ellesmere Port
Printed and bound in Great Britain by
Cox & Wyman Ltd, Reading

ISBN 0 09 971750 6

OXFORDSHIRE
COUNTY
LIBRARIES

For all of the victims and my steadfast supporters:
Joel Jones, Margurite McKinney, Judy Lawrence Mahoney,
and David Maurer.

Contents

Preface by Philip S. Hicks, M.D.   9
Acknowledgments   13
Introduction   15

The Nature of a Serial Killer

1 The Serial Killer in Our Midst   25
2 The Phases of Serial Murder   42
3 The Disease of Serial Murder   59
4 Serial Killers Today   72
5 The Anatomy of a Serial Murder Case:
   The Murder, the Victims, and the Community   88
6 The Police and the Serial Killer   109

**The Personal Statements of Five Serial Killers:
Stories of their lives and crimes in their own words**

7 Henry Lee Lucas   152
8 Carlton Gary   176
9 Bobby Joe Long   186

10 Leonard Lake   203
11 Charles Manson and Serial Killers in Groups   214

The Unifying Patterns of a Serial Killer

12 The New Criminologists   233
13 Inside the Brain of a Serial Killer   264
14 The Serial Killer Profile   284
15 Conclusion   325

Preface

You are about to read a book which takes you into the bizarre and distorted mind of the serial killer. A relative rarity, the serial killer occupies the darkest side of human nature, fusing the most regressive regions of sexual and aggressive conflicts into his criminal behavior. This is the ultimate perversion, and, as such, stimulates our most intense interest and horror. Joel Norris captures, in this fascinating portrayal, the essence of the serial killer and those factors which have created him.

This is an important book. America is in the midst of an increasing crescendo of violence, affecting every element of our society. With few exceptions, we have responded to this with traditional American solutions: outcries for 'law and order,' stiffer sentences for offenders, and escalating demands for capital punishment. Our jails and prisons are literally bursting with inmates, in spite of frantic building programs. We have abandoned any ideas of rehabilitation. Our prisons are little more than warehouses, providing only token educational and vocational programs. Recidivism rates are high and showing no tendency to fall. The costs of building and maintaining our penal institutions is approaching the level where the taxpaying public will be forced to find other, more innovative solutions for the problem of criminal justice. Our 'out of sight, out of mind' approach is simply becoming too expensive.

As Dr. Norris so eloquently describes in this book, criminal behavior is no simple matter. It is an exceedingly complex 'common final pathway' for disorders of the biological, psychological, and social aspects of human existence. I am in complete agreement with Dr. Norris when he defines serial killers as a public health problem. Unlike many other public health problems, however, we have not put resources into research into the causes of criminality and its prevention. Unfortunately, the field of criminology has little prestige within the scientific community. There appears to be apprehension on the part of many professionals who might otherwise consider working with criminals. Some express a fear of being victimized themselves, while others, perhaps less forthrightly, attribute the fear to their spouses. Statistics, however, consistently indicate that the risk of assault upon staff is far greater in mental hospitals than it is in prisons. Psychiatrists, like myself, who have chosen to work in penal institutions, find them full of the most fascinating examples of psychopathology. We see our inmate patients as the products of complex, yet understandable, interactions between nature and nurture. The majority are personality disordered individuals, true developmental disorders, with features which are traceable to inherited and environmental influences. Some are even amenable to psychotherapy. Most have some association between their offense and alcohol or drug use, while some have demonstrable brain damage. Of the latter group, a very high percentage have never been diagnosed, in spite of medical screening before their trials or during incarceration. Of these, a significant number have neurological impairments which are clearly related to their criminal offenses. It has been my experience that organic brain pathology is vastly underdiagnosed in the prison population and plays a much larger role in criminal behavior than we have previously thought. It is gratifying to note Dr. Norris' awareness and sensitivity to this generally neglected area.

Reading *Serial Killers* has been, for me, a true 'busman's holiday.' The author has, in his literary research, discovered those elements in the serial killer which constitute his tragic uniqueness and has shared with us these important insights. If these insights were to stimulate a greater awareness in the public of the need for research into the causes and treatment of criminal behavior, his work would, indeed, be historic as well as informative, stimulating, and entertaining.

–Philip S. Hicks, M.D.
Chief Psychiatrist
California State Prison
San Quentin, California

Acknowledgments

Many people are to be thanked for assisting in this effort. First and foremost are the three victims' families, who readily shared with me their grief and outrage. Rather than becoming vengeful people who only sought the executions of the murderers, these families were eager to understand the factors that motivated the killers. And today they are actively supportive in seeking ways to prevent future serial murderers from preying upon defenseless victims. I would also like to thank the families of the killers, as well as the killers themselves, who have shared their particular kind of pain.

Recognition and appreciation must extend to the medical and scientific experts who read the first drafts of this manuscript, and contributed their efforts to making sure that all the information was accurate and up-to-date. I also thank scientists such as Vernon Mark, Paul New, Jan Brunner, Sarnoff Mednick, Jonathan Indik, Robert Thatcher, and William Walsh, who have contributed to the medical and scientific opinions of the serial killers that we studied in the course of this book.

Thanks also go to the following friends and assistants, who, in the process, have learned more about serial murderers than they ever wanted to know: Connie and Jeff Ichihashi, Michael Eisenbach, Peter Corsi, Jeffery Robbins, Tom Pacheco, Judy Hanson, Susan and Roland Moussa, Linda Monez, and Gerry Vics.

I acknowledge also the help of other writers and editors along the road to completing this book. I was fortunate to first share this task with Brad Darrach, and Richard Burgheim of *Life* magazine. Special gratitude goes to Texas journalist Nan Cuba, Sheriff Jim Boutwell, Captain Bob Prince of the Texas Rangers, Clementine Schroeder, and the doctors and the hospitals in Dallas who performed the neurological testing on Henry Lucas.

Also to be thanked are my New York literary agent Carol Mann and her assistant Nancy Hogan and Jim Fitzgerald and Laura Nixon of Doubleday.

Finally, I would like to thank Bill Birnes, the coauthor of *Serial Killers: The Growing Menace*. Besides being an expert with words, Bill was chosen as coauthor because of his many years of experience working with the National Endowment for the Humanities in Washington, D.C., first as a Fellow, and then as a Judge. The NEH, by promoting the development of new pedagogies and funding the testing of new ideas outside the bell jar of the undergraduate classroom, has become known as a bipartisan model of social change that encourages inter-disciplinarian approaches to traditional problems. I knew that Bill Birnes would appreciate the growth, and the subtle roadblocks that prevent government, mental health, and criminal justice professionals from under-standing the nature of the problem that is confronting all of us.

It is my hope that the efforts of all my colleagues, during this task, will stimulate new research into the study of prevention of extraordinary violence and serial murder.

–J.N.

Introduction

I am a trained counseling psychologist. I have worked as an educator to the defense and appeals teams of several convicted killers in Georgia, some of whom were multiple killers. I taught supportive counseling techniques to inmates and prison guards at the Atlanta Federal Penitentiary, was a consultant to the University of Georgia on prevention of violence, and addressed the members of the Georgia State legislature on juvenile justice reform. And after years of working within the criminal justice and corrections systems and within the professional milieu of mental health and academia I have been witness to a vast chasm of misunderstanding between the most violent people in our country and those mandated by their chosen professions to understand and control them. I was fascinated by this fact. How could people who were responsible for dealing with the most violent elements of our population so completely misunderstand the people they were trying to control? There were no easy answers. Finally, after several years of intense community work, I took a sabbatical leave to reorganize my thoughts, regroup my energies, and undertake further research into the issues. This book is the result of that research.

The misunderstanding between those who commit violent acts and those who are supposed to apprehend, try, and institutionalize them manifests itself in a variety of ways. First, the justice system does not concern itself with the underlying motivations of the killers. Prevention of crime is not the issue here; punishment is. The trials of the multiple killers on whose cases I worked had more to do with calming the public's appropriate, but misplaced, rage; with the style, personality, charisma, drive, motivation, and financial and political strength of the attorneys involved; with the agenda of the court; and with the pervasive influence of the media. Chance and the legal technicalities of state statutes and judicial precedent were more beneficial to the attorneys on both sides than were any of the psychiatric explanations of the defendants' motivations. And the juries in these cases were simply ill equipped to understand the complex issues that formed the underlying structure of the killers' aberrant psyches. Simply stated, all the evidence wasn't in the courtroom when the cases were presented to the juries, only the evidence that floated on the surface of the arguments.

At the University of Georgia, while helping to devise a core curriculum for the development of creative therapy programs to study the prevention of violence and some forms of mental illness, I had the opportunity to discuss my observations with faculty members in a variety of academic fields. These professors were in a critical position to formulate policy for research, demonstration, and training projects both at universities and at state facilities. They were also able to select target populations for research and could influence the way violence would be studied for generations to come. Yet almost none of them had ever been inside a prison or interviewed a killer face to face. They were fascinated by my death row stories and would talk for hours about the subject of multiple and violent homicide, theorizing and speculating about motives and causality. But unfortunately their natural curiosity and their almost intuitive understanding of this unique prison population did not translate into the public and competitive arena of academia. To voice an intuitive theory about convicted killers or to present a member of this deviant group to an elitist board of regents or other academic policymaking groups, or even to suggest that convicted killers be used as target subjects for research, demonstration, or training projects, was risky to the professional future of the individual expert as well as to the program he or she wanted to develop. Consequently those who were in the best position to inform professional opinion about the true causes of multiple killings and other episodically violent offenses were too afraid for their reputations to get involved with the real issues of the problem.

At the same time the general public was enraged by society's growing vulnerability to violence. They wanted protection from criminals, and they wanted to see justice done in the courtroom. However, in the glare of media publicity that made multiple killers larger-than-life characters, the issues of prevention and motivation got lost and were replaced by demands for vengeance and retribution. It was easy to see why no academic or political figure would stake his professional livelihood on a program that might be perceived as 'coddling killers.'

Yet with each killer I met I saw a growing number of ill individuals, albeit people with no obvious disease. As a group, they all looked spent, drained but calm, as if they had recently experienced an internal storm. In the cages of the institutions where they were housed the inmates looked at peace, even though they were on trial for their lives, were serving life sentences, or were waiting on death row for their appointment with the executioner. Obviously they were physically and psychologically damaged people, some more than others. Almost all of them had scars on their bodies, missing fingers, evidence of previous contusions and multiple abrasions on and around the head and neck area. And they had permanent scars from accidents, fights, knifings, bullet and shotgun wounds, and burns; many of which had been inflicted by the killers' own family members while the killers were still at a young age. All of the killers talked about the desire for freedom even while they seemed to be 'at home' in their prison environments. More than once, after a particularly grueling interview with a killer, the attending guard would put his arm around the inmate in a knowing and fatherly way and say, as he was taking the killer back to his cell, 'Come on, son, let's go home.'

Almost all the killers I met were repeat offenders, and some were serial killers. They all spoke about how offensive prison life was, but through their behavior they had yielded to and embraced a particular lifestyle that ensured that an institution would become their permanent environment. It intrigued me that intelligent individuals would repeatedly make choices in their lives that would lead them to such an environment. Had they lost their free will in making such a choice? One such killer said to me: 'As soon as I leave the prison and breathe the air of freedom, I am like a parakeet out of its cage – out of control – and will do anything to get back in the cage.'

Some of the killers had been psychotic, but few had been judged legally insane because they had passed the litmus test, known as the McNaghten rules, which are used to determine whether one was capable of differentiating between right and wrong. The McNaghten rules came to American jurisprudence from England in the 1800s. Basically they state that if a person can intellectually understand the difference between right and wrong and the consequences of his behavior, then the person is not insane. This definition is the cornerstone of the concept of legal insanity and therefore informs all perspectives and theories about violence in our country. It causes me great concern that the most progressive society ever known to humankind, with all of the medical and scientific advances it has made since the turn of the century, continues to rely on such an antiquated and completely inaccurate definition of human behavior. To premise a legal definition of insanity on the McNaghten rules is just like applying nineteenth-century medicine to treating cancer or AIDS.

I also found that the media were interested not in the generally violent person but in the 'superstar killers' such as Jean Harris, Charles Manson, and Ted Bundy or in murder stories with a hero who had escaped or a detective or a parental victim who had saved the day. Because I was from Georgia and the Atlanta Child Murders case was still on everyone's mind, I proceeded with preliminary research into that case and the evidence against convicted murderer Wayne Williams. To my surprise, I discovered six additional serial murder cases in Georgia that took place in the same four-year span as the Atlanta tragedy. Upon further investigation, I discovered that the syndrome was not only indigenous to Georgia but was nationwide. It was at that point that I decided to focus my research on the most ultimately malevolent group of people on the spectrum of violence in American society: the serial murderers. In January 1984 the FBI announced that there was an epidemic of serial murder in America. And this coincided with my observations that serial murder and other severe forms of episodic aggression was a form of disease that had to be identified and diagnosed before it engulfed all of our social institutions. Accordingly, in August 1984, I published my first article on the subject in *Life* magazine.

During the next couple of years I had the opportunity to interview several accused and convicted serial killers face to face and to learn their own personal stories of violence and pain. I began my odyssey in my own hometown and eventually became a consultant to the defense team of Carlton Gary, the 'Stocking Strangler' of Columbus, Georgia, and the convicted killer of elderly women in my own childhood neighbourhood. I saw Ted Bundy and interviewed Bobby Joe Long on Florida's death row and Henry Lee Lucas in Georgetown, Texas. Kneeling in Lucas' jail cell and participating in prayer sessions with Henry and his confidante, Sister Clemmie, became as routine as hearing the killer's grandiose confessions and his recantations of those confessions just one year later. We learned to expect the unexpected.

I interviewed Joseph Kallinger at Farview Prison in eastern Pennsylvania and worked with his biographer Flora Schreiber, the author of *Sybil* and *The Shoemaker*. I witnessed the unique bond that had formed between Schreiber and Kallinger even though they came from different backgrounds and had led vastly different lives. I spoke to the relatives of victims of serial murderers as well, including Doris Tate, mother of Sharon Tate, and RoseAlyce and Charles Thayer, and the Fentons whose daughter was raped and murdered by Gary Schaefer in Springfield, Vermont. Experiencing their pain and understanding the ramifications of their irreversible trauma was an important step in evaluating the effects that serial murders have on their communities. Then in Quantico, Virginia, I met the 'supersleuth' agents of the Behavioral Science Unit of the FBI and was impressed by their fierce dedication to their task and fascinated by their skill in identifying the emerging patterns of commonality from murder case to murder case which allowed them to develop skillful techniques of apprehension. Yet I was also concerned because they did not understand how the patterns they had developed could be used by other professionals for the purposes of preventing serial murder.

Although the stories of the individual killers were

different, the patterns of parental abuse, violence, neglect, childhood cognitive disabilities, and alcohol and drug abuse were virtually identical. Now, four years later, after more than five hundred interviews, many hours spent in libraries and on the telephone collecting anecdotes and symptoms from the histories of serial killers, I am releasing my initial findings with *Serial Killers*. The highlight of the research that I hope will encourage others to examine new evidence in this field has been the overwhelming interest of the individuals I have met along the way. Other writers, experts from a wide range of related medical and psychiatric disciplines, serial killers themselves, families of victims, and both prosecution and defense attorneys have contributed more information and recommendations than a single book can contain.

What you are about to read will shock, terrify, sadden, and sometimes repel and enrage you. This is not the story of one serial killer, nor is it only the documentation of the disease of the serial killer. It is an investigation of a disease that is running rampant in society and threatens to overwhelm our juvenile justice, criminal justice, and correctional institutions. As you will find, this book acts as a mirror of the fine line that separates each one of us from yielding to the primal, instinctual, animal behavior that lurks beneath the veneer of psychological self-control and social convention. But as the conditions of society become more stressful, those social conventions will break down even further and the controls will give way. This is why the Surgeon General of the United States has called domestic and social violence one of the newest public health risks to the future of society. And as long as we treat violence – and especially serial murder – with an eye-for-an-eye attitude of personal vengeance, our body counts of victims of serial killers will expand exponentially with every passing decade.

The Nature of a
Serial Killer

1

The Serial Killer in Our Midst

At first it was concern that rippled through the Wynnton section of Columbus, Georgia, in the unseasonably warm autumn of 1977. Ferne Jackson, a sixty-year-old white widow, popular and from a socially important family, a public health teacher in the Columbus schools who had lived alone for years in this most exclusive neighborhood of Columbus, had been found dead in the bedroom of her house. She had been beaten violently about the face and head, sexually assaulted, and finally strangled to death with her own nylon stocking, which the police found still wound tightly around her neck. Finally, her attacker had pulled the covers up over her bleeding and half-naked body. The detectives from forensics at the crime scene noted that the killer entered the house through the rear sliding glass doors, surprised Mrs. Jackson in her bedroom, struck her until she could offer no resistance, twisted the stocking around her neck, raped her, and then strangled her. The killer then took her keys, stole her car, and left it abandoned in the Carver Heights section of the city, a black neighborhood in the flat lowland that separates Wynnton from downtown and the Chattahoochee River. It was a violent and ugly crime, and it broke on the evening news like a summer thunderstorm. That was on September 16.

On Saturday, the twenty-fourth, Jean Dimenstein, a seventy-one-year-old white spinster, was found beaten, sexually assaulted, and strangled with a stocking in her bedroom just four blocks away from where Ferne Jackson lived. Her car had been stolen and driven to Carver Heights, and it was parked just a hundred yards away from where the police had found Ferne Jackson's car four days earlier. One killing in the white-brick, well-manicured suburb of Wynnton was tragic enough, but two killings within days of one another, both stranglings of older women who lived alone, were enough to echo a pattern to the people of Columbus. They had seen this type of killing pattern on the evening news: body counts after the Richard Speck killings of student nurses, the continuing news of the violent deaths of young girls in the Seattle area, and the persistence of murders and rapes that were the hallmark of cities like Atlanta, Los Angeles, and New York. But now it was happening in the quiet city of Columbus.

Under pressure to find the murderer quickly, the police first arrested Jerome 'Duck' Livas, a mentally deficient who was a convenient suspect in another murder, and quickly announced that he was confessing to the murders of the Wynnton victims. But just as Wynnton had begun to relax from the tension, eighty-nine-year-old Florence Scheible, legally blind and confined to a walker, was also found strangled to death in her bedroom. Like the other victims, she was a white woman who lived alone and, like the others, she had been attacked by an intruder who broke in, bludgeoned her with his fists, raped her, and then strangled her to death with one of her own stockings and, prior to leaving, covered up her body.

Four days later sixty-nine-year-old Martha Thurmond was found dead in her home, strangled as well. Ironically, the throwbolt locks she had installed to protect her after the Scheible murder were put in backward, and the murderer had picked them with ease. This time, however, the killer didn't even touch her car. The police and Columbus residents then realized that robbery had clearly not been the motive for the crime.

The continuing pattern of identical murders that persisted even after the arrest of the police's only suspect weakened the case against Livas. The district attorney, however, refused to release him until two weeks later when, in an exclusive interview with Carl Cannon, a reporter from the Columbus *Ledger*, Livas confessed to the murders of both Presidents John F. Kennedy and William McKinley. The story broke in the paper the next day, and a red-faced Ronnie Jones, the director of the robbery and homicide division of the Columbus police, who had announced on morning television weeks earlier that the police had caught the suspect, admitted that the hunt for the real killer was still on.

By the end of 1977, after another murder victim — seventy-four-year-old Kathleen Woodruff, widow of George 'Kid' Woodruff, a member of the Woodruff Coca-Cola family — had been found raped and strangled with her scarf in the parlor of her house on exclusive Buena Vista Road, the panic about a killer on the loose began to change the community. There was now the realization that the crimes were not burglaries first and murders second; they were, in fact, violent, sexual attacks with murder as a primary motive. Secondly, after the killer had changed his pattern by not stealing the cars of his victims, it became obvious to the entire city that he was monitoring the news reports of his crimes and had altered his course of actions only to confuse the police.

In a once aristocratic neighborhood the stately white-columned mansions, built by Wynnton's founders before the Civil War, now became fortresses protected by deadbolts and elaborate burglar alarms. In the daytime police dogs sniffed for clues among the blossoming azaleas and along the tree-shaded streets while patrol cars became the sentries of the night, their whirling blue lights a blur as they crisscrossed through the dark neighborhood streets. Little old ladies carried revolvers neatly tucked into their purses on their way to church on Sundays, and an entire community had become fearful, suspicious of any new face.

Gradually the local Columbus police, the prosecutor's office, and the newspaper and television reporters who were tracking the case came to realize that the elusive phantom who was seemingly striking down these old women at will was not a traditional murderer as most people have come to understand murderers. Now the local police, the Georgia Bureau of Investigation, and the FBI were beginning to assemble a profile of such killers based on similar evidence patterns in Seattle, where college student Ted Bundy was in the midst of his career as a serial killer of young coeds; in Chicago, where John Gacy, a $200,000-a-year building contractor, had been killing young boys and burying them in his basement for five years; in California, where Ed Kemper had engaged in a killing spree of eight women; or even in the neighboring city of Atlanta where Wayne Williams was serving out his sentence for the kidnapping, sexual abuse, and murder of more than twenty-five young boys, the investigators now were coming to believe that they had a different type of murderer on their hands.

The dead women in Wynnton were part of a larger national pattern – victims of apparently motiveless killers whose methods and activities make them almost un-detectable. Not really a traditional form of murder, as most police and criminologists understand it, this crime is actually a form of disease. Its carriers are serial killers who suffer from a variety of crippling and eventually fatal symptoms, and its immediate victims are the people struck down seemingly at random by the disease carriers.

THE SERIAL KILLER IN OUR MIDST

It is the disease of serial murder that is rapidly becoming an epidemic in American society today and one of the patterns of violence that the office of the U.S. Surgeon General has called one of the top-priority issues of public health.

Wynnton was not accustomed to being a community of victims. The residents here were descendants of the planters and textile mill owners who rebuilt Georgia out of the ruins of the Civil War. The women who had been killed were Southern archetypes, matriarchs, and wealthy and influential standard-bearers of the city of Columbus who for years had funded charities and community service events. More importantly, they had been the domestic employers of the Columbus working-class and black populations. Striking out against the Wynnton matrons was to strike out against a symbol of the old South, the heart and soul of the community itself. As the Columbus residents read of the Atlanta Child Murders taking place just over a hundred miles away, they agonized over the strangling murders of their own mothers and waited for news of the next victim.

The murders continued. A short time after Ruth Schwob had successfully fought off her attacker in the early morning of February 12 and triggered a burglar alarm in her home, only two hundred yards away seventy-eight-year-old Mildred Borom was being beaten, sexually assaulted, and strangled with a window blind cord in her bedroom on Forest Avenue. The murderer, only minutes ahead of the local police who had responded to the burglar alarm, had not only eluded capture but in the midst of his interrupted frenzy had walked just a few doors down the street to attack his next victim. This boldness, the sheer audacity of a killer who could enter, rape, and murder while the police were up the street questioning one of his victims, raised the level of general panic to the point where an exodus of older women from the community had begun.

Three days later Don Kilgore, the county coroner, announced that 'negroid' pubic hairs were found at the scenes of the crimes. With the announcement, an ensuing public debate pitted the coroner and the police department against the local chapter of the NAACP. Racial tensions in the Columbus area began to flare and the Ku Klux Klan announced that it would patrol the streets of Wynnton to protect the women. The racial implications were considered all the more serious because what the police had suggested – a killer who crossed racial lines – conflicted starkly with a profile that the FBI had already begun to create. The coroner's announcement was at variance with Ruth Schwob's tentative identification of her attacker as Lyle Gingel, a young white man, the emotionally disturbed son of a popular radio personality.

At the end of March the police received a letter from a copycat killer threatening revenge on black women if the killer of the white women was not caught. The writer, who called himself the Chairman of the Forces of Evil, implied that he was a white man avenging the deaths of the Wynnton matriarchs. The police feared that he would become a copycat killer who reacted to the news of the serial murderer by committing his own homicides. One day later their fears proved to be valid. The bodies of two black prostitutes, Gail Faison and Irene Thirkild, were found on the grounds of the military reservation adjoining the Army's Fort Benning, and the Columbus chief of police agreed to negotiate the killer's $10,000 ransom demand on the lives of future victims. When the police and the Army's Criminal Investigation Division at Benning arrested Private First Class Henry Hance, a black man who would later be convicted of another murder and implicated in a third, the police knew that the pattern of secondary violence had already begun.

It wasn't until after another murder and after the cost of the investigation had exceeded a million dollars that the murders finally stopped. The Columbus police in desperation had even interrogated Wayne Williams, the suspect in the Atlanta Child Murders, but he had no connections to the crimes. It wasn't until six years later, when Carlton Gary was finally arrested in Albany, Georgia, on robbery charges and fugitive warrants, that the Stocking Strangler was found. After confessing to being present at the murder scenes, Gary was charged with rape, burglary, and murder in three of the Wynnton stranglings, and three years later he was convicted and sentenced to death.

Now, more than ten years after the first murder, Carlton Gary is still in jail, awaiting his appeal and subsequent trials that will cost the state in excess of another two to three million dollars to finance. Bud Siemen, his defense counsel, has told the court that Gary will readily admit to all the charges if he is allowed to plead insanity and remain institutionalized for the rest of his life. However, because of the sensitivity of the community and the nature of the murder victims, Siemen charges, the state will be happy only after Carlton Gary has been executed in the electric chair. The appeals process alone may take another three to five years and cost Georgia an additional million dollars if it has to go to the United States Supreme Court. This, I might add, the case of the Columbus Stocking Strangler, is only one serial killer at work in one community.

Other communities besides Columbus have known the panic that washes over people when a murderer moves into the area and victims first disappear and then are discovered in shallow graves, one after the other. In Texas and the neighboring panhandle states, more than three hundred people died, allegedly at the hands of Henry Lee Lucas. Even though questions still remain about the truth and accuracy of Lucas' early confessions, which he later recanted, some of them are so graphic and lurid that even the police refused to believe them. It was reported by the Texas Rangers and law enforcement officials nationwide that he killed hundreds of men, women, and children whom he did not know except for the few brief hours when he had stalked, tortured, put them to death, mutilated their bodies, dismembered them, and buried their remains. In Atlanta an entire community was frozen with terror as each week more and more bodies of its children were found sexually assaulted and buried in the area around the Chattahoochee River. The police in Seattle were baffled for years while they searched for the killer of a score of young, attractive women who had seemed to offer no resistance to the person who took their lives. It wasn't until Ted Bundy was finally arrested in another community that the Seattle killings stopped. It took another series of murders in Utah and then later in Florida, to which Bundy had escaped, to finally bring him to sentencing. Even after their convictions and sentencing, questions still remain about the full extent of their crimes, and families wonder whether their children who have been missing for years will ever be listed among the killers' victims.

Currently among the group of serial killers who are most prominently in the public eye and under police and FBI investigation are Richard Ramirez, also known as the 'Nightstalker,' a cat burglar by trade who indiscriminately killed anyone who happened to cross his path and discover him while he was in the act of robbing a house; an unknown killer on the loose in southern Los Angeles who has already murdered at least twenty prostitutes and is the object of an intense manhunt by the LAPD, and the 'Green River Killer' in Seattle, who has also murdered more than twenty prostitutes and buried their bodies along the banks of the Green River, which runs just outside of the city limits. When one adds to this list the 'Tylenol Killers' and a multitude of copycat killers who strike whenever a serial killer enters an area, the list grows seemingly without limit.

These killers belong to a newly identified class of criminals called serial murderers, motiveless killers, recreational killers, spree killers, or lust murderers whose numbers are increasing at an alarming rate every year. In 1983 alone, according to the FBI, approximately five thousand Americans of both sexes and all ages – fifteen people a day and fully twenty-five percent of all murder victims – were struck down by murderers who did not know them and killed them for the sheer 'high' of the experience. The FBI calls this class of homicides serial murders and their perpetrators recreational or lust killers. The FBI describes them as the most cunning and sinister of all violent people. Almost impossible to capture, diagnose, or predict using ordinary investigative methods and perversely attracted to the police who are pursuing them, serial murderers dance just beyond their pursuers' reach from state to state, retreating into the background, then springing up again in a different part of the country to begin another series of seemingly motiveless killings.

Addicted to the act of murder as if it were a drug, serial killers compulsively and silently troll for their victims amid shopping malls at twilight, darkened city streets, or country roads in isolated rural communities. They are motivated by a force that even they don't understand. Once they have sighted a potential victim, they begin to stalk with a dogged relentlessness that does not cease until the victim is cornered and the trap is sprung. Like tormented beasts of prey, serial murderers do not commit simple homicides. They often torture their victims, taking delight in the victims' agonies, expressions of terror, cries of despair, and reactions to pain. Then, in a period of marked depression that follows the high of the murder, the killers plead for help from the police or newspapers as did Richard Herrins, a serial killer in Chicago in the early

1960s, who wrote in lipstick on a dressing-room mirror above his victim's head: 'Catch me before I kill again.' Always hidden in plain sight, the killers ask to be caught, promise to turn themselves in so that they can receive therapy, but vanish again only to emerge after the next murder.

What makes a serial killer? What are the roots of this extraordinary violence? Why was a murderer like Ted Bundy so difficult to catch? What enabled Henry Lee Lucas to elude the police for more than ten years as he moved from state to state, leaving in his wake scores of his victims buried in mass unmarked graves. Why does Carlton Gary, the Columbus Stocking Strangler, even today admit to being present at every Wynnton murder but cling to the story that it was someone else – one of his known aliases – in the house with him every time who actually committed the crime? Are these individuals supercriminals who are able to outsmart the police at every turn or is the nature of their crime fundamentally so different from other types of crimes that local police forces are unable to control it?

Unfortunately for all of us, serial murder is different in kind from any other type of crime. Only recently have the police, the FBI, the courts, the medical profession, or any agency of government fundamentally accepted this fact. Most murders are committed for specific, identifiable motives. A fight between two people suddenly turns into a homicide when one of them draws a lethal weapon; lovers in the midst of a violent confrontation strike out at one another until one of them lies dead; a burglar suddenly freezes as the lights in an apartment or store are turned on and fires his weapon at the first person he sees; or the passions in a family confrontation suddenly explode into violence. Police can solve any one of these homicides within days or even hours. The motives are straight-forward. The victims have a clearly traceable relationship with the murderer, and the murderer himself is so filled with remorse and guilt that he makes it easy for the police to find him. Moreover, the overwhelming majority of murders are committed by individuals who are 'novice' killers. They have little or no evasive skills, and their only reaction is to run away in panic after leaving a crime scene littered with clues and witnesses. If they run fast enough and long enough, they believe, they will eventually be safe. It is only the weight of the crime itself that undoes them in the end. Were they the least bit practiced in the crime of murder or had they planned their escape route in advance and prepared a safe hiding place, they might elude capture just long enough for the trail to turn cold and for other murder cases to occupy the attention of the overworked homicide squad. Armed robbers who commit murder are also relatively easy to track down. Those who flee from state to state still leave clues that make their capture a certainty once the FBI joins the chase. And in cases of contract murder – gangland slayings and political assassinations – the motives are clear and the police need only find the killer to close the books.

Even mass murderers differ fundamentally from serial killers. First, mass murderers are almost always caught by the police. Some examples are: James Huberty, who killed more than twenty-five people at a Los Angeles McDonald's; Richard Speck, who killed seven nurses in Chicago; Charles Whitman, who killed more than ten people from the University of Texas tower almost twenty years ago; and most recently Juan Gonzales, the Staten Island ferry slasher who hacked his way through a crowd of Fourth of July celebrants. They differ from the serial killer in that they have a more tenuous camouflage of normalcy. Some experts say these mass murderers are more apt to have obvious psychotic neurological symptoms that are very easy to diagnose than the serial murderers. In fact several lawsuits are currently pending in cities around the country by victims who claim that the hospitals who released these individuals before their final acts of violence are liable for the damage the killers inflicted.

The serial murderer is an entirely different criminal. First, the serial killer is practiced and accomplished at what he does and can cloak himself with a mantle of normal, acceptable behavior. After all, most fully emerged serial murderers have been engaged in the crime for years. Even newly emerged serial murderers have been fantasizing for lifetimes about committing their crimes. The actual event itself has been rehearsed over and over again, just like an escalating masturbatory fantasy. Literally hundreds of potential victims have crossed the killer's path and have been the unwary actors in an internal psychological drama.

Second, the victim may be missing for months or even years before being discovered. It is only after the victim's discovery that the police begin the homicide investigation. The sheer volume of missing persons in a given jurisdiction might be so great that the police spend more time defending the community against a siege than tracking whatever clues might still linger in the area. Then it is only by chance, a random encounter between a police officer on patrol and a killer caught at the scene of the crime, that a suspect is apprehended. The relationship between the victim and the murderer, when the victim finally turns up, might be so fragile that the police are unable to comprehend it. Carlton Gary was convicted for killing only those white elderly women who reminded him of the type of person his mother had to work for when he was growing up, and Ted Bundy bludgeoned only those attractive and confident young women who reminded him of the fiancée who had rebuffed him. Not even the most farsighted of police investigators can put together these types of clues until after the killer has been caught and profiled.

36

THE SERIAL KILLER IN OUR MIDST

Most traditional killers flee to avoid capture. Professional and contract killers know how to fade into the background quickly and have planned their escape routes beforehand. Those killers who strike down a family member, a child or a spouse, out of uncontrollable violence are more afraid of what they've done than of the police and quickly turn themselves in. Serial killers, however, are like wild animals. They are fascinated with the remains of their crime. They visit the graves of their victims and attend their funerals. They lurk in the shadows, camouflage themselves with all of the trappings of normalcy, and dog the heels of the police as they relive the crime through the efforts of the investigators. The Green River Killer in Seattle telephoned a homicide detective's wife and taunted her about her husband's ineffectiveness, and Ted Bundy often confronted the police officers who followed him and asked them about the progress of their investigation. More often than not the killer has been in the custody of the police or a mental health professional prior to the discovery of his crimes. The enormity of his confession in those earlier situations, however, is usually so unbelievable that the authorities simply let him go, preferring to investigate a more traditional type of criminal.

After running out of vulnerable or archetypal prospects in a given area – young children, elderly people living alone, young women without escorts, prostitutes of both sexes, derelicts, gays – the killer moves away, trolling for victims in another city or state where fear has not yet gripped the populace. Often, in this new area, reports of missing persons or identifiable traits of the murder victims are not relevant to the police who suddenly find themselves confronted with a series of disappearances or bodies turning up in unmarked graves. Few homicide investigators will check the unsolved murder reports from localities two or three states away, and only recently has there been a national network of unsolved homicides. Even the FBI, unless specifically authorized to investigate, will respect the territoriality of the local police department. Thus a killer like Henry Lee Lucas who does not have the kind of public involvement with his victim that can be tracked by the authorities can strike in Texas, Oklahoma, New Mexico, and Arkansas without fear of being trapped by converging police departments. By the time the pattern of his crimes has become clear, he usually has long since left the area or is in custody on another charge.

Killing his victims at the rate of two or more a month, year after year and often for decades, the serial murderer commits his crimes in numbers vastly disproportionate to those of the traditional murderer. Since 1960 not only have the number of individual serial killers increased but so have the number of victims per killer and the level of savagery of the individual crimes themselves. The FBI has estimated that there are at least five hundred serial killers currently at large and unidentified in this country. Their toll on the rest of society is enormous.

However, as if this statistic were not bad enough, consider the fact that the epidemic of serial murderers is spreading. Passed on from generation to generation in the form of child abuse, patterns of chronic childhood malnutrition, drug abuse, and alcoholism, serial murder is actually a disease that is thriving in American society. In the last twenty years the United States, with only five percent of the world's population, has produced seventy-five percent of the world's serial murderers. Of the 160 serial killers who have been captured or singled out by law enforcement authorities over this period, at least 120 were found in the United States. As the influence of American culture spreads to less developed countries, the fear is that, unless checked somehow, the disease of serial murder will spread as well.

THE SERIAL KILLER IN OUR MIDST

The serial murderer in an episodic frenzy can strike without warning. He often preys on the most vulnerable victims in his area and then moves on, leaving the police to find the missing persons and search for traces of the scant clues he has left behind. Because his killing is not a passion of the moment but a compelling urge that has been growing within him sometimes for years, he has completely amalgamated this practice into his lifestyle. It is as though he lives to kill, surviving from one murder to the next, stringing out his existence by connecting the deaths to his victims. Without this string of murders, he feels he will fall apart, that he will disintegrate psychologically. The remainder of his life is devoted to maintaining the mask of normalcy and sanity.

Between crimes, he quietly slips back into the fabric of society. He lives and exists in plain sight from day to day, but on the sly he is observing the police who are busily trying to assemble clues but never seeing the larger picture. The serial killer meantime is waiting until the next convenient stranger crosses his path. The new victim may have a particular way of smiling, a certain style of hair, a familiar perfume or cologne, an air of confidence, or even the style of their house may trigger the murderer and move him quickly into his stalking phase. Whatever it may be, it only takes an instant for the killer to size up his prey and begin stalking. He may follow his unwary victim for days in an internal, one-sided foreplay to murder, memorizing their licence plate, waiting for them to cross an intersection where he is waiting for them, watching them in the rear-view mirror of his car as they leave from work every evening. He waits until they are alone or until he can introduce himself, lure them into his confidence, and spring the trap.

The serial murderer, unlike the traditional criminal, is addicted to his passion. He is suffering from a disease that is terminal, not only for his numerous victims but also for himself. He is his ultimate victim. On his own initiative, the serial killer can no more stop his killing than a heroin addict can kick his habit. Suffering from waves of primal pain and fear of the deepest nature after his most recent killing, an unusual set of defence mechanisms emerges. He simply forgets his crime as well as the victim. Soon thereafter, the urge to murder comes upon him again. He may loathe what he does and despise his own weakness, but he can do nothing on his own to control it. Perversely, he wishes for death, and the threat of the gas chamber, the electric chair, or the lethal injection is only an inducement to keep committing murders until he is caught and put to death. This is why, upon apprehension, so many serial killers readily confess to their crimes and beg for punishment. In retrospect, many police investigations reveal that a serial killer had been in custody one or more times, confessed indirectly to the crimes under investigation, and warned their interrogators that they would kill again. They were not believed by the authorities and released. Most serial killers are only partially aware of what they are doing, and because they have reduced their victims to totemic objects their recollections of the actual murders are very sketchy and vague. Most police investigators dismiss the pleas for help and the inexact descriptions of the crimes as the ramblings of attention-seeking cranks who are incapable of committing murders on a mass scale.

Like John Wayne Gacy and Ted Bundy, the overwhelming majority of serial killers seem on the surface to be normal-looking individuals who go to work or school, come home, and blend into their environments. They might even be married and lead routine lives in their communities. But in reality they are walking time bombs ready to ignite at just the right combination of events. For Bobby Joe Long in Florida, it was the sight of a barfly looking to be picked up by one of the men who frequented the singles clubs along the North Tampa 'strip'; for Ed

Kemper, it was the sound of a voice that reminded him of his mother; and for John Gacy it was the threat of any young man who challenged his authority.

An individual who is on the verge of becoming a serial killer may seem like a dormant volcano. No one knows that beneath the usually bland exterior is a psyche in turmoil, reliving the years of physical and emotional abuse heaped upon him by his closest relatives. He may be an epileptic or someone with serious brain damage who has been able to cover up his impairment for most of his life. But at some point all of the elements that combine to form the active serial killer reach a critical mass, and at just the right stimulation – a sight, a sound, or a smell – the individual slides into his trolling phase and the search for a victim begins.

2

The Phases of Serial Murder

A serial killer's addiction to his crime is also an addiction to a specific pattern of violence that becomes the killer's way of life. Each serial murderer has incorporated the act of killing into a ritual of psychological survival in which the particular victims, the preparations for their capture and torture, the moment of death, and the disposition of the remains each have an element of perverted significance to the criminal's behavior. This reliance on ritual is an across-the-board identifier of the serial murderer and sets him apart from his traditional counterparts. The sequence of ritualistic acts is the killer's way of building up to the 'murder high' and the emotional and sexual orgasm, the explosion of power, he experiences at the moment of the murder itself.

Criminologists who have studied serial murderers have broken the ritual into seven key phases:

1. The Aura Phase

This is some form of withdrawal from everyday reality that indicates the beginnings of a behavior change. First, time seems to slow down. Sounds and colors become more vivid. Odors become more intense, and the killer's skin now becomes sensitive to even the slightest pressure.

42

What now replaces the reality of day-to-day existence is a compulsion to find a companion, at first in fantasy, who will act out a role in the killer's primal ritual. The aura phase can last only for a moment or two, or it can last for months. In such a hallucinatory state, the killer is completely cut off from any stimuli until the aura phase has passed and he begins the search for his victim. Serial killers who experience such types of hallucination exist only in a world of their own creation and react to the invisible stimuli that only they individually can experience.

At the very beginning of the aura phase some serial killers can still verbalize their feelings and report that they are losing their grip on reality. At this point they can be treated by a therapist, and the murder cycle can be short-circuited. However, the vast majority of serial killers cannot verbalize this sensation, and once they enter the aura phase they do not reemerge until after the crime has been committed.

The aura phase can also begin as a prolonged fantasy. In this mode, the killer acts out the thrill of the crime in his own mind. He progresses from one step to another step, exciting himself as the vision reaches its climax. In this mode, the fantasy can play itself over and over again in the killer's mind for weeks or even years at a time. Every stranger who crosses his path can become a performer in that fantasy until an emotional trip wire is snapped, the fantasy becomes real, and the trolling begins. If the aura phase begins as a fantasy such as this, the killer is possibly reachable through intervention. He is able to describe what is happening around him, and through expressing his fantasy he can defuse his compulsion.

The aura phase once entered, however, is like a portal between two realities. On the one side is the reality that all of us, even the most neurotic, react to and inhabit all of our lives. This is a world of normalcy, of social convention in which laws are obeyed and rules observed. However, on the other side of the portal is the killer's reality. It is a world of compulsion, a world dominated by the replaying of the fantasy of violence in which there is no social convention or obedience to rules. It is a world in which everyday choices no longer exist because on this side of the portal the killer is simply a biological engine driven by a primal instinct to satisfy a compelling lust. The ritual of killing has become bound up with an automatic survival mechanism, almost as if the murderer had become a single-celled creature reacting to an overpowering chemical stimulus.

Passing through the aura phase, the serial murderer is translated into a different kind of creature. Whatever is human in him recedes for a while, and he enters into a shadowy existence, a death in life in which law and threats of death or punishment, morality, mores, taboos, or the importance of life itself hold no meaning. Although prosecutors, jurors, and society may eventually hold him accountable for whatever he does, he has in fact lost all power of reason, inhibition, and control. He attempts to medicate himself with large quantities of alcohol or drugs, but, like pouring gasoline on a fire, these create an opposite reaction and only feed his lust. He will not reemerge into the world of the living until after the hallucination has broken or the ritual has been acted out.

2. The Trolling Phase

Having entered into a compulsive stage, the killer now actively begins searching for his next victim. His earlier observations, fantasies, and perverted needs direct him to the likeliest spots where the fatal stranger will cross his path. Each serial killer has different favorite spots. He only has to troll like a fisherman spreading his net, plying back and forth across likely areas for abduction: the parking lots of suburban shopping malls; darkened city streets where single people are apt to travel at night; the student centres and coed dormitories of a large university campus; the playgrounds of elementary schools, schools for the deaf or retarded, or the rural roads where he has noticed that young children or coeds sometimes walk home from school.

Trolling does not consist of random or accidental patterns. It is an unconscious compulsion, a deliberate form of cruising for the likeliest prey. Some killers find themselves staking out certain territories where the most vulnerable victims are to be found. John Gacy looked for a certain type of teenage boy in the demimonde of male hustlers. Ted Bundy searched for pretty coeds on the Seattle University campus where he was a law student. Once he had made his escape from Utah to Florida, he quickly sought out new victims on the college campuses in Tallahassee. Carlton Gary preyed upon elderly women. He chose the Wynnton section of Columbus in his fantasy of robbing from the rich and giving to the poor and trolled the streets until he spied the right kind of house where his wealthy potential victim lived. Then he would stake out a house for days before he gained entry.

The trolling phase is a series of compulsive, frenzied, and paranoiac behavior patterns in which the serial killer becomes very alert and focused. Although at this point he is no longer functioning as an individual in the real world, he is nevertheless instinctively reacting to everday stimuli. It is as if, once the serial killer has passed through the aura phase and into the trolling phase, there begins to operate a new level of behavior programming which directs his every move. Ted Bundy, for example, although compelled by a lust to have a momentary intense relationship with his victim before he killed her, was able to appear charming and ingratiating. His arm strapped up in a false sling, he lured his victim into his car by asking for help with books, packages, or even the hull of a sailboat. Those victims who escaped reported that Bundy never seemed to be out of control until he actually struck. Similarly, Henry Lee Lucas often managed to strike up casual conversations with his victims, sizing them up for the kill.

The latter part of the trolling phase involves the identification and stalking of the victim. Once he has identified his intended prey, the killer begins his pattern of stalking from a distance. Carlton Gary kept watch on his victims' houses for weeks, stalking these elderly women as he travelled through their neighborhood delivering drugs and meeting young women for sexual encounters. He memorized his victims' schedules and habits. So when he did finally strike, he was able to move through the area silently, knowing what entrances could be penetrated without much trouble, and knowing how to leave the scene quickly after the victim lay beaten and strangled upon her bed. He knew which women in Wynnton lived alone. He attacked only widows or spinsters, women who reminded him of the mother he never had and the rich white women who employed his aunt and grandmother as domestic servants. At the same time, Gary believed that these lonely old women's absences would not be noticed until they were found in their houses, hours or days after he had left the crime scene.

Henry Lee Lucas trolled together with companion Ottis Toole along the desolate interstates that crisscross Texas. He found his victims in bars, standing by their cars at gas stations or rest areas, and alongside the roads, hitching a ride. Once he caught sight of a woman in a solo circumstance he would follow her until she was isolated. Then he would abduct her at gunpoint and take her to the spot where she would be humiliated, tortured, mutilated, and finally killed. Lucas revealed that he let a lot of potential victims go without harm. However, if a woman challenged him, resisted him, insulted him, or if her looks, voice, or body movements reminded him of his mother in any way, he would feel an involuntary chill and 'she was as good as dead.' Lucas claims that there are still scores of victims he has murdered who have never turned up and never will until he shows the police where the bodies are buried.

Richard Begenwald, another recently convicted serial killer, stalked his victims along the country roads of affluent New Jersey suburbs. Spotting pretty high school cheerleaders as they walked home from school, Begenwald tracked them day after day until he knew which ones would be alone in isolated spots and which ones had to walk the last stretch of road with no companions. It was then that he would strike, freezing his victims at first in the glare of his headlights. Then he lured them into his car with offers of rides. His next step was to spring the trap, overpowering them quickly and violently, finally savoring the moment of death and his moment of triumph. He then would either bury their bodies in a remote section near the murder scene or transport them in his trunk to his mother's house on Staten Island. There they would be buried in her backyard.

Most homicide cops report that it is the killer's stalking phase that most unnerves a police department once a pattern of serial murders has been established in an area. While the killer is stalking victim after victim, the police have to sit back and trace the few if any clues they have. The problem is compounded by the sensational nature of the news of each murder that appears on television every evening. This sometimes inspires the serial killer who is tracking both the police investigation, as Carlton Gary did, and the media reporting, as Ted Bundy did, to change the pattern of his crimes to throw both the police and the media off the trail. In the process the killings just keep on happening, bodies keep on turning up, and the police wind up looking as though they are completely ineffective and their investigations are getting nowhere.

For example, in Atlanta during the child murders investigation, the official criticism of the police department became so intense that a special task force of 'superdetectives' had to be assembled from the nation's largest cities to help. Even then there were jurisdictional fights among the neighboring city, county, and sheriff's departments. There was friction among the local and federal officers on the case, and the hunt for the killer went on for months before an agent from the Georgia Bureau of Investigation on special stakeout detail happened to notice Wayne Williams on the Chattahoochee River bridge.

Bob Keppel, one of the Seattle homicide detectives who investigated the Ted Bundy murders before Bundy relocated to Utah, complained that it was the knowledge that a killer was out there, actively pursuing his next victim, that was the most disturbing thing about the case. The police were always two giant steps behind the killer – first searching for the missing person, then identifying the dismembered and partially decomposed body – always following a trail that had turned cold long before they uncovered it. It was Keppel's experience tracking Bundy that convinced him that the police couldn't be reactive when trying to solve a serial murder case. They have to be preemptive. They have to be able to predict the killer's probable next moves from a behavior profile that they develop. The types of victims he chooses and the condition of the bodies after the murder are two important factors they must evaluate. Once they know what type of victim is most likely to be stalked, they can mass their resources in a specific area. It was Keppel who helped form the Behavioral Science Unit at the FBI. This unit assembles a character profile of a potential serial killer from the gathered information and assists local police forces through their interrogations of likely suspects.

3. *The Wooing Phase*

Most serial killers disarm their suspects by winning their confidence and luring them into a trap. Ruth Schwob, for example, the only victim to have survived the Columbus Stocking Strangler, remembered a feeling of erotic pleasure as Gary raped her and began to strangle her while she was in a twilight state between life and death. John Gacy, the Chicago building contractor who killed scores of young boys and buried them in his basement, accomplished this by promising his victims jobs in his company, cash for sexual favors, and even fatherly warmth and understanding. Once they had agreed to accompany him to his home office or to a job site, Gacy had them in his power. If the boy seemed to be just looking for money to tide him over, Gacy usually gave him money, had sex, and let him go. However, if the boy challenged him or tried to con him, Gacy then overpowered the victim with a blow to the head, bound him, raped and sodomized him, tortured him, and then killed him. Serial killers such as Ottis Toole who prey on young children routinely lure them away from shopping malls, their own backyards, or schoolyards to remote locations. Most young children do not fear strangers who offer them candy or promise to take them to their parents, and they readily follow such a person. Ted Bundy, who was a part-time law student in Seattle, had an ingratiating, boyish manner that charmed his female victims into thinking they were helping a friendly stranger with a broken arm. Bundy was adept at insinuating himself into the confidence of his victims by reversing the typical courtship pattern. It was the victim who was strong, healthy, and almost patronizing toward the good-looking stranger who approached her in the parking lot or on the beach. The murderer was injured, self-effacing, and embarrassed in his request for assistance. In fact one of the most startling aspects of most serial killers is that they are neither repulsive or even merely off-putting. They do not terrorize their victims into submission, they actually seduce them before turning on them.

When homicide detectives finally begin to uncover a pattern of serial murder, one of the first things they notice is that the victims rarely seem to have struggled against their killers. As Seattle's Bob Keppel realized from the few clues he was able to assemble and from the statements of those coeds who escaped from Ted Bundy, the victims willingly placed themselves in Bundy's power without realizing that they were in danger. The serial killer is often very selective about the type of victim he chooses and is able to relate to that person with little difficulty. As a result the victims are either taken in by the killer's charm and manners, or they believe his story, or they don't listen to their own instincts. It is only those who resist from the outset who have any chance of escape.

4. Capture

This event can be as sudden as the locking of a car door, a sudden break-in through a window, or a quick, well-timed blow that renders the victim dazed and helpless at the killer's feet. It can also be as gradual and terrifying as a conversational monologue fraught with innuendos about the violence that is about to happen. The killer waits until he has the victim alone and then he begins his ascent to a psychological high. The trolling and stalking phases served to heighten his expectation of the event itself, and the capture, when the victim has finally been ensnared in the trap, is the penultimate moment. This is the moment he savors because he believes that he has closed off all possibility of the victim's escape and can take all the time he wants to prepare the victim for the ritual that will follow.

The way the capture is effected differs widely from serial killer to serial killer. Carlton Gary struck quickly at his defenseless victims once he had broken into their houses. He threatened them, raped them, and then strangled them with one of their own nylon stockings, the slick cord from a window blind, or a silk scarf, and then covered their exposed bodies. Ted Bundy kept charming his victims, maintaining the veneer of the courtship, until he reached one of his 'safe places,' killing fields where he was completely isolated. Then he bludgeoned his victims to death and bit into their flesh. Henry Lee Lucas talked to his victims once the capture was completed. He went into detail describing what was about to happen and took delight in the terror he was inflicting, even before he began the regimen of physical abuse.

5. The Murder

Until the day she died Ruth Schwob, the only victim to have fought off the Columbus Stocking Strangler, believed that her assailant behind the ski mask was not Carlton Gary but someone else. Even when confronted with the evidence of the killer the police had accused, Ruth Schwob did not identify him but incriminated Lyle Gingel instead. That was how effective Carlton Gary's camouflage was, even during the moments when he should have been the most exposed. Ruth Schwob's description of being surprised in the intimacy of her own bedroom and of the sexual assault by her businesslike attacker is one of the few descriptions police have of what it is like to be the victim of a serial murderer.

To Ruth Schwob, the killer behind the ski mask was invisible, a faceless man who raped and abused his victims as if wreaking a terrible vengeance upon them for sins of omission they had practiced in the course of their daily living. These older women, the matrons of Columbus society, had looked through their black domestic employees as if they were invisible. They omitted them from their catalogue of human beings, and in Carlton

Gary's fantasy he was repaying them for that. Mrs. Schwob described the sexual violence to the police as an almost tantalizing torture that evoked memories of distant pleasures. Yet she knew, as she fought off the man tightening the stocking around her neck and struggled to reach the emergency trip buttons of the burglar alarm, that she was meant to be the next victim of the man the newspapers had called the Columbus Stocking Strangler. Although she did not realize it, Ruth Schwob was playing a role in the killer's private vision of his own hell. She was the matron Gary's family had to serve in order to eat. And now she was the focus of his revenge. Yet she never realized who the man was behind the ski mask.

For Carlton Gary, Ruth Schwob's failure to identify him was just as it should have been. He was meant to be invisible to his victims because it was invisibility itself that was at the core of his pathological addiction to murder. As his lawyers are quick to point out, the violent sexual assaults and strangling murders of the six elderly white women in the oldest and most exclusive neighborhood of Columbus point to a pattern of crime that goes well beyond the typical murder. It is a ritual in which Carlton Gary is reenacting an event over and over again. The murders are secondary in Gary's mind; the event being reenacted is primary. Gary can't even admit remembering the actual killings, insisting instead that he watched while someone else committed the crimes. By bringing the defendant's biopsychosocial case history into court as evidence of his incompetence to stand trial, his defense counsel had hoped to show that in Carlton Gary's consciousness he was never really there. They will argue that, in much the same way that he was never really visible throughout his childhood years when he watched his grandmother and his aunt carry out domestic chores for the very women he killed, he was just as invisible when he broke into their homes and raped them.

THE PHASES OF SERIAL MURDER

To these matrons of Wynnton, as were most blacks in the 1950s, Carlton Gary was invisible. From the narrow windows of his own existence, plagued by physical abuse and rejection by his father, malnutrition, and a destructively negative self-image that was reinforced by everything around him, he watched while most of his female relatives trudged up the long hill from the center of Columbus to Wynnton to work for women he would later kill. Their power in the community was unchallengeable, and in Carlton Gary's view they comprised their own pantheon, making the economic and social decisions that translated the lives of Gary's relatives into hope or hopelessness. But most frustrating of all to an abused but intellectually gifted black child growing up in Columbus was that he was absolutely invisible to the matrons of Wynnton. Not that they weren't kindly, churchgoing, charitable women; they were all that and more. They were the epitome of what a Southern lady should be, but the antithesis of what Carlton Gary's mother actually had been. They simply looked right through Gary and other black males as if they weren't there at all. Thus when, after twenty years, Carlton Gary emerged as a full-blown serial killer, he struck from behind a mask of invisibility, ripping away at the very sex of the women who dominated his childhood but who looked right through him, and strangling them with their own articles of clothing.

Carlton Gary's example illustrates the fundamental similarities that unite all serial killers: the murder phase is a ritual reenactment of the disastrous experiences of the killer's childhood. Only, this time, the killer tries to reverse the roles occupied in his childhood experiences. In this way he can almost magically cancel out his earlier suffering and reestablish his own power and identity. A Carlton Gary can strike while invisible, but this time he is the initiator who wreaks the revenge and rights all perceived wrongs.

53

Similarly, John Wayne Gacy, who was a sickly and effeminate child and who was also abused as a child by his violent, alcoholic, and castrating father, struck at the genitalia of the boys he had trapped in his basement. While strangling them slowly, he recited the Twenty-third Psalm and urged them to be brave in the face of torture and death. It was not the immediate death of the young boys that Gacy sought, it was the prolonging of the process of death. Through this ritual Gacy sought to reassert his own vision of a masculine identity that had been squashed down by his father.

Joseph Kallinger, in an almost identical ritual, had his cokiller son, sixteen-year-old Michael, cut the penises off their two male victims while they were still alive. Joseph's later confessions revealed that his mother had ordered him to hold his open palm over a flame until the skin began to smolder. If the young Kallinger cried, he was savagely beaten. This, his mother told him, would make him strong. Men shouldn't cry; they should be able to bear extremes of pain, and in bearing their sufferings silently they will become strong. This perversion of the ideal of the laconic male hero motivated Kallinger throughout his career as a serial murderer. The more his victims, one of whom was his son, screamed in terror and pleaded for their lives, the more delight Kallinger took. The death of the victim was almost anticlimactic to the process of torture and slow death. The moment one of his last victims, Kallinger's own thirteen-year-old son Joey, took his last breath and said, 'Daddy, please help me,' Kallinger had an orgasm and the hallucination broke.

Other stories of serial murders exceed even the wildest violence of the drive-in movie bloodbath. Henry Lee Lucas and Ottis Toole burned their struggling victims with cigarettes and white-hot metal. Lucas confessed that he burned and cut into the most private parts of his female victims and forced them to watch as he sawed off their fingers and toes. The act of mutilation was the high point of the ritual for Lucas, who himself had been burned and scarred by his mother when he was a child. He had been forced to watch his mother have sex with multitudes of strange men who had turned upon him with violence after abusing his mother. Thus Lucas, when he emerged, turned that same violence on women who reminded him of his mother. Ottis Toole, the homosexual who had been abused by his father and raised as 'the Devil's child' by his Satanist grandmother, turned that abuse on children and homosexual men. The confessed murderer of Adam Walsh, whose story has been documented on national television, Toole assaulted his helpless victims sexually, killed them, dismembered them, and ate parts of their bodies.

The moment of murder itself is the emotional high for most confessed serial killers. At this instant, when the victims were dying at their hands, many serial killers report an insight so intense that it is like an emotional quasar, blinding in its revelation of truth. In those seconds of acting out the absolute pinnacle of their own anguish, some report spontaneous orgasms, a sexual release so complete that it is clearly their moment of triumph, a powerful statement of their own existence when they can face the collective demons of their past without the least trace of fear.

6. *The Totem Phase*

As do most moments of intense insight, the serial killer's triumphant vision of truth fades rapidly after the victim is finally dead. The murderer's fantasy has been so all-consuming that he is drained after the crime and begins to slide quickly into depression. Some serial killers try to preserve the intensity of the murder, to prolong the feeling of power and triumph over their pasts, by attempting to preserve the body through a ritualistic dismemberment of the dead victim. Either the victim's genitals are cut off and carried away, or the limbs are severed, or the head is removed. Serial killers have eaten parts of the victims' remains, carried off parts of the body with them for later preservation in jars or scrapbooks, buried parts of their victims' bodies in isolated 'sacred' spots, or shown them to their subsequent victims. This is the totemic phase in which the dead victim has become a symbol of what the murderer had hoped would have been an emotional triumph. The victim has been transformed from symbolic creature to symbolic trophy, an object which, the murderer hopes, can transmit to him the fleeting feelings of power and glory at the moment when his private ritual reached its climax.

Many of the killers hold onto the moment of vision by taking Polaroid snapshots of the murder. Leonard Lake shot a series of video tapes of the moments leading to his victims' deaths. In California serial killer Edmund Kemper killed his mother, the woman whose voice had dominated his every thought throughout his life, as his final act of murder; to symbolize his victory, he cut out her vocal cords, burned them, and threw the remains in the garbage disposal, and brought her head back to his apartment where he used it as a dart board for several days. However, these parts of victims' bodies or photographs of the murder have no magical qualities that can be transferred, and the emotional high of the murder quickly fades.

7. The Depression Phase

Ted Bundy confessed that he never really had got what he had hoped for out of the murders. In fact, he reported, they had actually left him with a feeling of emptiness and hopelessness, as if he could never ultimately achieve the emotional release he was trying to reach. Kallinger reported the same type of depression, as did Henry Lee

Lucas and others. The reasons for this lie in the emotional premises of the murder itself: the killer is simply acting out a ritualistic fantasy. There is no more healing salve of reality in the ritual than there is in the false identity of the victim in the killer's mind. The tragedy is that a helpless individual had to be slaughtered as a form of sacrifice to the killer's own past. But, once sacrificed, the victim's identity within the murderer's fantasy is lost. The victim no longer represents what the killer thought he or she represented. The image of a fiancée who had rejected the killer, the echo of the voice of the hated mother, or the taunting of the distant father: all remain vividly in the killer's mind after the crime. Murder has not erased or changed the past because the killer hates himself as much as he did before the climax of emotion. And even during the course of the murder the killer finds out that it is only his own past that is acted out. He has failed again. No real power is ever achieved, and the killer is left feeling as empty, forlorn, and damned as he had throughout the entirety of his life. Instead of reversing the roles of his childhood, the killer has just reinforced them, and by torturing and killing a defenseless victim, the killer has restated his most intimate tragedies. He becomes the victim and remains unfulfilled and unsatisfied. And in this depression phase not even the newspaper headlines announcing the discovery of another one of his victims is enough to help him recapture the power he had experienced.

For days or weeks after the most recent murder the killer will inhabit a shadowy world of gloom in which he feeds on his own sorrow. All the while he is going about the business of life as if he were normal. Then, sick of the crimes he has committed, he may send a confessional note to the police or he may even call the local newspaper to ask for help. He may even be lucid about his own affliction. But soon the fantasies begin to assemble in his mind; his uncontrollable urges begin to overtake him again, and, driven by a lust for murder, he starts up the car again and drives off into the night to seek out the trolling grounds where his next victims will unwittingly congregate. Again, an unwary stranger will cross his vision, enter his corridor of death, and the killing ritual will once more be carried out to its inevitable conclusion.

3

The Disease
of Serial Murder

To understand the enormity that the problem of serial murder poses for society's institutions, multiply the Carlton Gary killings in Columbus, the Ted Bundy killings in Seattle, Utah, and Tallahassee, and the Richard Ramirez Nightstalker killings in Los Angeles and San Francisco five hundred times. Add to this the more than three hundred confessed killings by Henry Lee Lucas, the crime sprees of John Gacy and Ed Kemper, and the revelations of child sex abuse cases that are turning up in cities all over the country and the scope of the problem seems endless. However, it doesn't stop there: the problem is spreading and has escalated every year since 1959. At present the FBI estimates there are at least thirty-five serial killers on the loose and under investigation by the Bureau. Moreover, local police are still trying to solve ongoing serial murder cases in the Green River area of Seattle, a string of prostitute murders in Los Angeles, murders of elderly black women in Atlanta, murders of redheaded women throughout Florida, and a series of slayings of male derelicts in San Francisco who have been found with the sign of the pentangle etched into their flesh.

Only in the past few years have professionals begun to

understand the process through which such ultimately malevolent individuals have been created in each generation. After these professionals come to understand how the episodic killers have been shaped by patterns of child abuse, pathologically negative parenting, brain injuries resulting from physical traumas, inherited neurological disorders, chronic malnutrition, chronic drug and alcohol abuse, and toxic poisoning from environmental pollutants, the true nature of the medical/social epidemic will become clearer. What public health officials now know is that the cycles of violence in all of its forms that have been spawned from the previous generation feed upon themselves in each successive generation. Parents who abuse their children, physically as well as psychologically, instill in them an almost instinctive reliance upon violence as a first resort to any challenge. As each generation teaches the next generation to react with violence and as this is reinforced and compounded by the media, the patterns of violent behavior spread, consuming increasingly greater numbers of victims.

Until only recently, the linkage among violence in the background of an offender, a pattern of substance abuse, forms of psychomotor epilepsy that seem to debilitate – even momentarily – a person with a record of sex abuse or child abuse, and a pervasive self-destructive type of personality has gone unrecognized by criminologists and doctors as a form of medical syndrome. People who display this syndrome have historically been categorized as either sociopaths or psychopaths and have been relegated to the care of the criminal justice system. Under this system, they are treated as though they have volition and were capable of managing their own behavior. They are treated as though they were within the range of normal human existence, yet had willingly become deviant. This is not the case. Serial murderers are nonpersonality types who seem to come alive only during the episodic cycle of murder. However, because the criminal justice system concentrates on apprehension and punishment rather than on discovering the causality of violence and preventing its spread, individuals who display this type of medical syndrome have slid through the system untreated. And as a consequence the infection has been allowed to spread through society like a plague: the emerging serial killers are the carriers, transmitting the syndrome from one generation to the next, and six thousand Americans per year are their primary victims and the syndrome's most visible casualties.

Our evaluations of serial killers show that each of them has an amalgamation of symptoms that point to a type of disease that can actually shape their behavior patterns. It is a disease that some experts say can be prevented ninety percent of the time. During the period when they are experiencing episodic explosions of violence, these serial murderers are out of control. They are unable to own any sense of right and wrong and have a significantly diminished ability to judge objectively their own activities. They have lost their free will. They are in the grip of a form of episodic frenzy that does not fit traditional legal descriptions and cannot be evaluated by traditional criminological or psychoanalytical techniques. Their condition lies beyond insanity. When placed in the custody of an institution, however, be it prison or a hospital for the criminally insane, a medical treatment facility, or any place where systematic rules govern the daily activities of the inmates, there is a marked improvement in their behavior. It is as if, having no internal structure to their lives, the killers amalgamate the rules system of the institution as a form of external skeleton. Thriving in this controlled environment and sustained by any improvement in their diets and receiving frequent counseling, the killers become mercurial or placid, bonding closely with male or female authority figures, jail ministers, lawyers, and biographers, and they tailor their confessions to fit the needs of their interrogators and the requirements of the moment. By then, however, they tend to lose their sense of the past and to confuse the events of their lives. It is almost as if the murders never took place, as if a part of their consciousness has been shut down, and they begin to function like other institutionalized patients who rely on their external environments for all sentient activity. And almost all of them are markedly guiltless, as if the moral responsibility for the crimes they committed had been borne by someone else. However, when the appropriate feelings of remorse return, the grief and sadness have more to do with the tragedies of their own lives than with the lives of their victims.

The prevalence of these repeated patterns in all of the case histories of the serial murderers we have studied, the overwhelming similarities of their modus operandi, the primal qualities of their violent behavior, the similar patterns of brain dysfunction and learning disabilities that each of them evidences, the similarities in the results of the biochemical tests that many of them have taken once in prison, and finally the remarkable consistency of their reactions to institutionalization lead to the conclusion that serial murder is a form of disease. To be sure, this is not an illness that fits into traditional medical categories, but, until the work of Breuer, Freud, and Jung, neither were psychoses or neuroses. Serial murder is an illness that has eluded detection because it very conveniently slipped between the cracks of most diagnostic schema. Because many cases of minimal brain damage and lesioning due to forms of psychomotor epilepsy are not confirmed conclusively until after the brain is examined in an autopsy, a diagnosis could not be made. Also, because the murderers themselves seemed to be fully aware of the nature of the charges against them and even admitted their guilt, traditional insanity defenses could not be mounted. And because the episodes of truly psychotic hallucinatory behavior by some were controllable in an institutional setting – often the first stable living environment many of the killers ever experienced – the actual playing out of the murderers' dream visions never took place. Finally, and most importantly, many murderers wish for death and several have attempted suicide. They welcome it as a final solution to their agony. Therefore, rather than defend themselves against the murder charges, they embrace the death sentence as the ultimate murder episode in which their fantasies of self-destruction – fantasies that have driven them throughout their lives – are consummated.

Serial murderers share a significant number of common medical-psychological patterns that include evidence of possible genetic defect, soft signs of brain damage resulting from injuries or other physical trauma, severe chemical imbalances brought about by chronic malnutrition and substance abuse, an absence of a sense of self which is the result of consistently negative parenting or nonparenting, and an almost hair-trigger violent response to external stimuli with no regard for the physical or social consequences. One of the most significant common behavior patterns is a failure to perceive punishment as a deterrent to their actions and a fascination with police procedures and the officers who are pursuing them. Carlton Gary even dated a female deputy sheriff while he was actually committing the Wynnton murders. He led a double life as her lover and she was unaware of his actions. The psychophysiological mechanisms that keep most people from immediately acting on violent or negative impulses is simply absent in them. Once the killing begins, they are unable to control their behavior no matter what the circumstances are. However, in the specific instance of serial murder, this period of loss of control is episodic. During these episodes the criminal's behavior repeats a ritualistic pattern of trolling, stalking, wooing, capture, torture, murder, recapture, and postmortem depression.

Between the episodes, the absence of a sense of self allows the criminal to fade back into society as a common individual. Some killers are actually hypervigilant do-gooders. For example, during his killing spree John Gacy entertained children in hospitals. Ted Bundy worked on a suicide hotline and wrote a manual for rape crisis intervention.

This loss of control – the lack of rational behavior with regard to appreciating the consequences of personal violence, and the compulsive premeditation with regard to each successive victim – is what sets the serial murderer apart from other killers. As a result of scientific studies conducted by numerous institutions and individuals across the country on the causality of violence, we have developed the hypothesis that episodic aggression, which involves child and family abuse, rape, and serial murder, is inherently a disease and therefore treatable and preventable.

The key to detecting this disease in individuals is a recognition of the key behavioral patterns common to all episodic violent offenders in general and to convicted serial murderers in particular. First and most obvious is the subject's animallike, primal approach to the act of murder. The range can vary from a simple rape murder to ritualistic torture and dismemberment of the victim. In addition, many serial killers evidence a reliance upon hair-trigger violence as a first response to conflict or challenge. In the cases of both Henry Lee Lucas and John Gacy, encounters with strangers turned into murder when the serial killers felt challenged by the potential victim. Bobby Joe Long reported that after a serious motorcycle accident had left him permanently disabled and damaged a significant part of his brain he was unable to control his temper. Even the slightest annoyance, such as the tapping of a hammer or a sudden noise, would be enough to send him into a fury. Years later Long emerged first as a rapist and then as a serial killer who raped and tortured his victims before murdering them. John Gacy's story is very similar. Years before he killed his first victim, but always after a bout of heavy drinking, Gacy routinely sought encounters with young men in bus stations and other public places, offering them money and drugs, having sex with them, and going out to dinner. It was only years later, as a fully emerged serial killer, when any of his male sexual encounters offered him a direct challenge or confronted him in any way, that he lured the victim back to his house, where he tortured him and buried the body under his house.

This tendency to resort spontaneously to violence often turns up in abused or battered children. They, in turn, pass it along to their children in the succeeding generation. In fact, as Marvin Wolfgang has shown in a study of a cohort of males born in 1945, those people with violent criminal backgrounds often experienced violence in their households when they were growing up and were themselves victims of violent parents. A first resort to violence can also be indicative of a form of minimal brain damage, especially to the limbic region or the frontal lobe – the inhibitors of judgmental and primitive animal defensive reactions. Many serial killers who have undergone CAT or PET scans evidenced some form of significant damage to the limbic region of the brain.

Juvenile offenders who have committed violent crimes and homicidally aggressive children are particularly important in deciphering the developmental nature of this disease. For many of the most violent, this is not their first offense. An examination of their criminal records reveals a tendency toward violence that manifested itself from their first brushes with any authority. Often one or more parents have engaged in some form of criminal activity, and that violence has been a part of their backgrounds as well. Medical examinations of violent juvenile offenders tend to reveal a variety of physiological and neurological problems ranging from degrees of brain damage or dysfunction to nutritional deficiencies to forms of toxic poisoning.

Even at an early developmental stage, potential serial murderers show signs of pathology and grandiosity. Some experts say that the deficit occurs prior to age five. This is where skilled diagnosis is important and the most meaningful research has yet to be done. As full-blown sociopaths, they evidence no guilt nor do they see any necessary consequences of their actions. At their most violent and uncontrollable, serial murderers simply claim to block out any memory of their crimes and change their confessions to fit the needs of their interrogators and the moment. They have convenient but nonetheless real loss of memory and are able to lie with complete freedom about their previous crimes. This is what makes serial killers so difficult to interrogate and diagnose. It also makes them infuriating to their investigators. They can manipulate and even confuse the most skilled interrogator or diagnostician, even the lie detector operator. Everything they say must be documented by objective evidence because they will change the truth to conform to any situation. They are not plagued by a gnawing guilt that forces them into a confession. Their sufferings are internal and have little or nothing to do with any specific crime. For this reason, early intervention in the life of an evolving serial killer – while his pain and fury are still relatively close to the surface – is important. Once the entire architecture of violence has been digested by the emerging criminal, it will only objectify itself in its victims, and that is what sustains the murderer until the architecture collapses from its own weight and the murderer attempts suicide to end his own torment.

If primal displays of violence and a family background of violence are the most identifiable behavioral characteristics of the serial killer syndrome, history of head trauma, degrees of brain or neurological dysfunction, or forms of psychomotor epilepsy are important medical characteristics. Genetic factors can also play a role in the evolution of the serial killer syndrome. Because certain forms of epilepsy and brain dysfunctions can be inherited, the serial killer need not necessarily have received an injury or be a victim of a birth defect in order to have impaired brain activity. These physiological impairments directly affect outward behavior and the social controls the individual is able to exert over behavior. Even minor brain dysfunctions or minor damage resulting from injuries can result in a significant loss of control of violent tendencies. When this condition is brought about because of beatings received in childhood or exists in a highly unstable family background, the normal social conditioning that should have taken place doesn't, and the individual has no basis for controlling his emotions. His behavioral reference points are all internal rather than external, and he has no personality map to help him negotiate through the world. He is already losing control.

The final pathology components of this syndrome involve behavioral reactions to chemical imbalances resulting from malnutrition, substance abuse, and toxic poisoning. The first, malnutrition, results not only from an unstable family background in which the child's physiological development was impaired, but from continuing nutritional disorders and the resulting vitamin and mineral deficiencies. A diet that is severely lacking in any nutrients deprives the brain of fuel it needs to function. Deficiencies in iron weaken the system and deprive it of resiliency; deficiencies in mineral zinc and potassium can affect the hormonal system and place the individual in a chronic state of emotional turmoil; and deficiencies in vitamins B and C leave the body vulnerable to low levels of infection. In these situations, behavioral disorders such as hair-trigger reactions to outside stimuli are almost normal occurrences. These disorders can also result as reactions to an overabundance or deprivation of sugar and starch or to a serious deficiency in trace minerals other than zinc or iron. They can also result from physiological reactions to lead or cobalt poisoning, two environmental pollutants that have regularly turned up in laboratory analyses of blood taken from serial killers. This is why the clinical testing for a predisposition to commit violent acts should include laboratory analysis of the patient's blood and serum chemicals.

Substance abuse, either alcohol or drugs, also forms a major behavioral component of the serial killer's makeup. Most convicted serial killers are chronically heavy drinkers and narcotics addicts who are either drunk or high at the time they commit their crimes. The problem, however, goes well beyond a claim of temporary drunkenness. Alcohol has a residual effect on the brain and neurological system. Prolonged use of alcohol actually destroys brain tissue, rendering portions of the brain moderately impaired. During a prolonged drunken state, when the entire brain function is inhibited and social controls are lowered in general, there is simply no form of normal control exerted by the predisposed individual to prevent antisocial activity. During periods of episodic violence, alcohol only increases the level of the serial killer's disorientation and further separates him from reality. Much the same can be said for narcotics. They contribute to the serial killer's hallucinatory state and markedly diminish all brain functions. Henry Lee Lucas revealed that all of his murders were committed while he was drunk. Ted Bundy is a chronic alcoholic and had joined AA while in prison, and John Gacy became so violent while given alcohol in prison that he had to be placed in a straitjacket to prevent him from injuring himself. Most serial killings are committed while the murderer is under the influence of alcohol or drugs.

As a form of violence that is spreading in epidemic proportions and whose pathology is demonstrable medically, serial murder truly belongs to the areas of physical abuse that U.S. Surgeon General Dr. C. Everett Koop has designated as a critical issue of public health. The Surgeon General cited family violence, child abuse, sex abuse, substance abuse, and any crimes or homicides – all of which are components of the serial murderer's syndrome – resulting from these causes as public health issues that require a level of intervention from health care and social work professionals beyond the obvious involvement of criminal justice professionals. Rather than simply 'medicalizing' the problem of child abuse or rape, the U.S. Public Health Service is seeking a new form of prevention. By recognizing that violence is a form of disease, the Public Health Service can extend the responsibility for preventing these special types of crimes beyond the immediate level of the police and the courts and into parole boards, doctors' offices, hospital emergency rooms, school nurses' offices, and guidance departments in school districts around the country. By focusing the attention of the hospital or school social worker and even the local police juvenile officer on the case of a particular victim and examining the events surrounding the crime, the Surgeon General has suggested, the career of that perpetrator can be short-circuited before he can commit any more crimes or emerge fully as a serial or mass murderer.

Like physical diseases, most forms of family and personal violence are preventable. One of the first signs of the acceptance of this point of view is the Surgeon General's suggestion that violence is a disease that calls for medical intervention. Heart disease falls into this category as do many forms of progressive neurological diseases. Serial murder and many forms of violent behavior are similarly preventable if the person is identified and diagnosed in time. In many cases that diagnosis can be initiated by an emergency room physician or a school nurse who notices the patterns of bruises on a patient, the attitude of a woman who has been sexually assaulted, or even the behavior of an adolescent offender who has been apprehended by a school guard or a police officer. However, most professionals at an early possible point of intervention are so repelled by what they see, they simply turn away as if their own primal instincts were dictating their fear.

That fear and revulsion have to be addressed and overcome. Then, by making a preliminary investigation of the person's background and family environment, evaluating a subject's medical history, running a series of autonomic reflex and psychological recognition tests, checking a pupillary response to light, or even conducting a perfunctory medical examination, a doctor, nurse, or trained paraprofessional can see whether there is any reason to probe deeper. These tests and simple medical interviews can be performed in the space of an hour or two and require only that a health care professional evaluate whether the patient or subject is displaying any signs of uncontrollable hostility, psychological disorientation bordering on explosive violence or actual brain damage.

Further tests are always necessary to confirm any diagnosis. In the case of diagnosing a predisposition to episodic violence, the evaluation and appropriate clinical follow-through should be conducted by neurological specialists and clinical psychologists who have a knowledge of causes of violence and the applicable criminal law as well as court procedures for determining either insanity or functional incompetence during hallucinatory or fantasy cycles. This evaluation should include a thorough medical and psychological examination of the subject. Ultimately, new diagnostic tools will have to be developed from what we understand about the nature of episodic violent behavior to predict that form of violence in individuals. New training procedures will have to be developed as well to help physicians and other health care professionals to recognize the signs of an episodically violent person.

The premise of this activity is to provide a meaningful medical causality for the instances of episodic violence in any particular individual, determine the course of treatment, and, ultimately, save the lives of the victims of any crimes he would have committted. This level of intervention also presupposes that the causality of uncontrollable and episodic violent behavior is not only a lapse in volition but also a definable set of organic malfunctions – some genetic over three generations, some chronic, and some environmental – that, when combined with a history of violent upbringing and negative parenting in which the traditional polarities of reward and punishment and love and hate are reversed, results in a nonpersonality type – a nosferatu – an individual with no means of controlling violent impulses, who is incapable of functioning within a normal social framework. Everett Koop and his colleagues in the field of public health recognize that prosecuting individuals who commit extraordinary violent crimes solves only a minute portion of the problem. The issue is to recognize this form of violence as a disease and bring the full structure of the medical and legal establishment to bear on preventing its spread.

The biosocial case histories of recent serial murderers in the following chapters will validate this hypothesis and show how the disease manifests itself in specific individuals and how the system as it now exists prevents significant investigation and intervention in these individuals.

4

Serial Killers Today

The serial murder syndrome is not a new phenomenon historically, even though it has dramatically increased in American society since 1958 and is only just coming to the attention of the courts, the police, and the medical profession. In fact, throughout history, societies have recorded the crimes of individuals which look suspiciously like the crimes committed by serial murderers today. The stories of Caligula, Vlad Tepes, Giles de Reis, and Jack the Ripper are among the many legends about individuals who seemed to kill out of a blood lust for the act of murder itself and not from any other motivation. And certainly the many legends of vampires and werewolves that have circulated throughout Europe from the Middle Ages to the present seem to reflect a fear that some individuals lurk beyond the walls of society, preying on victims out of a necessity to kill. Where records have been kept, they often show that serial murderers seem to appear within the same extended family and that outbreaks of the pathology take place in each generation. Often the evidence of this pathology is manifested by an obvious physical abnormality such as an elongated middle toe, webbed skin between the fingers, or epileptic tremors. Many of these serial murderers belonged to families that held power within their societies, allowing the criminals to seek their prey at will until the family had the person shut away or the criminal eventually died.

Today, however, in the light of modern crime reporting statistics and the records of police investigations, a truer picture of the work of the serial killer has emerged, and the growing magnitude of the crimes and the extent of the violence of each individual crime now seems clear. The capsule descriptions in this chapter of some of the most active serial killers and their crimes since 1961 demonstrate how the level of violence continues to grow and how the murderers we are profiling fit into the general class of serial killers.

1961 — *Melvin D. Rees, Jr.*, was a jazz musician convicted of slaying a family in Maryland whom he had kidnapped from their car in a highway ambush. The mother, who was found with her dress pulled up over her head, had been strangled with one of her nylon stockings. Her little daughter had been beaten to death, and her husband was found a distance away from the car, his hands tied together with his tie. He had been shot through the head and the year-and-a-half-old child he was cradling in his arms when he was shot was suffocated when the weight of his body fell over hers. Rees was also a primary suspect in other killings in Maryland. After his conviction he asked for the death penalty but received life imprisonment instead.

1964 — *Albert DeSalvo.* Better known as the 'Boston Strangler,' DeSalvo held Boston in a grip of terror during his murder spree. A master of disguise, he gained entrance to his victims' apartments by pretending he was a plumber or a handyman. His compulsion to kill drove him to take greater and greater risks, even while he was living a normal life with his own family.

1966 – *Michael Lee Herrington.* In Milwaukee this twenty-three-year old tool and die maker confessed to the mutilation slayings of two women and another attempted murder over a period of three months. Herrington was married but had no children.

Suspect Unknown. In Cincinnati an eighty-one-year-old woman was one of five victims who were discovered in their homes with lamp cords tied around their necks. All of them had been raped. After ten months the murders stopped, and the suspect was never identified.

1967 – *Dr. Ronald E. Clark,* of Detroit, a former mental patient himself, killed his own patients by injecting them with lethal doses of sodium pentothal. He was also brought up on charges of sexual attacks on his patients and on children.

1969 – *Antone Costa* of Cape Cod was convicted of murdering three women whose bodies were found dismembered, mutilated, and buried in the sand dunes. The police are still officially searching for more bodies.

1971 – *William Pierce,* a Georgia prison parolee in Beaufort, South Carolina, was charged with his eighth and ninth slayings: a twenty-year-old housewife and a gas station attendant. Despite a report from a prison psychologist that said 'he may be dangerous to himself and others,' Pierce was placed on parole in 1970.

Edmund J. Cody was a truck driver who married nine times. He was charged with killing Letha Gay, his ninth wife, whose body was found strangled and decomposing in the trunk of his car. He is suspected of killing at least another four of his wives while the remaining four are still listed as missing. Cody is currently serving a life sentence.

1972 – *Benjamin Franklin Miller* of Stamford, Connecticut, was a self-ordained minister who preached on street corners. Charged with the slaying of five black women over a four-year period, he was known as the 'Bra Killer,' because he strangled the victims with their own bras. Miller believed himself to be another Billy Graham and was frequently invited to neighborhood churches to preach. It was there, police assume, that he met his five victims.

Charles Schmid, Jr., was called the 'Pied Piper of Tucson' by the police, who charged him with the murder of three teenage girls in 1965. Schmid admitted to strangling the teenagers and burying their bodies in the desert because it made him 'feel good.'

1973 – *Girard John Schaefer*, called the 'Sex Beast,' was connected to more than twenty murders in the Oakland Park area of Florida. Schaefer, who himself was an ex-police officer, was linked to the killings because jewelry, teeth, and articles of clothing belonging to the victims were found in the trunk of his car.

Herbert Mullin in Santa Cruz, California, was convicted of ten serial murders. This came as a shock to the community because in high school the killer was an outgoing, socially adept individual who was voted 'most likely to succeed.'

Edmund Emil Kemper, also from Santa Cruz, was charged with the murder of his mother and at least seven female hitchhikers. He had dismembered all of the bodies and preserved limbs and organs in a variety of ways. Kemper had a long history of mental illness and had been in and out of mental institutions throughout his life. After killing his mother, Kemper turned himself in to the police because he knew that he would keep on killing until he was finally stopped or killed.

Bruce Henderson Shreeves, an AWOL sailor, was linked to three murders in Spencerville, Maryland. Police said that the bodies were disposed of in a ritualistic way that connected the murders to one another and pointed to the work of the same killer.

Dean Corll, the 'Man with the Candy,' and *Elmer Wayne Henly* in Houston, Texas, together performed more than twenty-seven torture slayings of young boys. Corll lured the boys to his candy store, where he would have 'parties' during which he forced the victims to perform sodomy and other sexual acts. He would then kill them, sprinkle their bodies with crushed lime rock, and bury them. Corll himself was killed by Henly. According to Henly's story, Corll tied him up along with two other people. When Henly offered to torture the other victims if he were untied, Corll released him, whereupon he grabbed Corll's gun and shot him.

Julian Kennedy, thirty, of Lake City, Florida, was formally charged with the murder of a woman. During his confession to the police he admitted to thirteen other murders over a fifteen-year span.

His first murder, he explained, was part of an initiation rite into a motorcycle gang: he was told to beat a man to death with a chair and an axe handle.

1974 – *Larry C. Green*, *J. D. Simpson*, *Manuel Moore*, and *Jesse Cooks* claim to be members of a cult called the 'Death Angels.' Charged with committing the 'Zebra Killings,' a series of murders in which blacks killed whites, the cult boasted more than two thousand members and announced that its mission was to torture, mutilate, and kill white victims.

Joseph Kallinger, the 'Shoemaker,' along with his son Michael killed three people in New York. Kallinger claimed a mandate from God to torture his victims before killing them.

The *'Zodiac Killer'* murdered and sexually assaulted several children in San Francisco. Given his name by the police because he carved the sign of the zodiac into the bodies of his victims, the killer was never apprehended and the murder cases remain unsolved. The killer is believed either to have been killed himself or been confined to a mental institution. The murders stopped after a few months as mysteriously as they had begun.

Calvin Jackson, a former drug addict and ex-convict, admitted to raping and then strangling eleven elderly women in their New York City apartments.

1975 – *Thomas E. Creech*, in Wallace, Idaho, admitted to having killed forty-two persons over the previous eight years as a 'contract executioner' for a national motorcycle gang involved in drug trafficking or during cult worship. He also said he ranked eighth in the amount of victims killed by contract killers for the gang.

1976 – *Vaughn Greenwood,* also in Los Angeles, was indicted for murdering eleven skid row derelicts over a two-year period. He slashed the victims' throats and left a cup of blood on each of their bodies. He also sprinkled salt in a hoodlike design around the heads of the dead victims.

1977 – *Dr. Mario E. Jascalevich,* in the 'Dr. X' killings in Hackensack, New Jersey, murdered five of his hospital patients by injecting them with lethal does of curare, the African dart poison.

Patrick Kearny, who was a former aerospace engineer, and *David Hill* were convicted in the Southern California 'Trash Bag Murders.' The two killed more than twenty-eight homosexuals, wrapped up the remains, and dumped their bodies in the trash.

1978 – *Kenneth Bianchi,* the 'Hillside Strangler,' was convicted along with *Angelo Buono, Jr.,* of killing nine young women in an exclusive Los Angeles neighborhood.

Gary Gene Tison, in Florence, Arizona, broke out of prison, where he was serving a life sentence for murder, by his three sons. The four went on a three-week killing spree, murdering a two-year-old boy and his parents, a teenage girl, and a honeymooning couple. At a roadblock, two of the sons were captured, a third was killed by police, and Tison escaped into the desert. He was found dead of exposure a few weeks later.

Mary Rose Robatzynski, in Baltimore, was indicted

for killing four of her patients in the hospital's ICU by unhooking their life-support systems.

1979 — *Joseph Fischer,* was arrested in California for killing his wife, admitted to police that he'd killed nineteen other people at random in New Mexico, Arizona, Maine, Connecticut, and New York since being paroled from a California prison in June of 1978.

Suspect Unknown. In Houston, Joann Huffman and Robert Spangenberger were found dead in a park. She had been shot to death and he was discovered, decapitated, in the trunk of a car. The work was presumably done by the same murderer, and it was the second such murder in Houston in the same year.

Paul Bateson, an X-ray technician at New York University Medical Center in Manhattan, was convicted of murdering Addison Verill, a New York writer. Bateson claimed that he had killed a number of other men, dismembering their bodies and wrapping them in trash bags which he then dumped in the Hudson River.

John Wayne Gacy, a highly respected member of his community who owned a construction and building development company in Chicago, was arrested for the murders of thirty-three boys. In one of the most famous serial murder cases of all time, Gacy was accused of picking up the boys at bus stations or along the road, having sex with them, torturing and murdering some of them, and burying the bodies in the basement of his suburban home. His crime was finally reported by his wife, who complained of the putrid odors arising from beneath the house.

Theodore Bundy, in another famous murder case, was convicted of murdering two coeds in a Florida college dormitory and a twelve-year-old girl. He was also connected to numerous other murders in Seattle and Salt Lake City and was the object of a country-wide manhunt on a fugitive warrant. He was sentenced to death, but the sentence was delayed while his appeals are progressing through the courts.

Gerald Eugene Stano killed eighteen waitresses in Florida over a five-year period, and is currently on death row in San Quentin.

1980 – *Roy Lewis Norris* and *Lawrence S. Bittiker* were convicted of killing five teenage girls in the Los Angeles area, and are currently on death row in San Quentin.

Suspect Unknown in the case of a cult killer of seven hitchhikers in Point Reyes Station, California. The killer is still at large.

Carlton Gary commited nine murders of prominent women in the Wynnton section of Columbus, Georgia. Known as the 'Stocking Strangler,' Gary was able to elude the police until 1984. He was convicted and sentenced to death in 1986. The conviction and sentence are still on appeal.

1981 – *Suspect Unknown.* Termed the 'Skid Row Slasher' by the NYPD, this killer murdered eight derelicts and street people by stabbing them while they slept in alleys and doorways. The case is still open.

Suspect Unknown. In a related set of killings, a person called the 'Midtown Slasher' by the

NYPD murdered six Hispanic victims in the Times Square/midtown area of Manhattan. The case is still open.

Wayne B. Williams was arrested for the Atlanta Child Murders. These killings of young children in Atlanta kept the city in the grip of terror for more than a year, set local and state law enforcement agencies at odds with one another, and captured the front pages of newspapers around the country. Williams was convicted for the murder of one victim on purely circumstantial evidence, but his case has been reopened because new evidence has been introduced. The killings stopped after Williams' arrest, but many Atlanta residents feel that Williams is not the Atlanta 'Child Murderer' and that the real killer is still at large.

Carl Eugene Roberts of Houston, Texas, is the confessed killer of at least thirteen women. He was sentenced to sixty years in prison after a plea bargain with the county prosecutor.

Suspect Unknown in the deaths of seven black women in Atlanta. As the city prepared for the worst, many residents believed that the 'Child Murderer' was striking again at a new set of victims or that the Columbus murders of 1977 had spawned another killer of older women. The case is still open.

Suspect Unknown in the Richland, Georgia, slayings of three teenage girls who were found brutally beaten, sexually assaulted, and bound with twisted metal coat hangers to trees, where they eventually died of their wounds. The case is still open.

Suspect Unknown in the 'Sunday Morning Slashings' in Houston, where a serial killer murdered more than forty black women by stabbing them with a large knife. The case is still open.

Juan Corona, a contractor for migrant labor on California fruit farms, was convicted for the murder of scores of migrant workers and sentenced to twenty-five years in prison. He buried busloads of victims in mass graves after performing cultlike ritual murders.

David Bullock killed at least six people, including his business partner and an actor, on a Manhattan street corner. He told the New York state criminal court judge that 'killing makes me happy.'

Dale Robert Henderson, a drifter in Tavares, Florida, confessed to killing ten or more people in five states.

Joseph John Sullivan was arraigned in Syracuse, New York, for the murders of twelve people.

William Bonnin, the 'Freeway Murderer,' was convicted of killing ten young boys and men and abandoning their bodies along Southern California's freeways.

Bernard Burton Hunwick was arrested in Dade County, Florida, for a series of murders and confessed to being the head of a 'hit squad' responsible for at least a hundred additional murders.

Christine Falling was convicted in Florida of killing from two to five children by strangulation or suffocation while baby-sitting for them. She was a diagnosed epileptic who believed her victims were epileptic as well.

1983 — *Suspect Unknown* in the killing of four White Plains, New York, women within seven months. The killings suddenly stopped and the case is still open.

Henry Lee Lucas and *Ottis Toole*, both ex-convicts with histories of mental problems, were indicted in Galveston, Texas, for the murders of twenty-eight women.

Angelo Buono, Jr., an auto upholsterer, is convicted along with Kenneth Bianchi, the 'Hillside Strangler,' for killing nine young women in an exclusive neighborhood in Los Angeles.

Henry Brison was convicted in Chicago of the murders of three people during highway robberies. He is on death row along with John Gacy, whom he has sworn to kill as well.

Richard Begenwald killed four women and one man in New Jersey and buried them in shallow graves.

Charles Hatcher, charged with the murder of a four-year-old boy, admitted to the murders of sixteen other people.

Douglas David Clark, the 'Sunset Slayer,' killed six women in Los Angeles.

Suspect Unknown. The Galveston police and the Austin Hills Nursing Home Convalescent Center are investigating the deaths of twenty-eight geriatric patients. A nursing home employee is suspected.

Suspect Unknown. The 'Green River Killer' in Seattle murdered thirteen to twenty-one young girls and women and dumped their bodies along the banks of the Green River. The women were either runaways or prostitutes.

Suspect Unknown in the 'Dune Case' in Provincetown, Massachusetts, where police are investigating the serial killer who left the bodies of twelve young women in sand dunes. The case is still open at the insistence of the county prosecutor's office.

Genene Jones was convicted for three murders but is also suspected in the murders of sixty-one infants at the Bexar County Administrative Medical Center in San Antonio, Texas.

1984 – *Gerald Gallego*, a truck driver and bartender, was convicted of the kidnapping of a college couple, shooting the man in the head and raping and then murdering the girl. He was also convicted of killing four others in Utah and is suspected of another murder in Oregon and three in California. Gallego's father was also convicted of murder and sent to the electric chair in 1955. Gallego is currently on death row.

Debra Sue Tuggle killed her own five children and one of her boyfriend's children in Camden, New Jersey.

Joseph Paul Franklin, an avowed racist, was convicted of killing two black men in Utah. He is a suspect in the random slayings of eight other black men and four white women in seven states from 1977 to 1980. Franklin was a former member of the Ku Klux Klan and the American Nazi Party and usually ambushed his victims with a long-range rifle.

Robert Hanson in Anchorage, Alaska, confessed to killing seventeen women. He is a married man but told police that throughout his life he had a feeling of 'rejection by women.'

Calvin Perry, an eighteen-year-old inmate in Fort Wayne, Indiana, was found hanging in his cell after he admitted killing Dan Osborne, his wife, and their eleven-year-old son. He also raped and beat their two-year-old daughter and even clubbed their dog to death. Before his death Perry also admitted killing other people. Prison authorities suspect that Perry himself was murdered.

Christopher Wilder, in West Palm Beach, Florida, millionaire, was killed in a gun battle with state troopers. Wilder was linked to eleven sex slayings of women, four of whom are still missing.

Robert R. Diaz, a night nurse in Los Angeles, was charged with twelve counts of murder in the hospital in whose coronary care unit he was stationed. He injected his victims with ten times the normal dose of Lidocaine. He is now on San Quentin's death row.

Despite the apparent differences in the backgrounds of these individuals, overwhelming patterns of similarity do emerge. The most apparent similarity is the ability of the majority of the killers to lead relatively normal lives while pursuing their homicidal compulsions. Edward Paisnal, John Gacy, Juan Corona, Albert DeSalvo, and Ted Bundy all held legitimate positions within their communities that allowed them to navigate freely from place to place. Some used their camouflage to get in a better position to locate new victims. DeSalvo gained access to his victims by claiming that he had been hired by the landlord to check the plumbing. Once admitted to an apartment, he sprung his trap and strangled his victim to death. Both Paisnal and John Gacy lured people to their houses with promises of jobs, and both had rooms prepared for the torture and interment of their victims. And Ted Bundy, as a college student, had unlimited access to the lounges, dormitories, and other places where attractive coeds gathered.

Almost all of these killers chose their victims completely at random. In other words, there was no relationship between the victim and the killer other than the one that was established at the moment the victim entered the killer's sight. This is a pattern of critical importance because law enforcement authorities and homicide investigators rely on the relationship between killer and victim as the basis for solving murder cases. When a relationship is absent, as it is in most serial murder cases, the police are left without one of the most important clues in their examination of the crime.

Finally, there is growing evidence that each one of the killers on this list was 'sick' in one way or another. Our research shows that 88% have one or more symptoms. While not legally insane, according to the McNaghten test, each killer distorted reality so completely that he or she was able to keep on killing, for months or even years at a time, by amalgamating the act of killing into his or her personality. Eventually, many serial killers if not apprehended or killed, would commit suicide as a way of ending the pain and self-loathing. And, indeed, most serial killers do report that they have attempted suicide in the past or are actively contemplating suicide. To a person, each killer would readily admit that he or she is sick, and a large majority of the serial killers on this list have sought help for their feelings of homicidal sexuality at some point during their lives. Usually they reach out right before they begin their careers as fully emerged serial murderers.

SERIAL KILLERS TODAY

The similarities among the different killers suggest that they share a common illness, a common syndrome whose origins are not defined by social class, race, or environment. An understanding of the nature of that illness and the ability to detect the appearance of this syndrome in children are the first steps in preventing the spread of serial murder.

5

The Anatomy of a Serial Murder Case:

The Murderer, the Victims, and the Community

April 9 was the first really warm day of spring, Judy Zeitz remembered. It was a Saturday. Her ten-year-old daughter Rachel and Rachel's twelve-year-old friend Caty Richards had just come back from dance rehearsal at the Park Street school. Mrs. Zeitz had offered to let Caty stay over at the Zeitz house so Caty's mother, RoseAlyce Thayer, an artist and teacher, could have the afternoon free to paint. Rachel and Caty came downstairs from Rachel's room and asked for money to play arcade games at Athens Pizza just down the road. Mrs. Zeitz refused. She really didn't want them to go back out now, so late in the afternoon and so close to dinner. The girls bargained: Could they go if they found money on their own? 'It's okay with me,' Judy said. But she told herself that when they couldn't find any money they wouldn't be able to go.

The girls surprised her by managing to scrape together enough spare change to play a game. Mrs. Zeitz kept her part of the bargain and let the girls go. At first Rachel wanted to walk over on her friend's old crutches. 'No way,' Caty screamed at her, and Rachel put the crutches back in her room. Giggling, the two girls raced across the front lawn while Mrs. Zeitz watched from the living room window. 'They look so happy and well pleased with themselves,' she thought, probably because they had thwarted her lazy attempts to prevent them from going.

Caty Richards had been born to RoseAlyce Thayer late in life, her fourth child and first daughter. Her mother had divorced Caty's father and married Charles Thayer, a retired mechanical engineer who made toy sleds and cradles that RoseAlyce painted; they were sold at the quaint country stores that dot the Vermont countryside. Caty had a learning disability and, although she had an average IQ, she was emotionally much younger than her peers. As a result she was easily intimidated. Caty had also been the victim of harassment by an adult male neighbor for nineteen months prior to her death, and her own natural father had threatened to kidnap her. In fact Caty was so terrorized by male strangers that her mother requested that the school assign her only to classes taught by women. What neither Caty nor her mother nor anyone else knew was that she and her friend Tina Cross had also been followed for the past six months by a man named Gary Schaefer who was a member of a local fundamentalist sect.

Caty followed her friend Rachel over to the pizza parlour. But it was too crowded, and the lines in front of the arcade games were too long. The girls decided to walk back to Rachel's house along Route 106. It was four-thirty in the afternoon.

Gary Schaefer was driving his brand-new blue and white Pontiac J2000 along Route 106 north out of Springfield on Saturday afternoon, listening to his tapes and enjoying the first warm day of the new season. He passed two young girls walking along the side of the road. He thought he recognized one of them as his step-daughter, his ex-wife's child by her former husband.

'I wasn't really paying attention to where I was going or what I was doing 'cause I was thinking, just driving and listening to good music,' he remembered, 'when in my rear-view mirror I thought I saw Jodie. So I turned the car around and headed back towards Springfield and I went by the girls again. They were heading up Pedden Acres Road. So I drove into Pedden Acres and turned my car around and stopped and waited for who I thought was Jodie to come up to the car and she did. She walked right up to my car.

'I wasn't even paying attention to the other girl at this time. Not at all. I mean I know she was there, but I wasn't even thinking about anything about her at all. I was in the car, I had the window down and we talked about something, I don't know what we said. I don't even remember the conversation that went on. I know what they say that I said. I said, they said, I asked something about Joe Cerniglia or something like that. I don't remember saying anything like that. I could have, but probably did. I just don't recall. Then I remember opening the door and telling Jodie to get in the car or she was going to be in trouble.'

It was around 5 P.M. when Judy Zeitz, who had lost track of the time, was getting the girls' dinner ready. Rachel appeared at the sliding door with Linda Noyes, the Zeitzes' neighbor from down the hill. Rachel was crying and red in the face. 'Caty was kidnapped,' she kept repeating. 'She was kidnapped by a man in a blue car.' Vernon Zeitz jumped in his car and went back down the road to look for the blue car and Caty. His wife phoned RoseAlyce Thayer. Linda's husband had already called the police. 'I told Rose I'd come for her and for her to get some pictures of Caty.'

RoseAlyce was already on the phone by the time Judy Zeitz arrived. She placed a call to her son Ed but he was out. She left a message. She also called Charlie Thayer, her husband, who was at a meeting in Cuttingsville. She left a message there too. It was five-thirty. The two women drove to the police station, racing through a red light on the way, and began what was to be hours of interviews with the police. How did Caty get along with her stepfather? they asked RoseAlyce Thayer. What was her home life like? Where was Caty's natural father? Did she ever sneak out at night? Did she go out with older men? Was she sexually active?

RoseAlyce sat through the interviews while in a part of her mind she could see the image of her terrified daughter waiting, praying, and expecting to be rescued. 'I still have nightmares of Caty reaching out,' she said years later, 'crying for the police and for help.'

Rachel Zeitz leafed through police mug shots and gave a description of the kidnapper to the police artist for a composite Identikit sketch. 'The man drove a blue compact car like my mother's,' she said. He was wearing a red sweat shirt with kangaroo pockets and the numbers 1983 in white down the sleeve. He had orange-tinted glasses with oval lenses. Having driven past them a couple of times, he finally stopped the car on an S-curve, out of sight of the rest of the road and of the Noyes house only a hundred yards away. First he asked directions. Then he got out of the car, leaving the door on the driver's side open, put his hand in the pocket of his sweat shirt, and said, 'What if I tell you if you don't get in the car I'll shoot and kill you?' Caty bent forward and gasped. She made an 'uhhh' sound and started crying. The man spoke in a monotone, looking only at Caty as if he were trying to hypnotize her. Rachel ran toward the hill, and when she looked back Caty was already in the driver's seat of the car. There was something else about the sweat shirt, Rachel said. Joel DeLorenzo, one of her classmates, had worn the exact same one to school only the week before.

'I guess you know from what the other girl said and everything, I threatened to kill 'em if she didn't get in the car, but I don't remember saying anything like that. I'm not saying that I didn't say it,' Gary Schaefer told the police in his confession a year later. 'I just drove off. I didn't squeal tyres or nothing. I could have, I don't remember doing that. I don't think I would have. I just drove off. And I went back down the road and headed north, I rode out up Gassetts Road and got on 103 and headed towards Rutland. I was talking to her like she was my daughter. She must have been very scared and that's why she got in the car. I mean, I'm saying that she must have been because that's how she must have reacted. I don't know how she reacted. I would have reacted that way if I was a twelve-year-old girl or however old she was.'

Gary Schaefer asked the girl about school, about her friends, about how she had spent her day. They stopped for hamburgers, stopped at a gas station where she went to the bathroom, and finally stopped at a remote place where Schaefer used to visit when he himself was a kid. 'Used to hike up there, but I think I remember that's where I stopped. There was a garbage can and that's where we had our sexual encounter. It was the same thing that I always did with other girls. It wasn't anything different than any other time. It was oral, and then I rubbed myself between her legs. Never had any intercourse or anything like that. It never was Caty. I mean it never was Caty. Never saw her as Caty, never heard her as Caty, or talked to her as Caty, or anything like that. I mean I know it was now, but at the time it wasn't. It was Jodie, and it was the same kind of encounter, sexual encounter, that Jodie and I had all the time.'

Rachel Zeitz became annoyed when the police suggested that Caty Richards wanted to run away from home or that she had wanted to go with the man wearing the red sweat shirt. RoseAlyce was more than annoyed. She kept repeating: Caty was still a little girl; she still played with dolls; she was naive; she was always trying to be helpful; she trusted the law and the police, and she trusted her parents to come to her aid. RoseAlyce told Police Chief Peter Herdt that she and her friends wanted to start an immediate search. Her husband Charlie was a pilot, she said, and they had friends with planes. 'Please do an air search before dark,' she implored.

'Searchers will destroy evidence,' Herdt responded. 'We're already starting a search.' The harder RoseAlyce pressed, the more vehemently the police chief denied her requests. And, as night came, winter returned to Springfield in the form of a thirty-degree drop in temperature and a steady fall of icy rain. At ten that night, RoseAlyce remembers, she lost all hope of ever seeing Caty alive again. She knew that Theresa Fenton, the victim of an earlier and almost identical kidnapping in the Springfield area, had been found barely alive, abandoned by the side of the road. She died in the hospital the next morning. But RoseAlyce knew that Caty had been dressed in summer clothing and could not survive a night of freezing rain and snow.

The next morning Rachel was interviewed by the police again and by the state police and an investigator from the prosecutor's office. The police drove her to a number of parking lots, asking her if she recognized any of the cars or if she could find one that was the same color as the kidnapper's. Finally they drove her over to the DeLorenzo house. The police chief was already there, holding up a sweat shirt which Rachel had described to the police on the evening of the kidnapping. That was the one, Rachel said. That was just like the sweat shirt the man in the blue car was wearing when he told Caty to get into the car.

'I stopped the car. Got out and went to the bathroom. It seems to me that she followed me. I went to the bathroom, and I know she came up behind me, and that's when I lose all control. Changed it to be Dorothy, and it just changes to the cemetery and just changes to the – I get very scared that she is going to hurt me again and that I'm not going to let that happen and then I do the things to her that Dorothy did to me. It's – it's more than just that – it's not – it's just – everything. I lose control over everything. I mean everything just changes. It's not that I can start to breathe real fast and I get a rush or anything like that. It's just the whole scene changes and everything is different. I see myself getting hurt by my sister. I see that whole thing happening to me again, and this time I'm not going to let it happen like that.

'I make her lay down. I think she's on her belly. And I just do the same things to her that she – my sister – that she did to me. You see, it's not – it's not the little girl waiting there, I mean it's actually my sister that's there and that, I'm gonna, and I'm forcing her to do those things to me, just like she forced me to do 'em to her. And then I spanked her. It was all over and I spanked her.'

Schaefer forced Caty Richards to perform oral sex while they hid in a secluded spot just two miles from where he had originally forced her into the car with him. It was close to 8 P.M., just three hours after he had seen the two girls in his rear-view mirror. Schaefer confessed that in his mind he was spanking his victim, just like his sister Dorothy, he alleges, used to spank him after forcing him to perform oral sex with her. However, Schaefer wasn't actually spanking Caty Richards. 'I mean, it was, I was hitting her on the head with a rock, I didn't know that till – I mean I just didn't know that at the time. At the time I thought I was just spanking her. I hit her on the head with a rock and a lot of times. I don't know how many times. I know it was a lot.'

By nine-thirty in the morning on April 11, Caty Richards had become Autopsy #A4762, 'a lean white female wearing a bloodied, striped T-shirt with cerebral tissue around the back of the neck and on the shoulder portion. The shirt is pulled up above the breasts. There is a pair of mud-stained but new blue jeans on the lower legs turned down around the calves. There is a pair of blue on blue sneakers, the right sneaker of which appears to have been unlaced. The left sneaker is loosely tied. There is no sock on the right foot. There is a blue and white striped tennis sock on the left foot. There are five safety pins with various colored beads secured around the toe lacing of the right sneaker and a pin: I LOVE MAINE.' Caty Richards died at eight-thirty on the evening of her capture from severe brain injuries resulting from multiple blows to her skull with a blunt instrument.

She was so disfigured that no reconstruction was possible. Her coffin was closed at the funeral, and the only person to have seen her after she died was her brother Tom.

Gary Schaefer was sick on the morning after the murder. Thinking he had caught the flu, he had breakfast, threw it back up, shaved and showered, shined his shoes, and started off to church, where he was one of the leaders of the congregation. He still had no recollection of what had taken place the night before. 'Sunday. Sunday morning, I always pick my aunt up, my mother, and take 'em to Sunday school. I use my mother's car always and when I was going in – I was sick – I wasn't feeling good and I was headed towards the bathroom to upchuck.'

Beth DeLorenzo, Joel's mother and Gary Schaefer's cousin, had told the police that at about three in the afternoon on the day of the kidnapping Gary had stopped by on his way into Rutland to pick up some cars for the Springfield dealership where he worked. He was upset, she remembered, because he couldn't see his adopted daughter's baby, and he was also upset about his father's death, which had taken place just the year before.

'My cousin Beth stopped me, and told me that there was a little girl missing and that the police had been up to her father's house and they were looking for some guy with a red sweat shirt, and it was then that I knew that I had to have – I was somehow responsible for it.'

Beth DeLorenzo told the police that she had seen her cousin at church on the Sunday following the reported kidnapping. She noticed nothing different about Gary's behavior. He had asked her to go out with him. Suddenly she asked if the police had been over to see him yet. The police had already been to her house, she explained, questioning her family about the red hooded sweat shirts and telling her that the guy who had kidnapped the girl in Springfield had been wearing one of the shirts. Gary ran back into the church and vomited, DeLorenzo told the police later, and had to go home.

Schaefer drove the car directly into his garage, something he never did, and closed the doors. He cleaned the car so thoroughly that not a fingerprint, bloodstain, or any trace of Caty Richards remained in it when the police impounded it at two that afternoon.

'I always wear a red sweat shirt. I wore it a lot after I had gotten it. I knew somehow or other that I was involved in what was going on. I just – couldn't put nothing together in my mind that you know said that well you did this, and you did that, and you did this. It's just nothing – nothing clicked, nothing made no sense at all for me at all. I knew that somehow or another that I was involved. It's just – it's just a feeling that I had, and it was a bad feeling. You know I had my cousin drive me home.

'Then I went in the house, when I got back home. I know I went upstairs and sat at my desk for a long time trying to figure out what was going on. And I knew, I just knew that I was involved. I just didn't know what. I just knew that somehow or another I was involved in that little girl missing. That's all Beth told me, that there was a girl missing, and I knew that somehow or another, I was involved in it, but I just didn't know what.'

Caty Richards was found at noon on Sunday at the first location the police searched, an isolated stretch along Baltimore Road about two miles from where Schaefer had picked her up. People in Springfield who had scanners in their houses picked up the police call, and the news started to circulate through town even while Rachel Zeitz and her mother was still in church. 'When we arrived home, Rachel rushed up the stairs past Vernon who was coming down,' Mrs. Zeitz recalled in her statement to the prosecutor's office. 'He told me that Caty's body had been found. We didn't realize Rachel remained at the top of the stairs and heard us. She screamed, "No, no. It can't be. She can't be dead." '

The Thayers had not yet been informed. Finally, at two in the afternoon, still anxious that the family had heard nothing from the police chief, RoseAlyce called the station house. Indeed, she was told, Caty's body had been found. Now her daughter was the third young girl in Springfield to die after having been kidnapped.

Rachel Zeitz felt guilty about her friend's death. According to her mother, she felt bad that Caty had been alone when she died. Rachel felt she should have stayed with her friend, that she could have saved her, that she could have grabbed her hand and dragged her away, or that she could have yelled at Caty to run. She remembered that, even though it seemed as if she were trying to run away from the stranger as quickly as possible, she was going too slowly. She wanted to open her mouth and yell, but she couldn't. She blamed herself, and the blaming continues to this day.

Even four and a half years after Caty's funeral, Rachel still suffers from guilt. In June of 1986, her parents took her to see Caty's grave for the first time. She planted some flowers.

The abduction and murder of Caty Richards occurred against a background of the murder of another Springfield girl, Theresa Fenton, in 1981 and the abduction of seventeen-year-old Deana Buxton from Brattleboro the previous year. Even then, the police were pursuing leads to Gary Schaefer involving several abductions and rapes and including the murder of thirteen-year-old Sherry Nastasia, who lived in Schaefer's brother's garden apartment complex. However, the leads to Schaefer were tenuous, and police were proceeding slowly rather than have the case unravel in court for lack of a chain of evidence, although Deana Buxton had told the police about the kidnapper's blue car and the fact that he had driven her through the main streets of town in broad daylight after forcing her into the car. The Identikit composite made by Deana was almost interchangeable with the one made by Rachel. This was what led police directly to Gary Schaefer.

Five months later, in September, under pressure from a public letter written by RoseAlyce Thayer challenging him to stand by the precepts of his fundamentalist religion, Schaefer confessed to the murders of Catherine Richards and Theresa Fenton and to the rape and abduction of Deana Buxton. 'I am responsible for the deaths of Caty Richards, and Teresa Fenton. I do not feel that it is necessary to go into the details that caused their deaths, as I am sure you are or soon will be made aware of the circumstances concerning my state of mind,' he scrawled in a letter to William Bos, the state's attorney for Windsor County, Vermont. In December, Schaefer agreed to plead no contest to the sexual assault, abduction, and second-degree murder of Catherine Richards. In return for Schaefer's confession to the Fenton murder, charges in that case were dropped, although Theresa Fenton's parents were allowed to visit with Schaefer in his cell and hear his own confession of guilt until he requested the authorities not to have the Fentons visit again. Schaefer was sentenced to a term of from thirty years to life in January 1984 and is currently serving his time at the federal penitentiary at Leavenworth, Kansas.

RoseAlyce Thayer subsequently filed a complaint

against Peter Herdt and the Springfield Police Department for violating her and Caty's civil rights. She has charged, in a suit in federal court, that there was no search for the victim of this witnessed abduction for more than nineteen hours after the report of the crime and that she and her husband were physically prevented from initiating a search on their own or from the air. Mrs. Thayer testified before the Vermont legislature that the state needed a law that would mandate a centralized record-keeping facility for all missing children, so that a search for any missing children could begin immediately. The bill was passed by the Vermont state legislature in May 1985. RoseAlyce Thayer now travels throughout the nation speaking on behalf of missing children and their families; Mrs. Fenton has opened a bakery in her kitchen, and Mrs. Schaefer, Gary's mother, disowned him. The Christadelphian sect excommunicated Schaefer from the group.

The Springfield police department, although criticized by the state for its handling of the Caty Richards kidnapping, was publicly exonerated of any wrongdoing by the town officials. And RoseAlyce and Charles Thayer adopted a child, fifteen-year-old Cyndi, in August 1987.

The Caty Richards murder is like a microcosm. In it, we can see how murderer and victim came together, how each brought an individual past directly to the moment of encounter and the ensuing tragedy, and how those pasts helped create and shape the tragedy, and how the shock waves from the murder overwhelmed the lives of the families and friends that were involved, the police investigators, the courts, and even the state legislature itself. Unfortunately, Caty Richards was a prime victim. As a learning-disabled child, she was naive and emotionally immature for her age, and she relied on adults for direction and support. As a child who had been followed by an adult male neighbor for the year and a half previous

99

OXFORDSHIRE COUNTY LIBRARIES

to her encounter with Schaefer, she was already fearful. It was the act of confronting Schaefer after he had driven by her a number of times that put her at risk and meshed with Schaefer's own perceptions of her on the road.

By her own admission, Judy Zeitz had misgivings about letting the girls go back outside so late in the day. They were free-floating misgivings, to be sure, but misgivings nevertheless. However, like most parents, she didn't want to say no unless she had a concrete reason for saying no, and simply listening to her own instincts wasn't strong enough to take a firmer stand. Perhaps the presence of a visitor in the house and the combined impact of both girls' wants made Mrs. Zeitz more acquiescent than she would have been normally. And she was expending additional energy by watching Caty so that Caty's mother, RoseAlyce, could have the afternoon free to paint. She didn't know that a male neighbor had been chasing Caty near her mother's home. It was as if there just wasn't enough energy there to make the protest. Even she characterized her attempts at keeping the girls in the house as 'lazy.'

In the background, and seemingly out of mind, was the fact that over the past four years, in the immediate area two adolescent girls had been abducted, raped, and murdered, and one seventeen-year-old had been abducted and raped. She had the presence of mind to escape when her captor stopped for beer. Those other cases were not out of Chief Herdt's mind, however. When Judy Zeitz and RoseAlyce Thayer reached the police department after Rachel reported the kidnapping, the Theresa Fenton case file was upright in a holder on Police Lieutenant Chadbourne's desk. Also, aerial photos of the route that Schaefer had taken with Theresa Fenton lined the walls of the squad room. Judy Zeitz noticed that immediately and made the connection in her own mind between the Fenton murder and Caty Richards' abduction. RoseAlyce had made the same connection while riding to the police station in the car but tried to put it out of her mind. Unknown to both Judy and RoseAlyce at the time were the two other cases that remained unsolved: Sherry Nastasia in 1979, and Deana Buxton in 1982. The police had another opportunity to find the child murderer who had been eluding them for four years.

From the outset the police were aware of Schaefer as a potential suspect. They had a description of the car and had made a connection between the Deana Buxton case and Schaefer even though they had not positively identified him as the assailant. The police also knew that Caty Richards was a potential victim. Herdt had interviewed Caty Richards for one and a half hours after Theresa Fenton's death at the time when Caty was being harassed by the neighbor. The police chief knew what Caty was like.

RoseAlyce Thayer has also charged that the chief didn't want family members participating in the search. According to Judy Zeitz, the chief said that he didn't want 'amateurs' destroying evidence. If, indeed, the police had got a break in the three child abductions and two murders that had baffled them for the past few years, they didn't want to throw it away along with any chance of finding Caty Richards because someone had disturbed a vital clue at the crime scene. As in the Atlanta Child Murders, the Stocking Strangler murders, and many of the other serial murder cases around the country, the police are so desperate to find the killer and, once found, not lose him through the legal process that they might even compromise the safety of the victim so as not to compromise the integrity of the search, arrest, and eventual prosecution of the killer.

Once a suspect in the Richards case had been arrested and charged, another set of political and legal considerations were brought into play, for which the county prosecutor's office and the local police would later be criticized. William Bos found himself with a ten-year-old witness who positively identified Schaefer from a lineup as the man who forced Caty Richards into his car. Semen smears from Caty's body did not exclude Schaefer as the murderer, and Schaefer's alibi that he was in Rutland with his boss fell apart almost immediately. Bos knew that he had his man. However, he also knew that the links to the still open Theresa Fenton case were identical to those in the Richards case, and he wanted to make a further connection between Schaefer and the Nastasia murder and the Buxton kidnapping. And Donald Graham, Schaefer's public defender, was already moving in the direction of an insanity defense which would, at the very least, leave these cases pending for years during the appeals process, even if the state got its conviction in the Richards case alone. The public defender would have used Schaefer's insanity plea in a drug/arson case that the Navy had brought against him when he was in the service years earlier, even though the Navy psychiatrists found that Schaefer was sane at the time. Thus, with a drawn-out insanity trial in the offing, Bos felt that he had to move very deliberately and quickly to get a confession on all the open cases.

Then RoseAlyce Thayer went public with an open letter that baited Schaefer into his handwritten confession. Accusing him of being a 'series killer,' Mrs. Thayer charged him with the murders of eleven victims that he performed according to an established ritual. 'Mr. Schaefer follows this pattern laid down by so many others; he had a cleansing ritual, prior to the kidnapping, he had certain words he spoke to his victims, he had a particular type of weapon, a certain type of place to dispose of the body and he also took the traditional souvenirs of the victim.' She accused him of living a lie and being a member of a group of criminals who have become 'scorned rejects of society.'

She then turned to an attack upon his religious beliefs: 'Mr. Schaefer's self-justification is hidden behind an altogether transparent religious facade. His religion is a warped thing of his own decision, not truly related to the sincere beliefs of many members of the Christadelphian Church of whom I knew. It looks as though he has become flattered by the publicity which he has received. He is an egocentric person who has little regard for the pain being suffered by the members of his family church.

'Men like Schaefer are cowards who prey upon children who are too young, too innocent, and too weak to protect themselves; they are not real men, any man who will cause, or permit the death of a child to happen is not a real man. He is not a religious man, one who lives by the Holy Bible.'

Gary Schaefer responded quickly in a letter to William Bos by confessing to the murders of Theresa Fenton and Caty Richards and to the rape of Deana Buxton. He admitted that what he had been about to write was contrary to the advice he had received from his defense counsel but stated that he was more concerned about his religious beliefs than his legal defense. 'Contrary to what Mr. LeClair said about me not being a religious person, I am. And it is necessary for me to confess my sins in order that I may have any hope for God's mercy, even though I don't deserve it.' He concluded his confession by saying that, his legal defense notwithstanding, 'The only possible way that I can have any hope of having my sins forgiven me is to make this public confession of my sins and to follow what God commands me to do. I hope in doing so it clears up any questions Mr. Bos has concerning the three incidents in question.'

William Bos now had on his hands a public baiting of his suspect by the victim's mother and a confession so tainted that any competent defense attorney could have got it thrown out of court and have tied up the entire case in an appeals process for years. He might also have had a real fear that the forced confession could have been used as the basis for a mistrial. And, moreover, Donald Graham, the public defender, was a competent attorney. Graham believed initially that his client was insane when he murdered Caty Richards and that he was innocent of the Buxton rape. The crimes were dissimilar enough, he thought, that Bos wouldn't be able to use the Richards case as a pattern for convicting Schaefer of raping Buxton. Graham believed that there was no evidence to link Schaefer to the Nastasia murder or to the Fenton murder.

Whatever William Bos might have thought about the other crimes, he did not want to lose a conviction in the Richards case, especially because there was no doubt about Schaefer's guilt, only about his sanity. Bos was able to prove subsequently that Schaefer was competent enough to stand trial for the Caty Richards murder, and he negotiated a plea-bargaining arrangement with the defendant that allowed the state to close the books on the Fenton and Buxton cases as well as the Richards case. Bos came to believe, like Graham, that the links between Schaefer and Nastasia would never result in a murder conviction, although the case is still hanging over Schaefer's head many years later.

Schaefer agreed to plead no contest to sexually assaulting Catherine Richards and to murder in the second degree. He further agreed to plead guilty to the kidnapping of Deana Buxton and to provide full confessions to the Richards and Fenton murders. Lastly he was to admit his guilt to the parents of Theresa Fenton. In return, the state did not bring charges against him for the murder of Theresa Fenton. Even though Donald Graham argued that advances in the field of psychotherapy might eventually result in a complete cure for his client, the judge sentenced him to a term of from thirty years to life with the possibility of parole after nineteen years. Bos was confident, however, and predicted that, given Schaefer's record, 'he will spend the rest of his natural life in prison.' The prosecutor claimed that, with Schaefer safely convicted, 'parents in Windsor County should be able to sleep better.' In May 1986, after Governor Kunin signed a 'life with no parole' bill into law in Vermont, the chances of Schaefer's being granted parole in 2003 were greatly diminished.

What about Gary Schaefer? His sister Dorothy has conclusively refuted any accusations that she sexually abused her brother or struck him in any way. While rumours abound regarding the cultlike practices of the Christadelphian sect, the familial relationships among the members, and the charges of incest among family members that have arisen from time to time, there is no independent corroboration of anything that Schaefer described in his January 1985 confession. Schaefer's stepdaughter has also refused to comment.

If his revelations are true, and no one in Springfield doubts their veracity, then it is clear that Schaefer was insane at the time of the murders of both Theresa Fenton and Caty Richards. In both instances, he was perhaps acting out a hallucination of a ritual he claims he performed with his stepdaughter and which he claims was performed upon him by his sister. In his own mind, he was not committing a murder, he was spanking his sister in retaliation for the spanking he claims she had given him. Maybe his vision of a spanking was his way of blocking the ritualistic murder of his sister over and over again.

Schaefer's descriptions of cruising along back roads until he spotted someone in the mirror who resembled his stepdaughter is a valuable firsthand description of the onset of the hallucination and the switching from the trolling to the wooing phase of a serial murderer's cycle. Rachel Zeitz's description of the murderer's luring of Caty Richards, complete with his almost hypnotic stare as he ordered the girl he thought was his daughter into his car, is a frightening image of the intimate first encounter between the killer and his victim. In Caty Richards' case, it is all the more poignant, because she was the daughter of a man who had abandoned her when she was very young, plus the victim of a man who had followed her around in his car for nineteen months. Caty was also an emotionally immature, learning-disabled child who was more apt to freeze in terror than actively flee for her life. For Schaefer, she was the perfect victim.

Among the many tragedies of the Springfield child murders was the fact that everybody acted out his or her part with ballet-like precision. There were no false moves. Schaefer was afflicted with all of the symptoms of the prototypical serial killer. He was a loner, a man who was abused by and afraid of women, a hyperreligious individual who belonged to a cultlike Christian sect in which a strict, literal adherence to the Bible was its major precept. He admitted to having a drinking problem, and, furthermore, during the Deana Buxton rape, to which he confessed in 1983, he was under the influence of alcohol. Schaefer also had severe memory impairment to the point of blocking out the murders completely until months after incarceration, discussion with police and court officers, and different forms of counseling.

Gary Schaefer, like Henry Lee Lucas, Carlton Gary, and Wayne Williams in Atlanta, has become a symbol of the system and the local politics surrounding the serial murder crime and its impact upon the community. The serial murderer, once caught, becomes an important symbol of the way justice operates. A death sentence for serial killer Carlton Gary, for example, and the millions of dollars that the state of Georgia will spend arguing the sentence over the next eight to ten years throughout the appellate system, are far more important to the voters of Georgia than a summary guilty plea and a sentence of life imprisonment. For the prosecutor and the judge, the crimes against the matrons of Wynnton, though admittedly brutal, were far too heinous for them to come up with anything less than the strictest form of retribution under the law, even if that retribution might not be enacted for the next decade. The sentence itself was all that mattered because it was a political necessity. In this way, the murderer becomes a form of totem.

Wayne Williams was a similar gold mine for harried families of the victims of Atlanta. Although he was convicted only on circumstantial evidence in a case that involved the murder not of a child but of a young adult, Williams served as the focus for the fear and rage of an entire community. For the whites who administered the state's criminal justice system, Williams was conveniently black. For the black political establishment of Atlanta, Williams' conviction spared them from the specter of racially motivated violence had the perpetrator been a white. However, the Williams case may soon be reopened. He was too convenient, and at least one of the state's witnesses has recanted an important part of his testimony. The hunt for the Atlanta Child Murderer might have to begin all over again.

Perhaps the biggest firestorm of all has arisen over the revelations that Henry Lee Lucas has provided the Texas Rangers and state police from hundreds of jurisdictions across the country. Lucas' many confessions gave prosecutors the opportunity to close missing person cases that had been unsolved for years. Members of missing people's families were able, through Lucas' confessions to lay to rest their fears that a spouse or child might still be wandering in an unknown city. When the fears that Lucas had been prompted to confess to crimes that he had not committed surfaced, Lucas willingly admitted that he hadn't killed anyone except his mother. In other words, he became the person his interrogators wanted him to be. His reliability dropped commensurately.

Similarly, Gary Schaefer's case allowed the state to close the files on one additional murder and a rape. It solved the problem of the serial murders that had been threatening the Springfield area for five years. Gary Schaefer is off the street, and although he might be released sixteen years from now, after having undergone more than a decade of therapy at Leavenworth, for the present he represents a murderer who has been caught and convicted and cases that have been solved.

Schaefer, Lucas, Williams, Bundy, and Carlton Gary are all politically important to their respective jurisdictions because they all represent disproportionate threats to their communities. They have killed randomly; they have killed out of a compulsion that could make anyone into a victim. Consequently, the way the community adjudicates their cases is of vital importance to the sense of justice that keeps communities in balance. The serial murderer remains a threat to the community even after he is caught. His trial and sentence have to satisfy the victims' and the community's collective hunger for justice or neither the sense of loss nor the feeling of resolution will ever be satisfied.

The greater tragedy is that, because the serial murderer kills in such disproportionate numbers and because the community is paralyzed with fear throughout his reign of terror, the damage goes far beyond the families of the victims. Entire cities are traumatized when everyone becomes a potential victim. Even though the capture and conviction of the serial killer offers a resolution, people must come to realize that, for every serial killer who is finally caught, there are probably three more waiting to emerge.

6

The Police and the Serial Killer

Police homicide units are becoming increasingly more sophisticated in their investigations and tracking of serial murders. At first, detectives were strictly reactive. When a murder was reported, detectives gathered whatever evidence they could, traced the victim's identity, and tried to reconstruct the crime from what they could determine about the victim's movements during his or her final hours. If there were witnesses, they were interviewed also. Although this procedure works seven out of ten times in solving other types of homicide, it doesn't work so well in solving serial murder cases. The reason for this is simple: the serial murderer doesn't behave like other killers. His motive for murder is not dependent upon the particular situation or upon the individual victim; it is a chronic compulsion that drives him through an ever repeating pattern of violence.

The reactive homicide investigation depends upon the following to provide solutions to the crime: the weight of evidence, clues at the crime scene, the relationship between the victim and the murderer, involved witnesses or passersby, and finally the fear and guilt of the killer himself. In felony murder cases – in which the murder was committed as a secondary act – solving the first crime usually solves the murder case. Thus if someone were discovered during a breaking and entering, panicked, and killed the robbery victim, the clues that led the police to the burglar would also lead them to the murderer. The police in these cases will use informants to help them locate the stolen items. A large number of felony murders take place as adjuncts to drug deals that turned sour. These murders are also very traceable through informants or the network of street dealers in the neighborhood. Cases of family homicide or those in which the victims are related through friendship — these compose the largest single number of murders — usually rely on witnesses. Felony murders and family homicides also have well-defined motives that can be used to locate potential suspects. Once the police begin interrogating a suspect, a confession or arrest usually follows quickly.

Since 1980, however, almost twenty-five percent of all murders have been 'stranger' homicides in which the killer is not driven by any apparent rational motive and has no apparent connection with the victim. These serial murders are the ones in which the killer is compelled by forces beyond his control, and unless those forces are understood the killer eludes detection. Such cases are frustrating because the killer may be in the area for only a short time, run up a skein of victims, and move on. Worse, in rural areas that are not under the jurisdiction of a single municipal police department, many different jurisdictions might not routinely share information about unsolved homicides in their areas. The problems of one county sheriff are not the problems of the local police force in a different town. Hence, a killer might be seeking victims in three different counties in the same part of the country and never be the target of a combined task force investigation, until all of the homicide squads agree to pool their information.

Sometimes the connection between murders in different

locations is brought to the attention of homicide detectives not by the police but by outside concerned parties. In the Ted Bundy investigation, for example, the Seattle police had investigated and cleared Bundy on at least two separate occasions. Even after Elizabeth Kendall, his own fiancée, reported her suspicions to the police, the Seattle homicide detectives decided that Bundy was not a likely suspect. It was only after she informed them about a similar pattern of crimes taking place in the Salt Lake City area, where Bundy had relocated to attend law school, that they reopened the inquiry. Finally, after Bundy was charged in Salt Lake City with trying to elude police and being in possession of burglar's tools, the Seattle detectives began seriously to reconsider him as a suspect in the thirty-five murders of young women that had been unsolved for years.

It was through Elizabeth Kendall's assistance that Bob Keppel of the Seattle homicide squad was finally able to identify Bundy as the prime suspect in the area's unsolved murder cases. But Keppel never got his conviction. Bundy was convicted in Utah of the attempted kidnap of Carol DaRonch and was on trial for murder in Colorado when he escaped and fled to Florida. After Elizabeth Kendall read a news item about a rape murder in a sorority house on the University of Tallahassee campus, she notified the FBI that she thought the murderer might be Ted Bundy. They still didn't believe her and continued to doubt that he had gone to Florida until he was arrested there for the rape murder of a twelve-year-old girl.

In another case, the police and sheriffs' detectives in rural Texas were baffled by a string of murders along Route 35 until Henry Lee Lucas confessed to the crimes. His desire to conform to the wishes of the Texas authorities was so strong that he kept on confessing to murders he could not possibly have committed until, confronted with his own inconsistencies, Lucas recanted all of his confessions, even to the murders for which the police had corroborating evidence.

In felony murders, family homicides, and street crimes, the victim is often not isolated by the killer before the murder, nor is there usually any planned entrapment. The almost coincidental nature of the homicide is usually one of the factors that help the investigation along. This is especially true in felony murders when the killer never intended to kill the victim in the first place. In family murders that are committed out of passion or rage with little thought to the consequences, the abundance of clues, clarity of motive, presence of witnesses, and panic on the part of the murderer usually lead to a solution of the crime within twenty-four hours. The actual apprehension of the fleeing fugitive may take longer, but the weight of guilt acts as a ball and chain and usually forces the killer to turn himself in.

Getting confessions out of felony murderers and coincidental killers of friends or family members is also easier for the police to accomplish. Contrary to popular belief, most murderers do ultimately want to confess. It is only the hardened sociopath who is incapable of experiencing guilt and feels no need to express his remorse. The sociopathic serial killer falls into the twenty-five percent of all cases in which there is no prior personal connection between murderer and victim. The psychological basis for applying pressure on a potential murder suspect is not readily apparent. Even if the police have questioned the actual murderer during the course of the investigation, there is no immediate impetus for the murderer to reveal himself.

The crime scene itself is also a large issue in the success or failure of a murder investigation. Most crime scenes of typical homicide are not under the killer's control. Because he killed out of passion, fear, rage, or by accident, he was unable to isolate his victim or to make sure that there were no coincidental witnesses or passersby. In other words, he didn't consider clues. In most homicides, the medical examiner's autopsy on the recent victim provides invaluable clues that either help the police find the killer or at the very least shorten the list of potential suspects. As the former Los Angeles county coroner, Thomas Noguchi, has shown, the medical examiner's report indicates the probable cause of death, the probable time the death took place, whether that death was a homicide or the result of natural causes, and what weapons were most likely used. Medical examiners often advise police about the size and strength of the murder suspect, whether he or she is right- or left-handed, and whether the homicide was accidental, the result of a fit of passion, or premeditated. As Noguchi's examinations of the cases of Jean Harris, Claus Von Bulow, and Jeffery MacDonald have shown, a detailed and exacting medical examiner's report can provide the types of clues that can almost determine the outcome of the investigation right at the outset. However, the longer a body remains hidden, the harder it is for the medical examiner to find any clues that will identify a suspect. Also, if the body has been mutilated, cut into pieces, and/or buried for any length of time, it makes the investigator's job seemingly impossible.

Organized serial killers always maintain a high degree of control over their crime scenes. First, they familiarize themselves with the locale during the trolling phrase. They choose isolated spots where they can act out their fantasies in private. Second, they choose the likeliest spots for encountering potential victims. Side exits of shopping centres, streets that are particularly deserted during the night, bus stations where strangers tend not to be noticed, or lonely stretches of road adjoining populated sections of a town are the most common sites for serial killers. Third, they usually transport the victim or the victim's body to a different location for burial. This creates two crime scenes and often confuses the investigators until they either discover the common burial ground or establish a relationship between the scene of the abduction or murder and the burial site.

Leonard Lake and John Gacy maintained particularly strong control over their crime scenes. In Lake's case, the police weren't even aware of the existence of his crimes until they traced Lake's address through documents relating his ex-wife, Cricket Balazs, to her property in rural Calaveras County. There they found the bodies of persons who had previously been reported by their relatives as missing. John Gacy actually led a double life – a builder, happily married man, and member of many civic organizations, and a serial murderer – while he used the crawl space under his house as a burial ground. Henry Lee Lucas' murders were so random and committed in areas so rural that he often buried the bodies near where the crimes were committed. With the exception of Granny Rich, Lucas' final murder victim, the bodies were turning up as Jane Does ten years before he confessed to the crimes. In fact, until recently, Lucas had maintained that there were far more victims than have been discovered by the police, but that he had forgotten their descriptions or the locations of the crimes.

The serial killer's two most effective weapons are his mobility and his mask of normalcy. Essential to the serial killer's pathology is his compulsion to roam. He is a traveller who, although in his everyday life a resident of a particular city or town, during his episodes of limbic psychosis, seeks out places where the types of victims he preys on are available. John Gacy sought transient young boys with no connections to family or friends; thus the bus and train stations became his favourite haunts. Even if a serial murderer is killing in his own community, the number of murders that are committed within a specific time frame usually overwhelm the ability of the police to investigate each homicide properly. The amount of press coverage that a crime receives puts the police department's investigation squarely in the spotlight. Thus exposure actually helps a serial murderer to avoid detection. He simply changes his modus operandi for every crime. Finally, the fear that the murders arouse in the community has such a chilling effect on the public that the murderer is almost free to roam while the police spend their time calming fears, responding to crank confessions, and solving copycat murders. While the police are occupied in a particular community, the killer, who is never confined to a specific location, simply moves on to a neighboring municipality or state and continues his spree. He can always move back later. All the while, he monitors the police department's movements through reading the newspapers or listening to TV and radio news.

Because serial killers are sociopaths, they never develop empathic ties to their communities. For example, among Elizabeth Kendall's most shocking discoveries about Ted Bundy was the seemingly endless number of intimate girl friends and even fiancées who kept on turning up in Bundy's life, even though she and Bundy had been almost living together during their years in Seattle. Despite Bundy's repeated assurances, both verbally and in writing and both before and after his arrests in Utah and Florida, that he cared for Liz Kendall, he couldn't explain away the other women and continued to have relationships with them. Bundy was incapable of experiencing empathy for other people, especially those closest to him. This lack of empathy for individuals translates into a lack of empathy for the whole community as well. That is why a killer like Carlton Gary can be on the prowl in the neighborhoods of his own youth, committing murders, and yet not feel any guilt or remorse for the terror those murders are inflicting on the community at large. The same is true for the Atlanta Child Murderer, whether or not he is Wayne Williams, who witnessed the paralysis and confusion of Atlanta's black community while homicide investigators from more than half a dozen jurisdictions tried to solve the crimes.

Having no sympathies for the community means that the serial killer can easily live and work in any neighborhood, participate in community functions, and even, like John Gacy and Ted Bundy, be a community leader. This is an especially frightening aspect of the serial murderer syndrome because without any feelings of sympathy for the people he sees every day he is freed from the guilt that would eventually force the more traditional killer into giving himself up. A serial killer has no family and no friends. He perceives himself as a solitary stalker among his prey, fading into normalcy during the periods between his killing episodes, and emerging as a killer in response to electrochemical impulses deep in his limbic brain.

This same lack of sympathy enables him to wear a mask of normalcy as a camouflage. Gary Schaefer not only lived and worked among religious and family-oriented people in rural Vermont, he was a member of the Christadelphians. The members of this sect lived according to the fundamentalist interpretation of the Bible. Yet Gary Schaefer, whose family belonged to this church as well, lived the double life of a rapist and serial killer of young girls and a member of the church brotherhood. He lived this way until the very day he was arrested.

To most people, it is appalling that a person who was most trusted as a normal, civic-minded individual can turn out to be a serial killer. This aspect of the syndrome always baffles the police. Detective Keppel had Ted Bundy under investigation on at least two occasions and dismissed him from consideration twice – once after a Seattle girl reported that on the very day a murder had taken place she had been requested by a man named Ted who drove a VW Beetle and had a cast on his arm to help him load his boat onto a luggage rack and drive it back to his residence. She thought him just a bit 'strange,' she told homicide detectives later, and begged off. It was only after she read of the discovery of the body that she telephoned the police to tell them that it was likely she had been accosted by the murderer. One of Bundy's professors actually reported him to the police. The faculty member told the Seattle homicide detectives that he drove a VW. The police noted that Bundy was a prelaw student, had no prior police record, had been active in local politics and worked for some Republican candidates. He had also worked for local community and student groups. As a member of the community, he was a student whose schedules were highly structured, he had a steady long-term heterosexual relationship with a young woman whose daughter from a previous marriage lived with her, and he was well liked. He was too normal, they thought, clearly not the type of person who would go on a murder spree. Yet again and again his name was brought up, and this time by the very person he had been dating. The police questioned her but found that Bundy had not threatened her or her daughter and, in fact, had been the person who was more 'in control' than she was. Liz Kendall didn't take no for an answer. After she found plaster cast material in Bundy's closet she called the police again. But again the police refused to consider him as a suspect. He was just too normal.

A serial killer is a roamer. He eludes police detection and is always ten steps ahead of any pursuit. Or, when a serial killer is an upstanding normal member of the community whose comings and goings are on public exhibit, the police often don't waste their time investigating him. Almost all of the serial killers fit into one or the other category or even both at the same time. Carlton Gary, for example, was a roamer, dropping in, then out of society, and yet he was dating a female uniformed officer from the sheriff's department who was unaware of his activities while he was committing the Wynnton murders. Even though Gary had a police record, was a fugitive from other jurisdictions, and was dealing in cocaine and heroin, he was still able to maintain the semblance of a relatively normal heterosexual relationship.

Bobby Joe Long's description of the final days before his arrest exemplify the serial killer's well-tuned sense of survival. Long knew that because of the growing public clamor over the North Tampa murders the police were patrolling the area in greater numbers. He also knew that his own pattern of crimes, the places where he found his victims, and the types of victims he chose were a matter of public record. He had read about them in the newspaper. He also heard on the news that local and state authorities had formed a task force to catch him. 'At that point, I could have gone to Miami or even back to California,' he later explained from his cell on death row. 'I could have gone back to West Virginia for a visit. I could simply have walked away from Tampa and stopped picking up girls there, and I'd still be a free man today because the police had no idea who or where I was until I let McVay go and she went to the police.' Even then, he explains, he could have fled the area, but he didn't. He was steps ahead of the police. He was caught because he wanted to get caught. He wanted the murder spree that was killing him as well as his victims to stop, but he couldn't stop it himself. What is most important, however, is that the police couldn't stop him until he revealed his whereabouts to the task force by releasing his next to last victim. Then and only then did the police have the clues to establish his identity.

The critical factor that most police investigators fail to understand is that a serial killer is not an individual who has reached an equilibrium or who is in any type of stasis. He is a person with a disease in a process of development whose symptoms are changing. The skein of serial murders is just the penultimate stage of that disease. The final stage is his own suicide. Like a caterpillar that transforms into a moth that transforms into a butterfly, the serial killer also transforms. As a child, he is a mere victim. Like Charles Manson and Henry Lee Lucas, he is rejected by parents, deprived of any intimacy and sensory stimulation, beaten, malnourished, and abused. In extreme cases the child's own sense of self is so distorted that it is never established until much later in his adult life, if at all. It is interesting, for example, to see that two of the most infamous serial murderers in our study, Henry Lee Lucas and Charles Manson, were both forced to attend the first day of school dressed as girls because their parents or guardians felt it would be for their own ultimate good.

In his childhood, the serial killer acquires many of the scars he will later inflict on his future victims. If his deepest fears are aroused by a hatred of his father and a hatred of his own masculinity, he most likely will be a killer of young boys. Like John Wayne Gacy, he will act out an endless ritual of killing the boy that he was and torturing that source of weakness within himself. If it is his hatred of his mother and the fear of femininity within him that are aroused, he will most likely be a woman killer. Bobby Joe Long killed women he characterized as whores and sluts, women who, he said, manipulated men with their bodies. Although she has consistently denied that, Long claims that his mother had had sex with other men in the room where he as a child was sleeping and that she even forced him to sleep in the same bed with her until he was twelve. Or, like Gary Schaefer, if there was a little girl who aroused him, during torture he will become a killer of little girls and act out a ritual that was a part of his childhood fantasy of violent revenge.

Sometimes, as a child, the serial killer experiences physical injuries like concussions, fractures of the skull, and other forms of head trauma. He may have a genetic defect or a birth defect as a result of an accident during the pregnancy. Whatever the cause of the problem, this is a child who can have a disorder of the limbic region of the brain. It is serious enough that it will impair the way the primal neurological circuit functions for the rest of his life. It may result in a dyslexia, a reasoning or cognitive disorder, a form of deep psychomotor epilepsy, or a lesion in the hypothalamus that affects the body's hormone system. The child will not be able to control his rage. He will display extraordinary or inappropriate violence with almost no regard for those around him. He might be antisocial and extremely unhappy. He often will be accident prone, with an especially high risk of head injuries as he gets older. Finally, he will experience difficulties in perception and learning that will make his elementary school years a period of unbearable torture. In the schoolyard pecking order, he will be near the bottom, living in his own private hell.

This child will also be at high risk of confrontations with the juvenile justice system. He will display extreme cruelty to animals, excessive violence toward younger children and his younger siblings. He may be a fire starter who has no regard for the personal property of others. He will always be at the centre of accidents, collisions in the halls, or falls in the gym or schoolyard. This is the first emergence of the syndrome that may later claim the lives of five, ten, or three hundred victims before it claims the life of its carrier.

It is easy to lose track of a serial killer-as-child because he will have developed an uncanny knack for becoming invisible and fading into the background. Once he becomes aware of his own accident proneness, he will overcorrect for it and learn how to appear and disappear with as little fanfare as possible. However, the physio-logical forces set in motion during fetal, newborn, and early childhood periods will continue to develop. The malformation of his limbic brain, the disorder in the hypothalamus, or the discharges of electricity from his temporal lobe will continue to alter his behaviour. It will seem to him as if he is living out certain fantasies, he will find himself talking out loud to persons who exist only within his own mind, or he will find himself strangely unable to react to certain situations. He might not be able to make directional decisions and literally go in circles while deciding which way he wants to go. If he makes a choice, it will invariably be the wrong choice, and he will ultimately shrink from making any choices. But he will have his greatest difficulties when he tries to relate to other people. He may grow to hate girls because they are threats, and he may hate members of his own sex because he can't express the sexual feelings he has for them. While other preadolescents begin to explore relationships with one another, this preadolescent will retreat. Henry Lee Lucas was routinely killing animals and having sex with their carcasses by the time he was ten, and he had sex with his brother shortly thereafter. He committed his first rape murder when he was only fifteen. As a ten-year-old, Carlton Gary was already on the run, seeking out his mother and turning up unannounced at his uncle's Army base hundreds of miles away from Columbus, Georgia. He was already a street hoodlum by the time he was ten, robbing stores and starting fires. He had been tagged by the local police as a 'bad kid' before he reached his teens.

Charles Manson was in and out of reformatories before he reached his teens. He spent most of his life in jails and reform schools. He was beaten by guards, assaulted by other prisoners, and humiliated by every institution society could bring to bear. When one considers that Manson never had a father figure even remotely present except in jail, and that his mother was more often in jail for hustling sex than with her child, it is no wonder that Manson was at an extremely high risk of confrontations with the criminal justice system even before he turned thirteen. Like Henry Lee Lucas, Manson claims that he was punished, abused, and made to do things that no human being should ever be made to do. With no external structure that they could internalize, these two cult figures of modern murder were beyond anybody's definition of insanity by the time they were adults.

As Bobby Joe Long was reaching puberty, his body began to transform before his very eyes from that of a young boy into that of a young girl. Long, like many other members of his family, suffered from a chromosomal disorder, similar to Klinefelter's syndrome, that caused his glands to produce excessive amounts of estrogens that resulted in an enlargement of his breasts. Associated with an extra X chromosome on the male gene, disorders like Klinefelter's syndrome are also associated with different forms of psychological gender reversal, perceptual difficulties, and learning disorders. Long had an operation to remove the six pounds of extra tissue from his breasts, but his sexual disorientation continued, supported by his mother's manipulative behaviour and her sharing the same bed with her son. It wasn't until Long was thirteen and reaching masculine puberty that he no longer shared a bed with his mother. However, at thirteen, Long met the woman who would later become his wife. Thus, Bobby Joe long was nurtured by two women: his mother and his wife-to-be; and at age thirteen his mother handed her son off to his wife-to-be. Eleven years later Long became known as the 'Classified Ad Rapist' and assaulted more than fifty women in the Miami-Dade area. Less than ten years after that he would commit nine rape murders, bludgeoning his victims to death after raping them, driving around with the corpses still in his car, and burying them in shallow graves.

Almost all serial murderers have had a conflict with the juvenile or criminal justice authorities during their teenage years. After a period of incarceration or psychological hibernation during which the sexual and violent fantasies of the teenager often become full-blown hallucinatory experiences, the sexually aroused serial murderer emerges. He may begin by committing a series of rapes, as Bobby Joe Long did, or by tiptoeing up to the crime as Bundy did at first. Yet, ultimately, he will cross the line and commit his first murder. From that point on, driven by fear of what is within him as well as fear of the police who are pursuing the crime, the serial murderer eludes detection until the weight of his own morbidity causes him to collapse from within. For some serial killers, the fantasy itself must break, as it did for Henry Lee Lucas after the murder of his common-law wife, for Kallinger after the murder of his younger son, or for Long after the assault on Karen McVay. For some, like Charles Manson, the fantasy still hasn't broken.

What is important about this developmental process of the serial murderer from the police investigator's point of view is that it is impossible to see a complete picture of the criminal's motivation until well after he has been apprehended and diagnosed. The police might well have had this individual in custody once, twice, or perhaps twenty times over the course of his life, but they have failed to see the connection. Certainly Carlton Gary was well known to the Columbus police as Carlton Gary but not as the Stocking Strangler. The present police training focuses on the traditional murderer who is not compelled to murder, and who flees because he fears the police and prosecution. The serial murderer often seeks the very form of capital punishment that is being held over his head as a deterrent. He goes on committing enough crimes to ensure his own destruction.

The police have only the facts surrounding a murder on which to build their investigation. If it is an isolated murder, the case may go unsolved for years because the police won't be able to connect it with the ten or fifteen murders that have preceded it in other locations. If it is the first of a series of murders within a particular jurisdiction, the police often have to wait for a break in the case before they can solve anything. The breaks usually come only by chance. For example, even though the similarities between the murders in Seattle and the murders in Salt Lake City had prompted Bob Keppel to begin working with his homicide department counterparts in Utah on investigating Ted Bundy, this was the only common thread in both sets of murders. It wasn't until Bundy was arrested for trying to elude police and searched that he finally became implicated in both sets of murders. Keppel put all of the pieces together at that point, but he never arrested Bundy or got a confession. If the state of Florida has its way and executes Bundy for the murder of a twelve-year-old girl, Keppel will never prosecute him for the Seattle murders and neither will the homicide detectives who pursued him in Utah.

A homicide investigator looking over a crime scene must make a quick evaluation of the type of murderer he is dealing with. First, he must determine whether or not the murderer felt sufficiently in control of the scene to spend time there or whether he felt he had to flee immediately after committing the crime. A good detective will try to determine whether the scene had been arranged in anticipation of the victim or whether it was coincidental. If there are multiple crime scenes, an investigator looks for similarities among them. Both of Gary Schaefer's rape murders, for example, took place along similar stretches of deserted highway near where the victims lived. The victims of the Green River murders outside Seattle were all buried along the banks of the riverside, and the victims of the Hillside Strangler were all from the same Los Angeles suburb and buried in the hills just outside the city.

THE POLICE AND THE SERIAL KILLER

The police want to know if the murderer felt confident enough to spend time at the crime scene or whether he felt he had to hit and run. Most serial killers, police have found, are in complete control of the murder scene and spend the necessary time there to perform whatever rituals they must both before the victim's death and afterward. If the body has been placed in strange positions, either spreadeagled on the ground or propped upright – all of this can be determined from an autopsy and a thorough examination of the corpse – then the killer was confident enough that he would not be discovered. If the victim did not seem to have put up a struggle, then it is likely that she either knew the killer or that the killer gained her trust before the murder. If the victim has been mutilated, it is important to determine just when the mutilation took place. If the killer had to murder the victim first, then he was afraid to face her alive. If the multilation took place as a death ritual, then the ritual was an attempt to gain power over the victim.

Did the killer rape the victim before murdering her or afterward? This is one of the most crucial questions for the police because it helps them profile the killer. The killer who rapes his victims first and then murders them can maintain more control over them than the killer who has sex with victims only after they are dead. In the former cases, investigators surmise, once the thrill of the rape has passed, the killer is disgusted with himself more than with the victim. He tries to eradicate this revulsion by killing the victims, burying them, and erasing the crime. This is a killer who is perhaps a charmer, an individual who might woo his female victims into accompanying him somewhere before subduing them or tying them up. This most closely approximates the ways Ted Bundy, Carlton Gary, and Bobby Joe Long killed their victims. On the other hand, the killer who strikes first, takes the bodies to a remote location, and then has sex with the victims is less in control. He can face neither his victims nor the act of having sex with them. Therefore he kills first and performs whatever rituals he must after his victims' deaths.

If victims seem to be missing without a trace, then it is likely that the killer is exercising such control over the crime that the bodies might not be found for months. A news report of a discovered grave might be the event that triggers a flight reaction in the killer, sending him to a different location. On the other hand, the serial killer might like to keep the crime alive in his memory by reading about the dead victim in the newspapers and even visiting the site where he first found his victim. When many murders have been committed at the same site, it is likely that the killer periodically returns there even when he has no victim to kill. These are the types of clues police investigators must look for when searching for a serial killer.

If the killings took place quickly and without much ritual before the event, police surmise that the murderer is young, perhaps in his twenties, and that he wants to get the crime over with quickly. The murder itself is equated with a sudden orgasm so that the killer can experience it in reflection. Killers who take a long time with their victims are usually older, perhaps in their thirties or even early forties. They know what they are doing and have done it many times before.

How tentative was the murderer with the female corpse? Did the autopsy reveal semen inside the vagina or was it on the insides of the victim's thighs and around her pubic area? Did the killer achieve orgasm by actually having sex with the victim either before or after death, or did he simply ejaculate out of anticipation and then proceed to kill his victim in rage? By examining whether there were any signs of a struggle, investigators can determine whether the killer achieved his orgasm on the body after the murder or whether the act of struggling jolted the criminal into orgasm. These are two vital clues in creating the profile of the killer that will be used in interviews with witnesses and friends of the victim.

It is now clear to homicide specialists that most serial killers come from broken homes, that they were abused as children, and that the abuse came primarily from one parent. The degree of the intimidation and the type of destructive feelings the killer has for himself are usually manifested in some similar physical abuse of their victims. Ed Kemper was so intimidated by the sound of his mother's voice that after he killed her he cut off her head, removed her vocal cords, burned them, and put the remains down the garbage disposal.

If the killings and crime scene are all in the same area, it is likely that the killer is also from the same area. Police interrogators might have already interviewed the killer or might have had him in custody at one time and released him. Armed with a preliminary profile of the killer's personality, the police will fan out and interview all the residents in the area for descriptions of any strangers people might have noticed. They also look for anyone whose reactions conform to the profile they have developed. If the killer has been profiled as a white male in his twenties who seems to attack his victims and have sex with them after they are dead, the police will be looking for a shy person, perhaps someone who lives with his mother, who cannot easily confront them. If they find such a person they will direct the questioning toward his background, asking him where he was on the nights the murders were committed, asking for the names of people who can corroborate his whereabouts, and eventually try to shake a confession out of him. They understand what he must be going through, especially if he is going to kill again. They suggest that, by coming to the police, he will prevent himself from killing again and will get help. Police expect that that line of questioning will eventually pull a confession out of a suspect. However, when dealing with a fully emerged serial killer, the police are usually mistaken. Even the shyest and most disturbed serial killer would tend not to confess unless he was ready to end his own torment. He would instead become invisible, and if probed too hard he would leave the area.

The best weapon the police have against a serial murderer's sprees is their behavior profile. The psychological or behavioral profile, inaccurate as it may be, gives investigators the following basis from which to begin: it tells them whether to look for a younger man or an older one, a charmer who manipulates women or a withdrawn individual who kills almost immediately, a white man or a black man, a heterosexual or a bisexual, and finally whether it is a person who lives nearby or a transient who has just turned up in the community. Some profiles are so accurate that they lead police directly to a person they've already interrogated. Many times, as in the case of Albert DeSalvo, the Boston Strangler, they're not. Items such as body parts or specific articles of clothing that are missing from the victims are other key pieces to the puzzle. The killer may collect memorabilia from his victims, or he may have kept detailed records of each one of his murders in diary form. A serial killer is likely to have some perceptual disorder or learning dysfunction as well. The behavior profile might include the fact that the person is unable to spell or may routinely reverse letters. A sample of handwriting or any indication that the person has a learning disorder, a body tic or jerky movement, or a propensity to become easily rattled and short-tempered is noted in the profile. If the killer is especially savage with respect to the bodies of his female victims, police should look for evidence of feminine physical traits on the suspect. Does he have especially fine hair? Does he have an elongated or disproportionate body shape for a man? Are his features disproportionately delicate? This kind of hatred of the killer's own physical traits usually translates itself into the most horrific forms of mutilation of the dead victim.

With these behavior profiles in hand, homicide detectives can begin looking back over the people they've already interrogated in connection with other murders and as potential witnesses to this crime. If that proves unsuccessful, they can circulate their profile of the killer to other neighbouring jurisdictions and, of course, to the FBI to see whether unsolved murders by a person with a similar profile have been committed elsewhere.

The special task force is another administrative weapon police routinely use. If the crime is gruesome enough and if no leads to the crime turn up quickly, the police will assemble a special homicide task force. They might also assemble such a force immediately if the type of victim chosen, such as a child who has been sexually assaulted and mutilated as well as murdered, leads police to believe that this person will strike again in the community. The task force usually consists of detectives assigned to specific tasks: interviewing witnesses, fanning out and gathering information from people who live nearby or who knew the victim, responding to tips on the special phone number, gathering information from other jurisdictions, working with the FBI or other federal authorities, securing the crime scenes and going over the results with the forensics specialists, releasing information to the press, and coordinating with the district attorney's office. By combining the efficiency and maximum effort of a mobilized task force with the advantages of the psychobehavioral profile of the probable suspect, police are better able to marshal their resources against a killer who is psychotically motivated and protected only by his animal instincts of survival.

Finally, it is vital that police routinely utilize the power of electronic information gathering and retrieval. By computerizing modi operandi and establishing a national on-line network of missing persons and unsolved murder cases, police are able to compare similar cases not only among neighboring jurisdictions but across the entire country. A killer like Henry Lee Lucas, who thrived on the inability of police forces to cooperate on investigations from state to state, would be effectively thwarted because his possible whereabouts would be indicated by the similar types of crimes he committed. In fact, some criminologists have suggested that, if a national homicide task force were provided with the computerized reports of unsolved murders around the country, at least two thirds of those cases would be solved within the month. It took the kidnapping and murder of nine-year-old Adam Walsh and the efforts of his parents to create a national information hot line for missing children. Before that time, tracking missing children was a painstaking hit-or-miss process. Now there is at least some attempt to maintain an on-line information service similar to the services that track stolen vehicles and other property By expanding this same kind of data management and retrieval operation to unsolved murder cases, the police will be able to perceive patterns in the movements of possible suspects.

One of the most important recent developments in the battle against the spread of serial murder has been the formation of the FBI's Behavioral Science Unit in Quantico, Virginia. This is largely an information-gathering, processing, and dissemination facility that profiles probable suspects in murder cases. The unit was established with police officer Pierce Brooks, an LAPD homicide detective expert in the formation of special task forces, and Seattle detective Bob Keppel, who had spent four years in an unsuccessful pursuit of Ted Bundy. After having solved a serial murder case involving an American Indian torture ritual, Brooks realized that homicide squads needed a national information clearing house of unsolved homicides stored on a large central computer that could be accessed by local police departments. Such a database, he felt, would serve two purposes: it would help police find patterns to homicides they couldn't solve locally and it would alert them to serial killers who might be headed toward their jurisdictions. Although he tried to sell this idea to police chiefs around the country and to the federal government in 1967, he had no luck until he met Bob Keppel during the investigation of the Atlanta Child Murders in the 1970s.

At that time both Brooks and Keppel had been called in as consultants to the Atlanta Police Department to help form a task force to investigate the current wave of killings. The two detectives realized that their experiences as well as their work in Atlanta indicated a need for some type of national organization to manage information regarding serial killers and to get this data to the homicide detectives who were acting as front-line investigators. In 1981 the FBI agreed with Brooks and Keppel that the epidemic of serial murders showed no signs of abating, and the two detectives were hired as consultants to the Behavioral Science Unit it had established.

The Unit's first assignment was to begin developing behavioral profiles of killers. Special agents trained in social and behavioral sciences interviewed scores of apprehended serial killers to learn their methods and motivations and to establish the common patterns that appeared from criminal to criminal. They matched these to a killer's own confessions and revelations after he had been convicted and was serving time in prison. What the Unit learned about serial killings was enough to alert them to a far greater danger than either Brooks, Keppel, or the investigators imagined when they first started collecting data. First, they determined that, in order to profile the killer, they needed to profile the victim. As in the cases of Bobby Long and Ted Bundy, the first rape/murder victim usually sets the pattern for the entire series of crimes.

Long attacked only women who seemed to be prostitutes or hustlers. He used their preying on him to lure them into his car. In many ways they reminded him of his mother and his ex-wife, both manipulative women who dominated Long and his father. Bundy killed pretty coeds who reminded him of the fiancée who had rejected him years earlier. She, in turn, represented his mother, who had rejected him by giving him up for adoption, a fact that he never came to accept. Both of these men fit a pattern of serial rape/murderers: they did not emerge full-blown as killers, all of their crimes had discernible patterns, the clues that were present in their personalities and their pasts were readily observable to the trained eye, and they both had clearly reached out for help earlier in their lives before they began their killing sprees. And in an interesting footnote to these two cases, both of them changed their modi operandi toward the end of their killing sprees, possibly in an attempt to get caught and end their respective miseries.

It was this Behavioral Science Unit that first revealed how serial killers are compulsive trollers who travel in ever widening patterns to locate their victims. This trolling pattern appears very early in their careers, well before their first rapes or murders are committed, and is usually an indicator of escalating violence in the future. Neurologists have since established that the trolling pattern is actually a physiological mechanism within the limbic part of the brain that sets the individual in motion. He may be hallucinating during the trolling process, feeding himself with delusions of his own grandeur or hatred of others, or fantasizing about the sexual encounters he is seeking. The need to be on the move is one of the most important early indicators of a person predisposed to episodic violence. This fact alone was very important to the Unit.

The Unit also discovered that the serial killer has a clear history of abuse and that he was the victim of considerable abuse as a child, usually by his mother. Kenneth Bianchi (the Hillside Strangler), Ed Kemper, Henry Lee Lucas, Charles Manson, and Ed Gein – the model for Alfred Hitchcock's *Psycho* – all received extraordinary abuse from the dominant female figures in their lives with no male figure to exercise control or to whom they could turn. The male figure, especially in the case of Henry Lee Lucas, was so weak that the mother might have routinely abused him as well. In Carlton Gary's and Charles Manson's cases, the father was completely absent.

The Unit also detailed the types of sadism and brutality that serial killers, or 'lust murderers,' as they call them, display toward their victims. Because they themselves are afraid of the sex they want to engage in, they have sex with their victims only after they are bound, unconscious, or dead. Like Carlton Gary and Bobby Long, who strangled their victims into submission first, most lust killers can't confront the act of sex with a live, functioning person. Henry Lee Lucas routinely killed his victims first and had sex with different parts he had cut off their bodies. These killers don't see their victims as real or complete human beings, they are only carcasses, body parts that arouse the killers to an erotic fury. Whether it be the victim's breast, buttocks, genitalia, or other part of the body, it is what the victim represents that matters and not who the victim is.

And finally, the Unit's data revealed that serial killings are only one point in the life of a criminal who has been escalating toward this level of violence for many years. They stressed that individuals who may start off as voyeurs or peeping Toms and eventually break into women's homes to steal undergarments or similar artifacts can be considered candidates for serial killers in the future. Because the thrill of one level of arousal is too minimal to continue the stimulation, the individual requires an even greater 'high.' The theft of an article of clothing may be subordinated to a ritual in which the thief becomes an assailant and fondles the victim before stealing the garment. His fear of discovery or capture, however, may be too great, and he finds he must subdue his victim first before making sexual contact. When that fails to arouse him to his previous level, he will actually assault the victim before raping her, strangling her into submission or knocking her unconscious and then escaping. Finally, the full-blown serial killer will emerge, and his victims will be doomed by the random nature of their appearance during his violent episodes.

The Unit also found that a serial killer's cycles are much like a menstrual cycle. He drifted between episodes based upon his arousal and the need he felt to satisfy it. Actually, what the Unit still hasn't discovered is that the cycles are not *like* menstrual cycles, they are *forms* of a menstrual cycle in which the hormones responsible for arousal, violence, fear, and anxiety are generated according to a rhythm established in the hypothalamus. For those individuals who experience forms of psychomotor epilepsy or limbic psychosis, the cycles of behavior are akin to deep brain seizures that alter perception and behavior without physically incapacitating the individual. Bobby Joe Long reported that because of his actually growing woman's breasts when he was reaching puberty he was able to tell when the moon was full without looking at the night sky or consulting a calendar. He went on to explain that even on death row in the Florida state penitentiary the killers who cannot see the sky know when the moon is full because they begin to howl and fight among themselves. Since the menstrual cycle itself is controlled by hormones, it is natural that, if the area of the brain that controls normal hormonal function in the ductless glands is malfunctioning, the body's normal hormonal control system will malfunction as well.

To date the Behavioral Science Unit has consulted on hundreds of heretofore unsolvable murder cases and has provided police with accurate profiles of the potential suspects. It is still gathering information from interviews of apprehended serial killers and is computerizing their profiles and MOs. By disseminating these profiles and MOs to local departments and homicide squads, the FBI will begin to make a significant contribution to the tracking down of serial killers. However, until the juvenile justice system is brought into the same arena, and schools and emergency room doctors are made aware of the types of symptoms that show up early in a potential serial killer's life, law enforcement will only be playing a never ending game of catch-up with the problem instead of actually preventing it from spreading. This is why the Surgeon General cited the escalating levels of violent crime as one of the major issues of public health confronting American society. When the FBI and other government agencies that routinely deal with serial murderers and other forms of episodic violence turn their attention to preventing the violence before it becomes a crime, the corner will have been turned.

The Personal Statements of Five Serial Killers:

Stories of Their Lives and Crimes in Their Own Words

Henry Lee Lucas, Carlton Gary, Bobby Joe Long, Leonard Lake, and Charles Manson were all prolific killers during their careers. Each of their life stories typifies the basic constellation of physiological, psychological, chemical, and social patterns that point to the disease of serial murder. Each of their backgrounds illustrates a history of some degree of physical and emotional child abuse or negative parenting. Each personal statement reveals a medical history of varying degrees of head injury or diagnosed damage to the critical areas of the brain that control primal behavior responses or reasoning ability. With the exception of Leonard Lake, each serial killer on this list has a documented history of alcohol or drug dependence, with Lucas and Manson virtually living on chemical substances throughout most of their adult lives. Lake was a child of an adult alcoholic.

Tragically, each serial killer's life is out of his control. Lucas and Manson were so thoroughly abused during their early years that it is a wonder they even survived. And Lucas, Manson, and Gary spent the majority of their years in some form of juvenile or correctional institution. These men remember very little of a happy home life or family bliss whatsoever. When at home they were subjected alternately to severe beatings or absolute neglect. Their parents inverted the normal meanings of good and bad so that the children were told that all the evil things they were experiencing at home or in institutions were ultimately for their own good. Even Bobby Joe Long, who was not severely beaten as a child, was emotionally manipulated by his mother, who forced him to share a bed with her until he was thirteen. When Bobby wasn't in bed with her, one of her many lovers was, he claims, and Bobby was forced to compete with him.

Each of the killers on our list has manifested some form of congenital damage. Both Lucas and Long suffer from some form of gender misidentification. Lucas was made to dress up like a girl by his mother, who was a prostitute, and Long's hormone imbalance actually caused him to grow breast tissue, which had to be removed surgically, and to experience the emotional swings typical of a menstrual cycle. Even in prison, Long reports that his personality changes according to the lunar cycle each month.

Carlton Gary, Leonard Lake, Henry Lucas, and Charles Manson all evidence some form of learning dysfunction associated with congenital neurological defects. And Carlton Gary's webbed fingers and elongated middle toe are additional examples of the type of congenital disorder that can, given the other physiological, psychological, and social factors, result in a life of episodically violent behavior.

Each killer whose statement appears in this section has experienced the phases of the serial murderer in his own unique way. Lucas reveals that he had a long period of hallucinations during which he lost touch with reality while he was in prison in Michigan. He heard his dead mother's voice telling him to commit suicide and to commit murder, and when he asked for help from the prison medical authorities his request was turned down. Lucas, who claims that he was transformed into a lust killer in prison, spent periods during the next two decades constantly trolling for new victims. Always on the edge of violence, he explains that his killing episodes were always preceded by periods of heavy drinking after which he became almost stuporous. It was in this semistupor that he committed the vast majority of his homicides.

Lucas sought out hitchhikers, travelers, or other people who had become isolated by virtue of their being on the road. By offering them rides or striking up conversations at roadside service stations, he would make his first contact. Then, under the guise of offering a ride or giving directions, Lucas was able to lure his victim into his power. Once in his car, the victim was helpless. Lucas struck quickly, usually with his knife, killing his victim and having sex with the corpse. Then he buried the person in a shallow grave or jammed the body into a roadside culvert.

In those instances when Lucas had some attachment to the victim, he often tried to preserve a part of the body as a totem and visited the grave after the murder. However, his memory between episodes was affected by alcohol as well as by the extensive damage to his brain. During his recantation phase he alternated between amnesia and hyperamnesia – the memory of specific, tiny details that are dissociated from the larger event, which has always been forgotten.

Lucas claims his murders were always followed by periods of depression. He was never able to sustain the murder high, and, lapsing into subsequent alcoholic stupors, he trolled for his victims from Georgia to California. The depression finally became unbearable after he murdered Becky Powell, his common-law wife. He resolved never to murder again, but the next Sunday he killed Kate Rich, an old woman he had worked for as a day laborer. After he was arrested on a weapons charge in Texas months later, Lucas confessed to the Powell and Rich murders and to more than three hundred additional homicides in more than twenty-five states. He has since recanted his confessions and then recanted his recantation, but authorities still suspect him of more than a hundred murders. Lucas is on death row in Huntsville prison in Texas.

Bobby Joe Long's personal statement reveals that, although he was dominated by women throughout his life, he never struck back until after receiving severe head injuries in a motorcycle accident. He became hypersexual and fantasized about having continuous intercourse with every woman he encountered. Although he reported this symptom to his Army doctors, they dismissed it, and Long was not given any treatment. His newly discovered sexual dependence on women dovetailed with his lifelong emotional dependence on mother figures. Shortly after his divorce he became a rapist who lured victims into his trap by answering ads in the classified section of the local newspaper. This was his particular method of trolling. He would call the phone number in the listing, and if a woman's voice answered the phone, his sexual fantasies were aroused. He made an appointment to visit the seller. Once his victim was isolated with him in her house, he sprung his trap. He was not excessively violent at first. He threatened the victim with a knife, then simply tied her up, told her that he wouldn't have used the knife even if she had screamed. Long explains that he never consciously wanted to hurt his victims but that he felt compelled to commit the rapes by a force inside of him. He never understood it but was greatly afraid that the crimes would escalate unless he was able to muster the power to control his sexual urges.

As Miami's 'Classified Ad Rapist,' Long committed more than fifty assaults. During this period he also dated and lived with different women. Yet his sexual fantasies only became worse, and he found himself having delusions of violence as well. Finally he began a spree of murders in North Tampa's red-light district.

Feeling compelled to begin driving along the strip of singles bars outside of North Tampa in a hunt for a sexual companion, Long did not realize at first that he would be committing a murder. He was trolling, looking for girls who would be easy pickups for one night. His first murder even took him by surprise, he claims. He was picked up at one of the bars by a young Oriental woman who had actually lured him into a liaison. Once he had her isolated in his car, he turned on her and strangled her until she lost consciousness. The trap was sprung. Then he tied her up, took her to a deserted area outside the city, raped her, strangled her to death, and buried her. He fantasized about raping her for a short period after the crime, then the fantasies grew to a fever pitch once again and he went out trolling for another victim.

With each subsequent victim, picked up in exactly the same way in one of the singles bars, he became more and more depressed. He knew he was sick and needed help, yet he claims that he could not stop himself. When he tried to prevent himself from going out, he became so aroused that when he surrendered to the urgings he was more violent than he had been previously. And after each crime he felt depressed because he could not recover the feelings of sexual passion that had driven him to commit the crime. Finally, like Henry Lee Lucas, he left enough clues to allow the police to find him, and he began confessing to his crimes as soon as he was in custody.

Bobby Long kept a detailed newspaper clipping file about each of his crimes. These were his totems: by reliving the event through the news reports, he tried to recapture the feeling of passion and arousal that had almost, but never quite, satisfied his lust. When the totems and fantasies lost their power he would begin trolling along the same strip of bars for young women. With each crime, however, his depression over his own situation became more intense. When he was finally arrested, he explained, he felt a great relief that his life as a serial murderer had come to an end. He explained that he knew exactly what he was but that he had no control over the feelings that came upon him. He still believes that, had he received the help he needed when he requested it, the murders and the rapes might never have taken place. Bobby Joe Long received the death penalty and is on death row in Stark, Florida.

Carlton Gary experienced the phases of a serial murderer through phantom figures that he generated in his own mind. Like the other killers in this section, he was a severely abused and malnourished child who exhibited homicidally violent tendencies very early in his life. His pattern of trolling for victims, first as a mugger, then as a rapist, and finally as a killer, emerged very early. Like Long and Lucas, Gary complained to prison or medical authorities that he had visions of violent sex which he knew would soon drive him to a series of killings. His pleas for help were ignored. When he returned to his hometown of Columbus, a fugitive from New York, he plotted what he termed a series of robberies at the homes of elderly white women in the Wynnton section of the city.

Gary's confessions reveal that he was at the scene of every crime. However, he claims that he witnessed the crimes as they were committed by another person. Therefore, while never actually confessing to the homicides, Carlton Gary was able to reveal the details of the crimes as a witness and to provide the police with the facts they needed to charge him as the Stocking Strangler. Gary admitted to having mental blackouts and to using drugs. His statements to the Columbus police, however, reveal a person who has abstracted himself from the crimes so as to avoid the immediacy of the act.

Henry Lee Lucas in the county jail in Georgetown, Texas. He is posing here for a picture taken for *Life* magazine with a portrait he drew of his beloved 'sister' Clemmie. (Cuba)

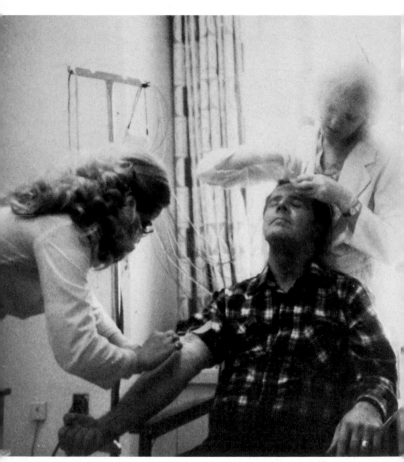

Lucas undergoing EEG testing. (Cuba)

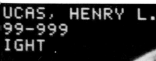

LUCAS, HENRY L.
99-999
IGHT

IDF#=135
SSN=100015
TR=1800 MS
TE=30 MS
TI=400 MS
EN=1/1

NSQ=4
SN=12/23

3-JAN-85   15:13:25

This photograph is the result of a magnetic resonance scan of
Henry Lee Lucas' brain. The arrows, which are in the
temporal lobe, point to a black area of spinal fluid
accumulations. Some accumulation in this area is normally
present, but the spinal fluid channels are widened at the
expense of the surrounding brain, more on the left side than
on the right. This may be a result from a past injury.
(Norris/Cuba)

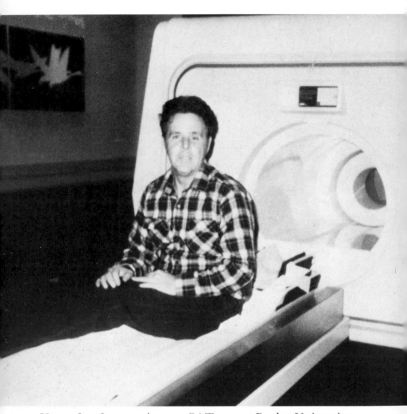

Henry Lee Lucas prior to a CAT scan at Baylor University Hospital in Dallas, Texas. (Cuba)

Defense attorney August 'Bud' Siemen and accused murderer Carlton Gary hearing the guilty verdict being read in the Atlanta courtroom. (Allen Horne/Columbus *Ledger-Inquirer* newspapers)

Carolyn David, Carlton Gary's mother. She had emotional and drinking problems all of her adult life and is the antithesis of the gentile white matriarchs that her son killed. (Allen Horne/Columbus *Ledger-Inquirer* newspapers)

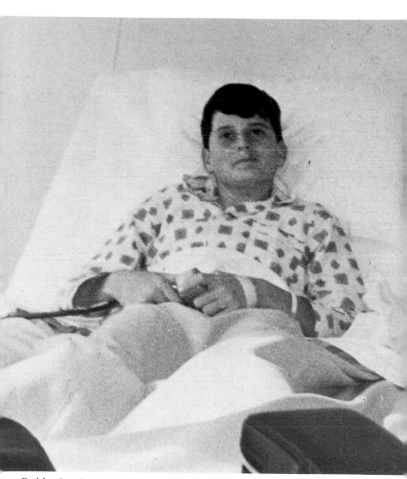

Bobby Joe Long at the age of twelve, recuperating in the hospital after having six pounds of breast tissue removed. Long remembers being terrified that he was becoming a woman. (Long)

Louella long, Bobby Joe Long's mother; Bobby Joe Long; his wife Cindy. These are the two women that Long blames for his untempered hatred of women. (Long)

Bobby Joe Long pictured with his wife Cindy and their two children during the time that Long was raping women. (Long)

Charles Manson, age thirty four, being led into court in
Independence, California, for a preliminary hearing on a
charge of possessing stolen property. At this time it was only
speculation that Manson was involved with the Sharon Tate
and LaBianca murders. (Wide World Photos)

Left: Leonard Lake as a young boy wearing an ROTC uniform.
As an adult, when he became a murderer, he also began
practicing staunch survivalists' techniques and preparing for
America's holocaust. (Norris)

Patricia Krenwinkle (Wide World Photos)

Right: Leslie Van Houten and Susan Atkins (Wide World Photos)

Tex Watson (Wide World Photos)

Steve Grogan (Wide World Photos)

Lerotha Harris, ex-wife of Carlton Gary, testifies of Gary's increasing abuse of her when they were married. (Allen Horne/Columbus *Ledger-Inquirer* newspapers)

Gary trolled for victims by 'casing' houses that would offer the least resistance to a break-in. He never remembered physically encountering one of his victims, but he remembered their being raped and killed. He watched from another room or from the street, but he was never there. When confronted with physical evidence such as pubic hairs that were at the crime scenes, Gary restated his admission that he was present at the crimes but claimed that he did not actually commit the murders. He was found guilty, sentenced to death by lethal injection, and is now on death row in Jackson, Georgia.

Leonard Lake's life is still shrouded in mystery because he committed suicide while in the custody of the San Francisco police on an illegal weapons charge. Most of what is known about Lake's crimes has been sealed by the courts in California because of extradition hearings against Charles Ng, Lake's suspected partner in the murders he is alleged to have committed. However, newspaper accounts of Lake's life, his career in the Marines, and accounts of his dungeon and torture compound in the rural Calaveras County hill country and interviews with his family reveal that Lake adhered to the basic pattern of the serial murderer.

Like Bobby Joe Long, Lake made contact with his victims through classified ads. He attracted Harvey and Debbie Dubs with an ad for the sale or exchange of video equipment. When they visited him in his isolated cabin, Lake sprung his trap, imprisoned them in an underground bunker, tortured them, executed them, and buried them in a troughlike grave on his property. Similarly, he lured Paul Cosner, an automobile dealer, to his property with the promise of buying a Honda if it were delivered. When Cosner delivered the car Lake killed him and took his driver's license and credit cards. Cosner's body was found in the same grave as the bodies of the Dubs family and Lake's other victims.

Lake's personal diary reveals that he was fantasizing heavily about the violence he was about to commit as he fled from Humboldt County to Calaveras County. His delusions of grandeur and his vision of a survivalist compound in which only the strongest and bravest would survive the coming onslaught shed light on his siege mentality that was isolating him from the rest of the world. His aura phase began with his flight from Humboldt and his setting up the compound on Blue Mountain Road in the small town of Wisleyville. He stockpiled guns and supported himself by making snuff videos and selling drugs. His trolling nets were the classified ads he placed and those he read in the newspapers. He expanded his net by contacting the friends and relatives of people he had previously killed and drawing them to his cabin, where he captured them. His male victims were summarily killed for their possessions. His female victims became the star players in the videos he made. The police uncovered many of these tapes, which contained torture sequences in which Lake and his partner Ng encouraged the women to scream for their lives and beg for mercy.

The videos were Lake's and Ng's totems. However, they did not stop at murdering their victims. They carefully dissected them and boiled the skin off the bones and encased them in plastic bags which they buried in troughs near the bunker. In this way Lake and Ng lived on the grave site with their triumphs, constantly spreading their nets wider and wider as more victims passed by.

Leonard Lake swallowed poison while he was being interrogated by San Francisco police detectives in connection with a stolen car, stolen property, and illegal weapons that were in the trunk of that car. Charles Ng, who was with Lake at the time a hardware store owner called the police to charge Ng with shoplifting, escaped while the detectives were questioning Lake. Ng was later apprehended in Canada and is being held there awaiting extradition for kidnapping and murder. Leonard Lake died in the hospital the day after he took poison.

Charles Manson and his family are perhaps the most infamous killers since the 1950s. His 'helter-skelter' murders of the Tate and LaBianca families and his commune family's involvement with scores of other murders throughout California in the late 1960s as well as with the attempted assassination of President Gerald Ford raised them to cult figure status. Yet clinically, Manson is very much like the other serial killers whose lives are reviewed in this book in that he suffered from the same patterns of abuse and head injury, had virtually no childhood bliss whatsoever, was institutionalized from the time he was twelve, was brutalized and raped by prison guards and inmates, and abused every type of psychedelic drug he could get hold of. He was also a drug dealer and contract killer. Manson's background differs from the other serial killers', however, in that he did not actually do any of the killings himself. His homicidal patterns were actuated by the other members of his group whom he inspired to commit the specific crimes.

Nevertheless, Manson reveals that he experienced the same types of phases that the other serial killers did. During his extended aura phase, which began under the influence of drugs in San Francisco's Haight-Ashbury section after his release from federal prison, Manson was constantly on the move. He joined a number of religious and Satanic cults to heighten the other-worldly sensations he was experiencing, gathered other rootless young men and women to join his family commune, curried favour with children of entertainers in order to get his music produced, and performed whatever tasks he could in order to make money.

As his hallucinatory experiences became more intense and his relationships with cults and pseudoreligious groups more extensive, Manson began to act upon his apocalyptic visions. His fantasies became reality, and he sent his family members out on missions to bring about chaos through demonstrations of brutal homicides. As Susan Atkins, Tex Watson, and Patricia Kenwinckle returned from each mission they brought vivid stories as totems to allow Manson to experience the violence vicariously. New evidence reveals that Manson revisited the murder scene at the Tate house the same night of the murders. All of the episodes merged into one long murder spree that didn't end even with the arrest and conviction of the leader of the family. Years later 'Squeaky' Fromme was arrested for the attempted assassination of President Ford, the last of the serial murder assaults committed by the Manson family. Manson's death sentence in 1971 for the Tate/LaBianca murders was overturned by the Supreme Court. He is currently serving a life term at San Quentin. He is up for parole every five years.

The personal statements in the five chapters that comprise this section represent the attempts of five individuals to reconstruct periods of their lives during which they were often beset by hallucinations and delusions and suffered from mental blackouts. Much of their reality was distorted by alcohol and drugs and their constant need to hide or stay on the move. Each of these killers was compelled to find new victims, and this explains their constant motion as they set out at the beginning of each episode of violence to seek victims.

What surfaces in each of the statements is the extreme hatred each person feels for the society around him and the isolation of having to cope with the violence and turmoil raging within. Henry Lee Lucas expressed it best when he claimed that he hated each and every day of his life. Each of these killers hated, and each sought the means to control the hate, to extinguish the fires that were consuming them, or to prevent themselves from inflicting violence upon those around him. None of them were successful, and each lived out his career as a serial murderer, destroying families and striking terror into communities as a consequence of his crimes.

There is no external logic in any of the following personal statements. No killer will explain what he did in any way that reveals a causality or a motive for his actions. Henry Lee Lucas kills Kate Rich partly as a consequence of having gone out drinking with her and partly out of a misplaced feeling of unhappiness after having killed Becky Powell the day before. There is no logic or motive to Lucas' action. Bobby Joe Long will feel no remorse for any of his victims.

Carlton Gary explains his actions to the police as if he were walking in a dream. The figures in Gary's confessions aren't real people, they are phantoms. There is the phantom killer who accompanies Gary to the hotel in Albany, New York, where he murders his first victim, and there is the phantom who accompanies Gary on each of his robberies in Wynnton, where each of the victims is raped and strangled. Gary feels no remorse for his crimes because, in his mind, he never committed the crimes. He is not lying; his mind does not accept the murders as something he committed.

All we have of Lake's personal statements are the videos and the snippets from his diary that the California courts have released. The real Leonard Lake will never emerge until after Ng has been brought to trial in California and the evidence is finally presented. From what we know about the individual who slaughtered animals and boiled them down into soup, Lake lived a life of fantasy. His delusional episodes were strung together to form one continuum. His world was populated by demons and warlocks – characters out of a dungeons-and-dragons game – and he was the warrior with an unlimited license to kill all those around him. Thus, Lake's tale is the most difficult to comprehend because he isn't alive to assist with the research.

The personal statement of Charles Manson reveals some of the darkest elements of human existence. He, like Lucas, fed upon his own hate of the world around him. His vision of the apocalypse was a violent bloodbath in which his victims were gutted and left to die like animals. Manson's statements, more than those of any of the other serial killers, express the feelings of a dead man. By the time Manson was interviewed in San Quentin in 1987, there is no single pattern of causality that emerges in his life. He is the ultimate victim, the bastard with no birthright, the emblem of his mother's shame, and her affliction. In the Bible-reading family into which Charles Manson was thrust like a curse, he was a focus of evil. Bartered away by his mother for a pitcher of beer when he was six, influenced by a rigid and militaristic uncle, sent away to reform school where his runt size made him the plaything of the guards and older boys, Manson could only absorb punishment. In the venom of his own words, he was raped, sodomized, beaten, and tortured by everyone who came in contact with him while he was in prison.

The statements of these killers have been placed within the biographical context of their lives. However any narrative that imposes a causality or reason for the crimes these killers have committed falls far short of the real horror of their separate truths. There is no rationale for their crimes and certainly no justification. And just as there is no rationale, there is nothing that society will gain from their executions. The threat of the electric chair or the hangman's noose did not stop Lucas from hating nor did the image of a needle of lethal poison being injected into his veins stop Bobby Joe Long's violent sexual fantasies.

The narratives place the killers' lives within a frame of

reality, but it is what the killers say about themselves that creates the greater reality. If to understand the implications of serial murder one has to hear about it in the killers' own words, then what these five murderers have to say must be said without prejudgemental interpretation.

7

Henry Lee Lucas

1. Also known as: none
2. Date of birth: 8/16/32
3. Place of birth: Blacksburg, Virginia
4. Place of arrest: Montgomery County, Texas
5. Date of arrest: 9/5/83
6. Charge: Illegal weapons, murder
7. Convictions: Murder, rape, kidnapping
8. Sentence: Eleven murder convictions, one
                           death penalty, serving six life
                           sentences, two seventy-five-
                           year sentences, one sixty-year
                           sentence
9. Current status: Death row, Huntsville, Texas

'I hated all of my life. I hated everybody. When I first
grew up and can remember, I was dressed as a girl by
Mother. And I stayed that way for two or three years. And
after that I was treated like what I call the dog of the
family. I was beaten; I was made to do things that no
human bein' would want to do. I've had to steal, make
bootleg liquor; I've had to eat out of a garbage can. I grew
up and watched prostitution like that with my mother till

I was fourteen years old. Then I started to steal, do anything else I could do to get away from home . . . but I couldn't get away from it. I even went to Tecumseh, Michigan, got married, and I started livin' up there, and my mother came up there and we got into an argument in a beer tavern . . . that's when I killed her.'

Henry Lee Lucas remembers very little of the actual killing. Both he and his mother had been drinking heavily that night. He remembers that during the fight with his mother, Viola, she accused him of having sex with his sister, ridiculed him in the presence of his new wife, and he began slapping her until she fell to the floor. When he went to pick her up, he found his knife in his hand and saw his mother stabbed through the chest. He took off and left her alone in the house, and she died in a hospital the next day. That fight with his mother was the culmination of a twenty-three-year nightmare during which Lucas was repeatedly beaten with sticks and, on at least one occasion, with pieces of a two-by-four timber, deprived of food until he was near starvation, and forced to watch his mother, a sometimes prostitute, have sex with scores of men. A neighbor's report confirmed Lucas' stories about his early years.

She had also beaten Lucas' father, Anderson Lucas, an alcoholic who lost both his legs when in a drunken stupor he fell under the wheels of a slowly moving freight train. He was a double amputee called 'No Legs' by the locals of Blacksburg, Virginia. This occurred before he met and married Viola, the daughter of a Chippewa Indian. Anderson Lucas made moonshine liquor, skinned minks, and sold pencils for a living. But he drank most of the moonshine himself and taught his son Henry how to mind his still. Henry Lucas' own taste for alcohol developed by the time he was ten. 'He hopped around on his ass all his life,' Lucas says of his father, who was also coerced into watching his wife have sex with a variety of men. He would watch until it made him sick; then he would crawl out of the dirt-floored cabin and lie in the snow. Finally one night in 1950, after he had taken all he could take, he went out the door and stayed in the snow all night. He caught pneumonia a few days later and died, leaving his youngest son, Henry, alone to face the mother's brutality. Henry even recalls being beaten by Bernie, his mother's live-in-boyfriend who lived with them in the three-room cabin.

Lucas' childhood was a mixture of horror and pathos, a virtual breeding ground for the type of violence that turned Texas Interstate Highway 35 into a mass burial ground for Lucas' future victims. Viola beat the child mercilessly with broom handles, sticks, pieces of timber, and any other weapons she could find. Her cruelty was such that she would not even let him cry. After beating him and telling him that what she had done was for his own good, she would prophesy that he was born evil. She went on to predict that he would someday die in prison. Her continuing violence began to infect every level of his existence. Henry Lucas' earliest memory, he claimed, is of his mother finishing up with a customer, then pulling out a shotgun and shooting the man in the leg. The blood spattered all over him in the process. This traumatic scene may very well have set the stage for his own fascination with spilling blood and the fragility of the human body later in his life.

Viola Lucas also liked to outfit her young son in girls' clothing. Lucas remembers that on his first day at school his mother curled his long blond hair and made him go to school in a dress. The teacher, one of few people in official positions of authority who came in contact with Henry Lee Lucas during his youth, was shocked. She took the responsibility for cutting his curls and dressing him in pants. Later this same teacher fed the malnourished youth sandwiches during school lunchtimes and took him home to her house, where he would receive the only hot meals he ever ate as a child. 'I think she was responsible for my first pair of shoes,' Lucas remembers. Years later, in a rare interview, his teacher described Lucas as one of the many impoverished and desperate West Virginia hill children in her classes. But, she revealed, he was especially dirty, smelled very bad, and was constantly tormented as an outcast by the other children.

As he grew older, the injuries he sustained from his mother grew in seriousness. One day, when he was too slow to fetch wood for the cabin stove, his mother hit him especially hard across the back of the head with a two-by-four. In his own account, Lucas claims to have remained in a semiconscious state for about three days before Bernie got scared and took him to a hospital. As an excuse, he claimed the child had fallen from a high ladder. After that incident, Lucas reports, he had frequent bouts of dizziness, blackouts, and at times felt as though he were floating in the air. Neurological examinations and X rays conducted years later confirmed that Lucas had sustained serious head traumas resulting in damage to those areas of the brain that control violent behavior and the ability to manage emotions.

Lucas claims that, as a child, anything that he liked or played with his mother destroyed. He remembers a pet mule that he kept. His mother, seeing him take pleasure in the animal, asked him whether he liked it or not. When he replied that he did, she went into the house, reappeared with a shotgun, and killed the mule. Then she beat him because of the expense she had just incurred in needing to have the mule carcass carted away. Incidents like this were responsible for Lucas' inability to love or admit to love and for his perverted emotions toward other living creatures. He became accustomed to the fact that there was little or no value to life and that people were no different from any of thousands of inanimate objects that populated his world.

After Henry's first serious head trauma, he received another injury about a year later. His brother accidentally sliced into his left eye with a knife. The wound punctured the eye, and for months Lucas could only see shadows and phantom images. His peripheral vision was seriously impaired as well, causing him to walk sideways so that he could see what was on his left. He was eventually returned to school where the teacher who had shown him so much kindness when he was younger, purchased special readers with large type so that Lucas could continue learning to read. Even this level of progress was interrupted when another teacher at the school, while striking out at another student, missed, accidentally hit Henry instead, reopened his wound, and caused him to lose the impaired eye completely. It was replaced with a glass eye that he still wears.

As a young teenager Henry Lee Lucas reported having sex with his half brother and with the animals whose throats the two would cut open before performing bestiality. He often caught small animals and skinned them alive for pleasure. He began stealing for food and money. 'I started stealing, I guess, as soon as I was old enough to run fast,' Lucas remembers, ' 'cause I didn't want to stay at home. I figured if I could steal, I could get away from home and stuff.'

He claims to have committed his first murder at fifteen. He cornered a seventeen-year-old girl at a bus stop, carried her up an embankment, and attempted to rape her. When she struggled and screamed, Lucas began strangling her. 'I had no intention of killing her,' he said thirty-three years later in an interview about his life. 'I don't know whether I was just being afraid somebody was going to catch me or what. That killing was my first, my worst, and the hardest to get over. . . . I would go out sometimes for days, and just every time I turned around I'd see police behind me. Then I'd be always looking behind me and watching. Everywhere I'd go I'd have to be watching for police and be afraid they were going to stop me and pick me up. But they never did bother with me.'

It was also at age fifteen that Lucas was first convicted for breaking and entering and committed to a reformatory as a delinquent. This began a pattern for the remainder of his life that stretched from state prison to federal prison to death row in Huntsville, Texas. He was discharged from the reformatory a year after having made what the prison report calls 'a good adjustment.' A year after his release he was again convicted of breaking and entering and sentenced to the Virginia State Penitentiary for four years. He escaped in 1956 and with a male companion stole a series of cars from Virginia to Michigan. Later in 1956 he was arrested on a federal charge of transporting stolen property across state lines and sentenced to a federal reformatory in Ohio. He was transferred back to Virginia to serve out his original sentence with time added for the escape. He was finally discharged in September 1959 and made his way back to Michigan to join his sister. It was in Michigan, just four months later, that he wounded his mother fatally with his knife. He fled the crime scene, leaving her bleeding on the floor. By the time Henry's sister found Viola Lucas fourteen hours later and took her to the hospital, it was too late. She died from complications resulting from the wounds her son had inflicted. Henry Lee Lucas was convicted and sentenced to forty years for second-degree murder.

In prison in Michigan and eventually in the Ionia State Psychiatric Hospital to which he was transferred on the recommendation of the prison psychiatrists, Lucas was diagnosed as a psychopath, a sadist, and a sex deviate. He was cooperative, though, telling his doctors that he sometimes heard voices telling him to do 'bad things.' He felt from time to time as if he were floating in the air, and claimed that he was sorry for the murder and rapes he had committed. The reports describing the inmate Henry Lee Lucas document a personality completely turned in upon itself. Incapacitated by an inferiority complex, Lucas was 'grossly lacking in self-confidence, self-reliance, will power, and general stamina.' There was also evidence of a 'general preoccupation with sexual impotence, the same which is believed to exist as only another reflection of his deflated impression of personal qualities in general.'

The person the prison psychiatrists described in July 1961, the schizophrenic Henry Lee Lucas who had been so brutalized by his mother that he eventually could achieve sexual potency only after he had killed his victim, attempted suicide several times in the Michigan State Penitentiary. First, he cut open his stomach with a razor blade. After that proved unsuccessful, he tried slashing his wrists. It was while serving time in the Michigan State Penitentiary in 1961, he claims, that he heard his mother's voice burning inside his head. 'I kept hearing her talking to me and telling me to do things. And I couldn't do it. I had one voice that was tryin' to make me commit suicide, and I wouldn't do it. I had another one telling me not to do anything they told me to do. That's what got me in the hospital, was not doing what they told me to do.' Lucas claims that he became a changed person in the Michigan prison. Where before he had killed only out of instant rage, he now became blatantly determined to kill as many people as possible. He was filled with hate and tormented by the sound of his mother's voice echoing inside his brain.

His multiple suicide attempts and his refusal to abide by prison routines prompted his transfer to Ionia State Hospital, where he remained for almost five years. He was eventually returned to the prison and his hallucinations continued. He used the prison records room to study the criminal cases of the other inmates. He immersed himself in the details of their crimes. During this time he studied the techniques the police employed in pursuing their investigations and developing leads. He learned how they used their suspects' mistakes to track them down. He studied police procedures so aggressively that upon his release he was able to commit crimes and escape the authorities with much greater ease. His new knowledge enabled him to predict the authorities' next moves. According to his own later statements, he had learned how to be a career criminal. 'I learned every way there is in law enforcement. I learned every way there is in different crimes; I studied it. After I got out of that hospital, they put me in the records room. And every record that jumped through there, I would read it, study it, and see how what got who caught.'

Lucas was recommended for parole in 1970 even though he warned the prison officials and the staff psychologist that if he were released he would kill again. He told them he was sick, that he was hearing a voice from the dead, and that the forces that had compelled him to attempt suicide while he was in prison would now compel him to kill strangers if he were let loose. The state of Michigan, however, was facing a prison overcrowding problem in 1970. The parole board released him even though he claimed not to have been rehabilitated. 'I knew I was going to do it!' he proclaimed years later in his Texas jail cell. 'I even told 'em I was going to do it! I told the warden, the psychologist, everybody. When they come in and put me out on parole, I said, "I'm not ready to go; I'm not going." They said, "You're going if we have to throw you out." They threw me out of the prison because it was too crowded. So I said, "I'll leave you a present on the doorstep on the way out." And I did it, the same day, down the road a bit. It wasn't too far away from it. But they never proved it.' Lucas found his first murder victim in Jackson, only a few miles away from the Michigan penitentiary. He killed her and left her within walking distance of the prison gate. The case wasn't solved until Lucas confessed to it in Texas.

In 1970 he began a killing spree that took him across much of the Southwest and into Florida, abducting children, raping young girls, and killing whoever was convenient. 'I was bitter at the world,' he claimed years later. 'I hated everything. There wasn't nothin' I liked. I was bitter as bitter could be.'

It was for the murder of his common-law wife, Frieda 'Becky' Powell, the niece of his companion Ottis Toole, that Lucas was finally apprehended and convicted again. Becky had first met Henry when she was nine and he was forty. He cared for her as if he were her father, providing her with food and clothing and generally raising her. He made sure that she went to school. In a ludicrous parody of normal parenthood, he even introduced her to his own skills and taught her the rudimentary techniques of his profession, including thievery, breaking and entering, and random murder. Soon the pair were no longer surrogate parent and child but common-law husband and wife and partners in crime. In December 1981, Becky was caught and sent to a juvenile detention home in Florida. Soon thereafter Henry and Ottis Toole helped her escape and all three of them began another killing spree across the Southwest to California where they eventually settled.

Henry used some of his prison-acquired skills as a laborer, carpenter, and roofer to earn money doing odd jobs. He worked often for the owners of an antique refinishing store in California in exchange for room and board for him and Becky Powell. In early March 1982 the owners of the antique store, Mr. and Mrs. Jack Smart, talked about going down to Texas, where Henry and Becky were to be paid to care for Mrs. Smart's eighty-year-old mother, Kate Rich. Henry and Becky and the Smarts bought tickets and left for Texas on what was to become the final chapter in Becky's life and the beginning of the end of Henry's freedom.

They were welcomed by Kate Rich, whose idea it had been to invite them to live with her, doing odd jobs around the house in return. The rest of the family in Texas quickly became suspicious of the two drifters and eventually forced them to leave. On the road while hitching a ride the pair met Ruben Moore, a preacher who led a small fundamentalist sect called the House of Prayer in an old converted chicken farm in Stoneberg, Texas. He also had a small roofing company and invited Henry Lucas and Becky Powell to join his group, live in one of the communal shacks, and have access to the group's kitchen in exchange for Henry's services as a roofer and day laborer. The same day that Henry and Becky met Moore they moved in.

Becky Powell quickly found a meaning in the group's religious practices. She attended Sunday services, made friends in the community, enjoyed the communal atmosphere, and even visited Kate Rich, who lived only ten miles north of there, whenever she could. The following August she decided that she wanted to start her life over again and return to Florida and the reformatory. After arguing with Henry, who wanted her to stay with him, she convinced him to take her back to Florida. The two left the House of Prayer in August 1982 and started hitchhiking back east.

A few days after they had set out the two drifters reached Denton County, where they could neither hitch a ride nor find a room in the local motel. Though it was a hot and muggy night, there was no rain so they decided to spread out their blankets and sleep in an open field. Henry started drinking heavily. Their bedtime conversation soon became an argument: Henry didn't want to go to Florida. For one of the first times in his life he was happy living at the House of Prayer. He liked Moore, he had friends in the religious community, and he also had legitimate work. Becky was adamant: she was tired of being a fugitive, always in danger of being caught and returned. Back at the reformatory in Florida she would be able to make a new start, clean her slate, and begin life all over again. She didn't want to leave Henry, but she didn't want to be on the run for the rest of her life either. Their voices got louder and their tempers rose. Each pushed the other closer to the edge until Becky slapped Henry hard across the face. That was his trigger: still there after his years at the Michigan penitentiary and the Ionia State Hospital and still just as fragile as the night in Tecumseh when his mother slapped him. Without thinking, he later confessed, he reached for his knife in his bedroll and plunged it deep into her chest. The blade penetrated her heart, and she died immediately. Henry Lucas said that he just looked at the little twelve-year-old girl twisted on the ground before him and wept.

Later, he remembers, he thought he should try to bury the body, so he removed her ring from her finger and then cut Becky into pieces. He put all but the legs in two pillowcases and placed her remains in a shallow grave. Then he tied a belt around Becky's legs and dragged them into the brush where he buried them. For the rest of that night and on several subsequent trips to the grave site he talked to Becky's remains. He wept, telling her that he was sorry for having killed her, and promised her that someday he would join her. His remorse over his reflex murder seemed to throw a switch somewhere in the psyche of Henry Lee Lucas. He was no longer interested in covering up his tracks with the same cunning as before. From that moment, his criminal career began to unravel. It was another nine months before he was finally apprehended. It was then that he would confess to the murder of Becky Powell and hundreds of other nameless victims.

After killing Becky, Lucas returned to Ruben Moore's

House of Prayer and casually reported that she had run off with a trucker on her way back to Florida. He then visited the widow Kate Rich one more time to take her to church services one Sunday evening in early September. Before church, they drove into Oklahoma for a couple of six-packs of beer. They drove around and drank and talked for hours until it was too late to catch the services, and then they decided to go home. On the way back to Ringgold, Texas, where Kate lived, they turned off the highway to a remote old pumped-out oil patch. In a sudden fit of rage, Henry stabbed Granny Rich to death there. Had she asked about Becky just one too many times? Had she argued with Henry about missing church services? Had she confronted the drifter about something he could not answer? Not even Henry is sure about what triggered him to kill her, but he did. He only remembers cutting an upside-down cross between the old woman's breasts, having sex with the dead body, and afterward dragging it into a culvert where he lodged it there with a two-by-four.

Granny Rich's children reported her disappearance to Montague County sheriff William Conway. He sought Lucas, who was the last person to have seen her alive. On and off throughout the next nine months Sheriff Conway questioned Lucas, pursuing him vigorously until Lucas fled the area. He traveled to California to visit Kate Rich's daughter. The police in California held him for questioning because of the bloodstains on his car seat. This, too, aroused suspicions, and the Smarts reported their fears to Sheriff Conway back in Texas. Lucas then traveled to Illinois, where he spent the remainder of the year unsuccessfully looking for legitimate work. Finally he returned to Texas where William Conway, having received the reports filed by the Smarts, wanted him arrested for Kate Rich's disappearance. It was at the House of Prayer that he was finally turned in by his friend

Ruben Moore for possessing a gun: a felony for an ex-convict. Henry was arrested in June 1983 on the weapons charge, and within weeks, after experiencing what he called a religious conversion in the cold and darkness of his jail cell, he began confessing to the murders of Becky Powell, Kate Rich, and hundreds of other victims.

Many of his confessions were found to be false, the police later concluded. Henry was a practiced liar and had been simply testing his interrogators. But also, because his own sense of self was so throughly absent, he would become a chameleon and conform reality to the perceived wants and needs of others. Many of the details that Lucas remembered and the descriptions of the burial locations proved to be right on target. From his jail cell in Texas, where he unwound a tale that would spread across the center of the country, his testimony began clearing up unsolved crimes in states throughout the South and Midwest. The deepest fears of hundreds of parents whose children had been listed as missing for years came to the surface. A large portion of these confirmed crimes involved the series of slayings along Texas Interstate 35 and in particular the lingering investigation into the grisly murder of a nameless victim known as 'Orange Socks.'

A motorist driving on I-35 on Hallowe'en had found the strangled, nude body sprawled face down and hugging the concrete along the side of the road. She was a pretty, reddish-brown-haired girl in her mid-twenties who had little scars around her ankles where she had evidently infected insect bits in childhood by scratching at them too much. She also had venereal disease. She was difficult to identify because not only did she have a set of flawless teeth, making a dental records trace all but impossible, but there was no evidence of surgery or of previously healed fractures. She wore a silver abalone-inlaid ring but had no pocketbook, no credit cards, and no driver's license. The identifying features were bunched-up remains of paper towels she had fashioned into a tampon and her stretched, dusty, pumpkin-coloured socks that had been pulled down around her ankles as if the person undressing her had left them on by mistake. She had also eaten just before she died. The sheriff dubbed the Jane Doe Orange Socks. She was just one of the scores of unsolved homicides along I-35, an area that by 1981 had become a dumping ground for the corpses of hundreds of murder victims. It stretched for five hundred miles from Laredo to Gainesville.

These random murders included an assortment of victims who had been sexually assaulted, sodomized, shot, strangled, beaten, and dismembered. No single pattern of murder emerged that investigators could use to group the victims together. The victims themselves puzzled the investigators. Some of them were women, some men, some teenagers, some middle-aged business-men; some were obviously hitchhikers, others were elderly women found in homes near the road, some were single women who might have had car trouble, and others were obviously vagrants bumming toward the Mexican border. There were no apparent similarities. The authorities had always assumed that the bodies were the victims of different murderers who had easy access to the area because it was wide open and not well patrolled. The murders were committed in a variety of ways, some by strangulation, some by gunshot wounds, but there was no unifying pattern that tied the crimes together except for the common burial ground. The police had no solution and no suspects. Many thought that none of the cases would ever be solved. That was until Henry Lee Lucas was taken into custody in 1983.

'Yeah, that one, she was a hitchhiker, and she would have been a strangle,' Lucas said after looking at the picture of Orange Socks's face. She was lying on her back at the edge of the macadam. 'I picked her up in Oklahoma

City,' he said into the videotape camera after having been read his Miranda rights by Sheriff Boutwell, who had interrogated the mysterious, glass-eyed ex-convict on Sheriff William Conway's wild hunch. 'Then we drove around awhile; we stopped and had sex . . . voluntarily. We had sex one time, and I wasn't satisfied. She put her clothes back on, and we stopped and ate at a truck stop. . . . We started to head back south, so we took 35. And after we got on 35, why, I asked her to have sex with me. Then she said no.' Even though Lucas' court-appointed lawyer stepped in at this point to advise his client that he was confessing to a capital crime under Texas law, Lucas wanted to continue. He had already attempted suicide himself numerous times, he claimed, now he might just as well let the state do it. That way he could pay for his crime and keep his promise to the dead Becky Powell.

'Well, we were talking about sex, and she told me, "not right now," ' he continued, remembering the scene with a vivid attention to detail. 'She tried to jump out of the car, when I grabbed her and pulled her back. We drove for a little piece further than that, and I pulled off the road because she was fighting so hard that I almost lost control of the car and wrecked. After I pulled her over to me, why, I choked her until she died, I had sex with her again . . . then I pulled her out of my car, and I dropped her into a culvert.' It was a wrap. The police felt satisfied they had their murderer. The camera and tape machine were turned off, the room lights were turned back on, and the book was closed on Orange Socks.

The following spring a San Angelo jury found Lucas guilty of the rape/murder of the Jane Doe female nick-named Orange Socks and sentenced him to die by lethal injection. Although Lucas' partner, Ottis Toole, later admitted to the murder himself and the whole case is undergoing a reexamination in light of some of the obvious lies that Lucas told in many of his other confessions, the Orange Socks murder and the hundreds of other stories that Lucas told about finding his victims and killing them shed light on the behavior of a serial murderer. Whether or not Lucas killed the hundreds of victims described in his confessions, he has become the center of a political firestorm in the Texas criminal justice system.

There is no doubt that Henry Lee Lucas murdered his mother, Becky Powell, and Kate Rich. It is also highly probable that he murdered scores, if not hundreds, of strangers along Interstate 35 in Texas and in a number of neighboring states. His descriptions of the victims, his drawings of their faces, and his hyperamnesia – an ability to remember even the slightest of specific details while forgetting entire blocks of time – point to a knowledge of the crimes that only someone at the murder scene could possibly recall. However, like most perpetrators of seemingly random or motiveless killings, Lucas has become the centre of the conflicting ambitions of state and country prosecutors, police departments from different jurisdictions, and politicians from opposing parties.

For Sheriff Boutwell and the Texas Rangers who have followed the case since Lucas' first confession to the Orange Socks murder, the prisoner has become the key to scores of unsolved murders. To the families of missing children and young girls, Lucas has been a source of peace, a criminal whose confessions have allowed families to release their lives from doubt and let grief and mourning finally fill the void left by the missing person. To local prosecutors, however, whose cases are based entirely upon Lucas' statements – confessions of a man already sentenced to die – he has been a source of embarrassment. They have to hope that his confessions are true so that they can close the books on their missing person cases and allay their fears that the real kidnapper may be still at large. In other words, the police and the prosecutors each legitimately need Lucas to be either a monstrous serial killer or a man lying to buy time for himself by fending off the executioner's needle until there are no more crimes left to confess to. And the prisoner at the centre of it all feeds upon the attention and thrives in its glow.

Lucas was tranferrred from his own private cell at a Texas jailhouse, where he had been confined since 1983, to death row at the federal prison in Huntsville. He has almost run out of appeals on his original convictions. While at Georgetown he had a heavy appointment schedule, made appearances on national television, held interviews for national magazines and posed for photographers, and was the subject of a series of detailed physical and neurological examinations. Yet he is still an enigma who has led police officers on wild goose chases across three or more states only to find that the murder victim Lucas so carefully described was still alive and well.

Henry Lee Lucas exemplified the type of deviant we have categorized as a serial murderer. According to his confessions which police have been able to verify, he committed at least three murders of unrelated victims within the space of six months. His actual victim count is probably much higher. Described as a sociopath with a debilitating character disorder, his real actions have defied traditional psychological labels and he has functioned at close to normal levels within certain types of highly structured communities such as prisons and hospitals. He was able to look back upon his own crimes with such a convincing sense of remorse that even the most experienced police officers and psychologists have been unable to explain it. At times they felt that they were manipulated. In reality Lucas' remorse was the result of his being confined to a stable environment. Completely institutionalized, Lucas is now on a stable diet, he has undergone psychotherapy in which his hallucinations and confessions of crimes were taken seriously for the first time, and he has claimed to have experienced several religious conversions. It is as if at Georgetown he had started to mature emotionally as a result of the forced structure of his prison environment. This is not a paradox. It is what typically happens when a serial murderer is finally incarcerated and begins to adjust to prison and his captors.

The complexity of Lucas' behavior and the layering of his different medical and psychological problems are the results of the years of abuse he suffered as a child and his severe brain damage. CAT scans and nuclear magnetic resonance tests done on Lucas reveal that the repeated head traumas he received during childhood damaged those sectors of his brain that control primal emotions such as love, hate and fear. Lucas' chronic drug and alcohol abuse also contributed to his criminal behavior by diminishing his voluntary control over his emotions and increasing the length and depth of his mental blackout period. He claims that he always drank heavily immediately preceding every murder. Furthermore, the high levels of lead and cadmium content in his blood indicate a nonresilient personality, one that is unable to cope with any negative stimulus. However, all of these factors – the brain damage, his savagely violent childhood, his substance abuse, and his nonresiliency – fused and automatically have turned Lucas into a serial murderer. Each aspect of his life would have contributed independently to a psychologically crippled adult were it not for the negative parenting that taught Lucas that life was without value and that he was a person of no worth in a hostile world. It was as if his mother's negative parenting, the constant reinforcement that Lucas was 'the child who would come to no good,' was a self-fulfilling prophecy. It was the single factor that acted as a catalyst, combining all of the other negative factors in Lucas' deviant childhood into the violent individual who could only relate to creatures who had died.

Lucas came alive only in the death of another being. He gained sexual potency after he had bludgeoned and strangled his sex partner into a coma or to death, and he then had intercourse with the victim's remains. He existed in the world of the living by subterfuge and camouflage and by trusting no one. He even turned on those who had been his companions, killing Becky Powell because she confronted him as his mother had. He killed Kate Rich for probably the same type of confrontation. He failed at everything positive in life, succeeding only at murder.

Clinical evaluations we conducted on Henry Lee Lucas after his murder conviction revealed extensive neurological damage to his brain. There were small contusions to the frontal poles that indicated a frontal lobe injury. There was damage to his temporal lobe and pools of spinal fluid at the base of his brain. There was an enlargement of the right and left Sylvian fissure at the expense of the surrounding brain tissue that indicated significant loss of judgmental functions and was the result of head traumas received after birth. Neurologists, commenting on the results of both the CAT scan and the nuclear magnetic resonance test, confirmed that the extent of brain abnormality indicated an individual who was not able to control violence with the same degree of success that people with more normal brains were able to do.

The neurological diagnoses are also supported by symptoms of hypergraphia, the inability to control one's self-expression through writing, painting, and speaking, and by periods of either blackout or grey-out in which the person experiences long periods of floating sensations and the inability to perceive different objects around him. The experience of floating sensations also indicates a form of deep sensory motor epilepsy that requires constant EEG monitoring for periods of from thirty-six to forty-eight hours to diagnose. The length of the test is necessary for the machine to pick up the telltale deep spikes of the seizures. In addition, Lucas' hypergrandiosity and hyper-religiosity are traits common to people who have incurred damage to their temporal lobes. The loss of judgmental ability, the loss of the ability to balance feelings against logic and sensory input, leads to a form of internal feedback in which the brain acts directly upon its own delusions. In other words, what the brain thinks it sees becomes reality. Lucas' extreme dealings with Satanic cults in Florida and Texas and his sudden conversion to born-again Christianity in jail only a few years later are examples of this symptom. Even after his conversion to Christianity, Lucas continues to lie and to manipulate those around him with an almost uncanny ability to sense what he thought they want him to say.

Toxicological tests also reveal that the high levels of lead and cadmium found in his nerve tissue, combined with the years of chronic alcohol and drug poisoning, destroyed a significant amount of cerebral capacity and left him with no physical or psychological resiliency. The three indicators of active cadmium poisoning – loss of dream recall, excessively strong body odor, and loss of sense of smell – are all well documented in Lucas' medical tests. In fact, the killer still does not remember most of his dreams and allegedly rode in a car for three days with the decapitated head of one of his victims without noticing the acrid odor of decomposing flesh.

Like all serial killers and most multiple murderers, Henry Lee Lucas demonstrated bizarre and violent sexual activity combined with a confusion regarding his sexual identity even before he committed his first serious crime. He claimed that he had sex with relatives, committed bestiality, and engaged in forms of necrophilia with parts

of his victims' bodies. He has killed, he has said, in order
to gain sexual potency because he was unable to have sex
with a living person who, just by being alive, challenged
Lucas' superiority and posed a life threat to him. Any
ability to rely on his own sense of being was so completely
destroyed by Lucas' mother that even today he realizes
that in order to have any relationship with a person he
must kill that person. And after he has killed his sex
partner, if the relationship has been positive in his own
mind, he mourns for the victim and for himself. If the
relationship was only sexual, he had coitus with the
remains and left them in a shallow grave or in a roadside
culvert.

'Sex is one of my downfalls,' Henry has said. 'I get sex
any way I can get it. If I have to force somebody to do it, I
do. If I don't, I don't. I rape them; I've done that. I've
killed animals to have sex with them and I've had sex
while they're alive.' Forced to watch his mother have sex
with her clients, and forced to wear girl's clothing to
school and to wear his hair in curls, Lucas developed a
hatred of women that has contaminated his entire life.
Even Becky Powell had only to argue with her up-to-then
protector, and in the next moment she lay dead from a
knife wound through her chest. And with the memory of
Becky's murder still playing back in his mind, Lucas
turned his attention to Granny Rich and killed her only a
few weeks later. Thus, he put to death the only two women
with whom he had any close relationship because he did
not have the personal resiliency to sustain those relations
in moments of confrontation.

For all of his childhood years and until his imprisonment, Lucas was chronically malnourished. His mother
forced both Henry and his father to scavenge for food on
the streets or in garbage cans while cooking for herself, her
customers, and her pimp. As a schoolboy, his teacher used
to provide him with sandwiches and an occasional hot

meal. Lucas' diet during the years immediately preceding his arrest for murder included a daily consumption of alcohol and drugs, five packs of cigarettes a day, and peanut butter and cheese. These years of malnutrition, especially during childhood, resulted in stunted development of the cerebral tissue as well as in impaired judgment and cognitive performance. It was only during his incarceration that his diet was stabilized to the point where he no longer suffered from elevated levels of blood sugar and severe vitamin and mineral deficiencies.

Throughout his life Lucas has demonstrated an escalating propensity toward violence, another important trait of the emerging serial murderer. As a very young child, he was a fire starter and was maliciously cruel to animals. As an older child, he practiced bestiality, rape as an adolescent, and single murder as a young adult. As a fully emerged serial killer, he has committed multiple murders, necrophilia, torture, mutilation, dismemberment, and totemic preservation of the remains of his victims. He has even admitted that, despite his conversion, he recognizes that he can exercise no control over himself, was grateful for the intervention of the criminal justice system for that control, and admitted on more than one occasion that if released through some quirk of justice he would probably kill again. He recognizes society's laws but maintains that punishment has no meaning for him because he has been through what no human being should ever have to endure. Even though he has been diagnosed as sane, Lucas knows that within him there is a darkness that nothing can reach.

'When I'm around people,' he explains, 'I feel tense, nervous. I guess it's because I haven't been around people. Most of the life I've lived has been alone. I have trouble talkin' to them; I always have. I don't think there's a doctor in the world that's going to go against another doctor's word. They say there's nothing wrong with me, so that's the way it is. I don't feel there's something wrong with me, I *know* it! People don't do the things they do unless there's something wrong with them. I just thought there's no way I could kill somebody, so it's not that. Something pushes me into doin' it. What other choice is there?'

Thus Lucas has lived his years in a kind of phantom world, in part because his brain was never able to process information in the same ways that healthy brains do, and in part because the normal conditioning that takes place when parents raise their children was twisted by his mother into an aberration in which evil became her version of good. The successive head injuries, the starvation of his brain through prolonged malnutrition, and the poisoning of the cerebral tissue from alcohol – which Lucas began consuming in large quantities by the age of ten – and drugs all combined to cause a progressive degeneration of Lucas' neurological system. The physical connections between the different areas of the brain, the hundreds of thousands of electrochemical switches that balance primal feelings of violence with logical, socially ordered behavior, simply didn't work properly. As a result, when pushed to a certain point, Lucas was incapable of controlling his own actions. When asked how he perceived his victim at the time of the murder, he explained: 'It's more of a shadow than anything else. You know it's a human being, but yet you can't accept it. The killin' itself, it's like say, you're walkin' down the road. Half of me will go this way and the other half goes that way. The right-hand side didn't know what the left-hand side was going to do.' But even more important, the combination of physiological, chemical, and psychological events resulted in a type of nonperson, an individual who was so far beyond the bounds of normalcy that the traditional categories used to describe deviant behavior no longer applied. Henry Lee Lucas, like the other serial killers in this section, belongs to the walking dead. He is a man who died emotionally and socially before the age of ten and for whom existence had become only a hunt to satisfy his primal urges from each moment to the next.

Typical of an individual who has never internalized any coherent patterns of social and emotional behaviour, Henry Lee Lucas dwelt in a world of shadows when not under the care of an institution. Once in prison or in a state psychiatric hospital he became docile, identifiable as a schizophrenic with a severe character disorder but certainly within the pale of human experience. He even attempted suicide on many occasions to end his own misery and to stop the voices that were reverberating in his brain. Finally, on death row in Huntsville, Texas, and living on an institutional diet, Lucas has responded. The structure of the institution has become an exterior emotional skeleton, a shell that supports discrete elements of his personality. Supported by the structure of this shell, some personality development can take place in Lucas. He senses the early feelings of grief, and he mourns for himself and for the person he will never become. But he probably will never honestly mourn for his victims. 'I feel each one of these victims I go back to; I got to go and relive each victim. It's like going back and completely doing the crime all over again. . . . I find myself many a time breakin' down and cryin'. Before I didn't have that. I didn't have feelings for nobody – a person was a blank.'

8

Carlton Gary

1. Also known as: Carl Michaels, Mike Gary,
                       Michael Davis, Michael
                       Anthony David
2. Date of birth: 12/15/52
3. Place of birth: Columbus, Georgia
4. Place of arrest: Columbus, Georgia
5. Date of arrest: 9/12/83
6. Charge: Murder, rape, assault, robbery
7. Convictions: Murder, rape, assault
                       8. Sentence: Death
9. Current status: Death row, Jackson, Georgia

'There was a cigarette stand and an elevator where John was standing. Then this white dude came down and asked us what we wanted. I told this white dude that we were looking for a Mrs. Polite, as we were looking for a dishwasher's job that was advertised in the newspaper. This white dude said it was too late to find anybody in the housekeeping department. The white dude went back to the desk and John and I got in the elevator. John worked the self-service elevator. I didn't pay any attention to what floor we got off but John pushed the button. The elevator

176

stopped, John and I got off and we walked down the hallway with John leading the way.

'While walking down the hallway, John put on his rubber gloves. He told me not to worry about my fingerprints as I had no record and they couldn't be traced. We came to this hotel room door. I notice that when John or Pop came to this door he had some kind of material jammed in the door lock. John went in first. I followed him. John turned to me and said, "Check out the bathroom." The bathroom was dark. I recall now that at this time all John had on were his Converse black All Star sneakers. I was in the bathroom. I looked around. I could see John in the other room and he was holding a flashlight and going through papers. Outside of the bathroom there was a door. I opened this door and it was a closet. I looked in the room where this closet was and John was holding a flashlight and he was looking through the dresser drawers. I noticed the bed was all messed up. I heard some people coming down the hall. I got scared. Now after the sounds stopped I seen John with his flashlight go over toward a door and I seen John direct the flashlight to this door at the bottom of which was a low, big trunk. John asked me to help him move this trunk. When the flashlight that John was holding shined on the trunk I noticed the head of a human being up against this trunk. The head of this human being was stretched out on the floor. There was a lot of papers thrown over the rest of the body to which this head was attached. I could tell this was the body of a woman, a white woman. I seen John reach down and grab this human head by the hair and throw it to one side. I did not step over the body but John asked me to help him put this trunk on the bed. I reached down and with my hands I picked up the trunk and with John helping me we put the trunk on the messed-up bed. John started to work on the lock of the trunk. There were some pots and pans and some household stuff in the trunk. Some of the stuff in the

177

trunk was wrapped up in papers. We searched through the stuff in the trunk. I picked up John or Pop's snow boots and I walked out of the hotel room. I walked around the hallway and down to the elevator. John was still in the room. I walked out of the Wellington Hotel and up to the corner of State and Eagle streets outside of the DeWitt Clinton Hotel. I waited there about twenty-five or thirty minutes and then John or Pop came up State Street and he joined me. We walked down Eagle Street to the Gulf gas station at Eagle and Howard streets in Albany, New York.'

In this confession to the Albany police department in July 1970, Carlton Gary under the alias of his alter ego Carl Michaels, described the murder of eighty-five-year-old Nellie Farmer, a prototype of the murders he would be convicted for sixteen years later in Georgia. Gary was never prosecuted for this, one of a string of robbery murders committed in Albany that even today are still open cases although the crimes were used to establish a pattern of behavior similar to the Columbus stranglings that helped a county jury convict him in 1986.

In his confessions to the Albany police and later to the Columbus police in the Wynnton murders, Gary admitted to being at the crime scene and participating in the burglary, but he implicated an accomplice who he said had actually committed the murders. In Albany, John Lee Williams, the man Gary incriminated while he was being held in the county jail, was convicted on his testimony and sentenced to Dannemora. The conviction was later overturned when Gary withdrew his testimony, and John Williams was deemed innocent and released. In Columbus, the jury found that there was no accomplice in the Wynnton murders and that Gary had acted alone, robbing the old women, bludgeoning them, raping them, and finally strangling them with a stocking or a scarf.

'He's always been a crook,' former Gainsville, Florida,

detective Homer McGilvray said about the young Carlton Gary, whose name seemed to turn up every time a crime was committed in the area. Gary himself told the New York State prison authorities that he never had a home and never had any parents. That was partially true. Having lived with his mother as she moved from place to place, later with his aunt, with his grandmother, or completely on his own when he tried to find his mother, Carlton Gary had never had a home. Before his first arrest as a juvenile, he listed fifteen different residences. From the time neighbors spotted him rummaging in garbage cans in Columbus for food while he was a very young child to his first arrest for arson at age sixteen, his life reads like a blueprint for violence and crime.

Carlton Gary had a gifted-level IQ and creative abilities that were overshadowed by probable developmental disabilities and the lack of any childhood bliss. His congenital disorders are evidenced by several minor physical anomalies, the obvious webbing of skin between his fingers and an elongated middle toe. While still in elementary school he was afflicted with at least one severe head trauma which left him unconscious and comatose on the schoolyard ball field. Rejected by his father, chronically malnourished as a child, and a heavy drug user through his teens, Gary had been charged with robbery, assault, and arson before he turned eighteen.

Carlton Gary became a person who combined opposites: a husband and a pimp, a killer of older women and a care giver for his older aunt, a thief and a benefactor. While committing the Wynnton murders and pushing drugs in the black neighborhoods of Columbus and modeling on local television, he was living with a female deputy sheriff who had no idea that Gary was leading a double life.

Gary never confessed to the murders. In fact, publicly he still maintains that he worked with an accomplice named

Michael Crittendon who cased the houses of intended burglary victims and who actually committed the murders while Gary hid outside in the bushes. The prosecution produced no witnesses to the murders, although a victim of one of the sexual assaults identified Gary as her attacker after undergoing a session with a hypnotist months after the crime. Even then her angry testimony, according to Gary's lawyer, Bud Siemen, was inconsistent and not strong enough to serve as the basis for charging Gary with rape and attempted murder.

What was the basis of the prosecution that was able to win a death sentence without even producing a single eyewitness to the crime? And what was the path itself that led Carlton Gary full circle back to Columbus after twenty years of guerrilla warfare with police and prisons in Florida, South Carolina, and New York? First, the case against Gary rested upon a repeated pattern of behavior that the prosecution was able to connect with the rest of the stocking stranglings and with the robbery murder in New York. Although the state only charged Gary with the murders of Florence Scheible, Martha Thurmond, and Kathleen Woodruff – largely on the basis of fingerprints left at the scene – they used the murders of Ferne Jackson and Jean Dimenstein to create a larger pattern of related crime. And they used the murder of Nellie Farmer in Albany to establish a lifetime pattern of similar criminal activity that stretched back seventeen years.

Carlton Gary had confessed to being at the three crime scenes. In a midnight ride, he accompanied the Columbus police to the victims' houses and demonstrated how he had gained entrance and where the victims were at the time of the murders. Although he blamed the actual murders on Michael Crittendon, who was later cleared by the police, Gary described how the murders were committed and how Crittendon had raped and beaten the women. The prosecution used these robbery confessions to place Gary at the scenes and at the times of the murders and used the results of semen tests to show that Gary could have been the attacker who had raped the women. Further laboratory tests indicated that 'negroid' pubic hairs found on the victims also did not exclude Gary as the assailant. Finally, the prosecutor was able to use Gertrude Miller's testimony as positive identification of the man who beat, raped, and choked her with a knotted nylon stocking in 1977, only four days before the first of the Columbus stranglings was discovered. Carlton Gary was found guilty by the nine men and three women on the county jury and sentenced to the electric chair.

'I don't have any parents,' Carlton Gary once said. And by most people's standards that was true. He never knew his father, a construction worker who eventually died in an accident, saw him only once when the boy was twelve. And his mother was always on the move each time she met another man. The young Carlton Gary moved with her sometimes and sometimes he was left with his great-aunt Alma Williams or with his father's sister, Lillian Nesbit. Soon Gary was moving from place to place, often without the knowledge of his mother, aunt, or great-aunt. He became an orphan of the streets, developing a keen instinct for survival that enabled him to ingratiate himself with women and adults or anyone else who could help him. His uncle on his mother's side, William David, remembered that he was once notified by the MP at the main gate at the Fort Lee Army post in Virginia – four days before Christmas – that there was a visitor for him. Eight-year-old Carlton was put on the phone. 'Unk, it's Gary. Come get me.' To this day, David cannot understand how his nephew got to Virginia by himself. William David enrolled him in school, but by the following spring he was shipped out to another uncle in North Carolina.

Without a real home or any parents to assume legal responsibility, a teenage Carlton Gary gravitated between his aunts Alma and Lillian in Columbus and his mother in Florida. In Fort Myers, Florida, after he had finally established a residence with his mother, he returned home from school one day to find that she and her new man had moved out of the apartment. And he was on the road again, a sixteen-year-old with no home, seeking his mother, who had moved to Gainesville. It was in Gainesville that he met his first wife, Sheila, and was convicted for fire-bombing a white-owned grocery store whose owner had prosecuted Gary's mother for refusing to make good on a bad cheque.

That wasn't the first time Gary had been charged with a crime. Six months earlier, he was charged with breaking and entering an automobile in Gainesville, and two months after that he was charged with another breaking and entering. Gary escaped from custody in Gainesville, and made his way north to Connecticut. He sent for his wife and the two lived and worked in Old Saybrook, New London, Hartford, and Bridgeport, cities and towns along the southern Connecticut shore. Then, after being charged with assaulting a Bridgeport cop, Gary and his wife fled across the state line to Albany, New York, where he began playing music in nightclubs and was finally arrested for taking part in the robbery and murder of Nellie Farmer.

In a deal with the Albany county prosecutor's office, Gary admitted to burglary and testified that John Williams murdered Nellie Farmer, a rape/robbery/murder that occurred just two months after Marion Brewer, another retired worker from the welfare department, was raped and strangled with a pillowcase in a hotel nearby. Gary was sentenced to ten years at Dannemora on the burglary charge, even after the state's case against John Williams fell apart for lack of corroborating evidence, and murder charges against Gary were never filed. He was released on parole after serving five years.

Four months later he was rearrested for breaking parole. A year later he was reinstated on parole.

Finally, after escaping from Onondaga County prison in New York in August 1977, Gary returned to Columbus, where he committed the stocking stranglings throughout the fall and winter of 1977 and into 1978. By April of that year he had stopped the skein of murders and begun a series of robberies of fast food restaurants in Columbus and South Carolina, where he was finally caught and convicted in February 1979, almost a year after the last of the stranglings was committed. And it was there in South Carolina that he confessed to the restaurant robberies in Georgia and to escaping from the Onondaga prison. Five years later Gary escaped again and was arrested in Georgia, where he was indicted one day later for the Stocking Strangler murders. He was sentenced to death in August 1986.

Carlton Gary's trial was almost a pro forma exercise to invoke the death penalty on the killer nine years after the crimes were committed and almost two and a half years after the suspect was arrested. The appeals process will take at least another six to eight years. And Carlton Gary may never face the electric chair and the state of Georgia may never get what it wanted from the moment the first Stocking Strangler victim was discovered. The real tragedy is that these murders need never have taken place had someone in either Onondaga or Syracuse taken Carlton Gary seriously when he warned that he was embarking on a path of episodic violence fifteen years earlier. He asked for help from a parole officer even then. His pleas were ignored.

In much the same way the road signs of Gary's potential for future violence were evident when he was a schoolchild rummaging through the neighborhood garbage cans for food or when he turned up unannounced at the front gate of the Fort Lee Army post. Like Henry

Lee Lucas, Carlton Gary was born into an unstable and violent home environment. His father was never present, and his mother drifted from new address to new address as easily as she moved from relationship to relationship. Gary was abused as a child not only by his mother but by the men she lived with. He was malnourished while growing up, and, as evidenced by significant signs and symptoms observed from preliminary medical and psychological interviews, he suffers from a minimal brain dysfunction.

Gary has had a history of severe brain trauma on more than one occasion, he has been a chronic drug abuser, and he has been treated for psychological problems as well. Throughout his youth he displayed a propensity toward violence and antisocial behavior. He has been convicted of arson, robbery, assault, sexual abuse, and multiple murder. And this pattern of violence and crime has continued unabated throughout most of his life. In fact he has spent most of his thirty-five years either in jail or as a fugitive from the police. However, unlike more traditional criminals, his murder victims have not been people he has known, they have been complete strangers whom he first raped and bludgeoned before finally strangling them with a scarf or stocking. And his skein of murders seems to have run in patterns: two or more elderly white women in Albany and then five elderly white women in Columbus. In other words, even without the extensive battery of physiological tests that were used to establish the benchmark symptoms for Henry Lee Lucas, Carlton Gary has displayed all of the outward manifestations of a serial murderer who mixed freely among people while he was committing his reign of terror.

The book on Carlton Gary is far from being closed. Throughout the course of the appeals process, and until his condition is diagnosed, his lawyers will seek to have the death sentence overturned on the grounds that a proper defense was prevented from being presented. If, in the process of these appeals, deep brain EEGs and CAT scans reveal organic abnormalities and skin and hair tests reveal high levels of mood-altering toxins, it will come as no surprise. The combination of physiological, psychological, and social abnormalities set against the pattern of his criminal behavior will reveal that he was an individual who was not in control of his behavior during the cycles of the Wynnton murders, and the missing puzzle pieces of Carlton Gary's life will finally come together.

9

Bobby Joe Long

1. Also known as: None
2. Date of birth: 10/14/53
3. Place of birth: Kenova, West Virginia
4. Place of arrest: Tampa, Florida
5. Date of arrest: 7/14/83
6. Charge: Murder, rape
7. Convictions: Murder, rape
8. Sentence: Death
9. No. of victims: Fifty (plus) rapes, nine murders
10. Current status: Death row, Stark, Florida

When Bobby Joe Long spotted the pretty young woman bicycling home from work in North Tampa, he had already decided he'd had enough. For seven months he had been on a wild spree of rape and murder that loosely followed the cycle of the full moon. He picked up 'loose women' in bars or on the street, drove them to a deserted stretch of road in the rural countryside around Tampa, overpowered them and tied them up, raped them, strangled them to death, and left their bodies along the side of the road. The local homicide detectives were stymied and assembled a task force of state police and special agents from the Behavioral Science Unit of the FBI.

'I knew when I let her go that it would only be a matter of time,' Long remembers from his cell on Florida's death row. 'I didn't even tell her not to talk to the police or anything. And before her, when I first read about the task force in Tampa, I could have gone to Fort Lauderdale or somewhere else and they would have never found me. I just didn't care any more, and I wanted to stop. I was sick inside. Doesn't the fact that I could have run and didn't count for something?'

During this entire period, Bobby Long lived and worked among the residents of Tampa, dated girls, worked at whatever jobs he could, and obtained a degree as an X-ray technician. He tried as best he could to satisfy a sex drive that had reached a level of compulsion. He knew that a part of his personality was no longer working. He knew that ever since the massive head injuries he had received in a motorcycle accident ten years earlier things just weren't the same inside him. He lost his temper easily. Loud or sudden noises sent him into a fury. He became violent with little or no provocation. He had lost all resiliency and couldn't roll with the punches the way he had before the accident. And he had an insatiable drive for sex. While he was still married, he had sex with his wife two or three times a day and masturbated at least five more times a day. He had fantasies of making love to his wife's sister and her friends. He had fantasies of group sex and of overpowering women. These fantasies started while he was still in the hospital recovering from the accident.

After each murder, in the solitude of his apartment in North Tampa in 1983, Bobby Long would sleep deeply for sometimes more than twelve hours, and upon awakening he would wonder whether he had only dreamed the murder or had actually performed it. He would walk across the street to the nearby Magic Market to get a newspaper to read whether he had only dreamed the murder or whether it was real. He read about the growing panic in Tampa with the discovery of each new body. He read about each girl's background, the mysterious victims who had worked the streets and bars in North Tampa, and their grieving families. If he could have had any emotions about his victims, he would have hated them. Ngeon Thi Long, a dancer in the strip bars along North Nebraska Avenue in Tampa, was the first. He knew she was a prostitute, and he detested women who were whores, who were aggressive, who had no allegiance to any man. In reality, he claims, he was sympathetic toward women. When he was the Classified Ad Rapist in Ford Lauderdale and Ocala eight years earlier and had assaulted housewives who placed 'for sale' ads in the newspaper, he felt pity for them. He explained that he didn't want to hurt them, and wouldn't have hurt them even if they tried to scream for help. More often than not Long would try to apologize to them during the assault. 'Many times we would just talk. You would be surprised what some of them told me.'

But by November 1983 it was different. Bobby Joe Long was getting progressively worse. He had already committed eight murders. He was disgusted with what he was doing, but he couldn't stop. Then he saw the girl on the bike. She had got off her late shift at the doughnut shop after midnight and was riding home. Bobby Long's reaction was almost instinctive. Any pretty girl out this late had to be trouble. She seemed too aggressive, focused as she was on pedaling her bike along the dark road. Long hid in the bushes and waited until she passed. Then he sprang out from hiding and knocked her off her bike. He overpowered her at once and tied her up.

But this victim wasn't aggressive. Long blindfolded her, put her in his car, and then began a twenty-six-hour odyssey with her that eventually led to her release. She was a true victim. Her family had no money and her stepfather was out of work and confined to a wheelchair. She told Bobby that he, too, had abused her when she was younger. Now she had to work the late night shift in a doughnut shop just to help support her family. And she was also a student. Long knew that she didn't deserve to die; she wasn't like the other girls. She wasn't a prostitute or a woman who used her body to manipulate men. He drove her around blindfolded for many hours and tried to talk to her the way he had spoken to his first rape victims eight years before. He explained that he didn't want to hurt her. He drove to a bank machine for cash, and she was able to peek at the dashboard and around the car from under her blindfold. Then he took her back to his apartment where she again was able to sneak looks at the interior and later give police an exact description of where she had been and what the place looked like. He raped her, but it wasn't the same for him as it had been before. Finally he drove her back to where he had first picked her up and set her free.

He knew that she would lead the police back to him as soon as she was released. He had also known it was near the end when the first police task force was assembled. But there was still a living part of his brain that couldn't continue the violence any longer, and it closed him down. His fantasy had exploded, and his skein of rapes and murders was coming to an end.

Two days later his compulsion came over him again. As he was driving along the outskirts of North Tampa late in the evening, he spotted a car swerving back and forth in front of him. He thought it was being driven by a woman and that she was drunk. He followed her. She almost swerved off the road, but then she noticed she was being followed. She pulled over to the side. Bobby Long stopped his car directly behind hers, got out, walked over to her car, and the two of them began a conversation. In a few moments she agreed to ride around with him, believing that he would drive her back to her car in the morning. Bobby noticed how big she was. He described her later as a hard-looking girl in cowboy boots. Not fat, but she had a large frame. He disliked her from the moment he saw her.

As soon as she got in beside him he attacked her. She screamed and fought back, kicking him in the shins and putting her boots through his dashboard. The two struggled until Long overpowered her and tied her hands. She kept on screaming, however, until he forced her to stop by squeezing her windpipe. She became quiet, and he began cruising with her. Every time she started to scream he squeezed her throat until she stopped. Finally he strangled her until she lost consciousness. She came to shortly thereafter and began screaming again. And again he strangled her until she lost consciousness. Bobby undressed her but found, as he looked at the stirring figure, that what had been a raging desire for sex had simply dried up. Finally she came to again and began to scream for help, and this time he strangled her until she died. He rode through North Tampa with the naked body of the dead Kim Swann beside him for hours. Nobody stopped him even after he'd pulled into a local gas station to fill up. Finally he drove the body to a secluded area outside of the city and pushed it out of the car. He had never even bothered to rape her. Four days later he was arrested for the rape and kidnapping of the seventeen-year-old, and the violent career of thirty-one-year-old Bobby Joe Long was now in the courts.

When the eleven-year-old Bobby Long was reaching puberty, he realized that his breasts were growing. It was embarrassing for him to look down and see his enlarged breasts filling out his shirt as if he were a young girl. All of his clothing became tight, and his figure started to change shape as well. Other members of his family had experienced this congenital dysfunction of the endocrine system and his doctor prescribed surgery. Long's mother recalls that the surgeon removed more than six pounds of tissue from her son's chest. That seemed to remedy the problem, but it didn't keep Bobby Long from experiencing a lunar protomenstrual cycle for the rest of his life.

'Even now,' he recalls, 'I can always tell when it's the full moon. I get crazy when the moon is full; I can't sit still; I have to pace; even the smallest thing sets me off. And I'm not the only one. All over the row, you can tell when it's the full moon, even if you can't see it from this hole. People start screaming and carrying on, you just know that it's a full moon.'

Long's fear of being transformed into a woman when he was reaching puberty paralleled the many problems he had relating to women throughout his life. When he was still a very young child his mother divorced his father and took the boy to Florida. They were very poor, Long recalls. They rented single rooms in boardinghouses where they both had to sleep in the same bed. Bob's perception and his mother Louella's memory vary greatly. His mother worked nights and dated a lot of different men, some of whom Bob claimed regularly visited her at the boardinghouse. Even though Louella Long, Bobby's mother, denies this, they both agree that she changed jobs frequently and kept them on the move from place to place wherever she could pick up new work. Therefore he was never in one community long enough to make any lasting friendships. He was always the new kid in the neighborhood and was forced to rely on his mother for most of his companionship. For Bobby Joe Long, this situation aroused extreme rage in him, especially when the attractive and seductive Louella Long had relationships with grown men.

When his mother wasn't working nights, Long remembers, he asked her to spend time with him at home.

Instead, 'she would never stay home. She would always go out. I used to ask her why she couldn't spend her nights off with me. Take me out once in a while. But she would go out and leave me with one of the neighbors.' Worse than the loneliness, however, was the fact that Long and his mother shared the same bed until he was twelve, at which time she married her second husband. For Long, it was awkward and embarrassing; for his mother, it was an economic necessity.

'I never undressed in front of him or did anything anyone would consider indecent,' his mother explains. 'We just didn't have the money to rent two bedrooms.' She also remembers that, because she worked nights and didn't get home until five or six in the morning, 'by the time I was getting undressed to go to bed, Bobby was getting up to go to school.' According to her, the two were actually using the same room in shifts: he would sleep at night and she during the day. She also denies ever bringing men over to where the two lived. 'We were very poor and had to live on the tips I could make waitressing or carhopping. There were times when I didn't even know where I would get the money for the next meal, not to mention the rent, and I was afraid we'd be living in the street. But no matter what Bobby Joe or anyone says, I was never a prostitute, and I tried to be a good mother.'

Bobby's father saw his son only rarely between 1956, when Louella left West Virginia with their son, and 1968, when she divorced her second husband. 'They would come back to Kenova on Christmas or some other times, and I would see them. But for the most part, I didn't see Bobby Joe at all when he was growing up.' During Bobby's trial, it was disclosed that during his young life, on several occasions, Bob Long, Sr., while visiting the family in Florida, would become violent and sexually attack Louella, sometimes using a knife. Even today, he speaks of his son from a state of severe grief. But it was

BOBBY JOE LONG

Bobby's mother who raised him and who became the dominant influence in his life. She remembers him as the 'perfect, cute little boy. He made good grades at school. Then he met Cindy.'

When he was thirteen, Bobby Joe began dating Cindy Jean Guthrie, the girl who lived with her aunt just a few blocks away from Bobby and his mother and the person he would marry seven years later. She became the other woman who exercised control over his life. 'Cindy and I were inseparable from the first times we began dating,' Bobby recalls. 'She would be over at our house, or I would be at hers. We were always together.' From time to time they would break up, date other people, but get back together again. Five years and two children later they were divorced.

Cindy behaved like Bobby Joe's mother. She was forceful and told him what to do. The two women also look very much alike. Both are thin and fair, they have similar voices, and both are aggressive and able to manipulate the men they want. And Bobby Joe had found Cindy at just the time his mother had married her second husband. In his own mind, it was a natural transition from one mother-son relationship to the next. Louella had established herself with a new partner, and so did her son. His romance with Cindy would last throughout the stormy times in Louella's second marriage, the trips back to West Virginia to visit her first husband, and constant fights the two teenagers had. It lasted through Bobby's first brush with the law on a breaking and entering charge that was eventually dropped and throughout high school and his enlistment in the Army.

Louella didn't like the attention Bobby gave Cindy, and even today the two women are bitter about one another. 'She was manipulative,' Louella Long says of Cindy. 'She was one of the cruellest people I ever knew. She never really had a mother or a family for that matter and was jealous of the family that Bobby had. I tried to be a mother to her and to help her with the children, but she never liked me.' She remembers that her son's performance in school, which had always been affected by his changing residences every few months, had still been above average until he met Cindy. Then his grades fell apart completely, and he never finished high school. In fact Louella even blames Cindy in part for her son's crimes. 'You have no idea how she changed him and how what she did ruined his whole life.'

Bobby Joe Long married Cindy after he had enlisted in the Army, where he was training to become an electrician. He had worked as an apprentice electrician while he was in school and he saw the Army as a way to get enough experience to become a licensed professional. However, all that changed six months into his enlistment when he was almost killed in a motorcycle accident on the way to cash a cheque. 'I must have been doing at least sixty-five or seventy when I broadsided a car. My Bell motorcycle helmet was shattered. That's what kind of force my head hit the car with. I don't remember a thing about it until I woke up in the hospital.'

Bobby Joe severely fractured his skull in the accident and remained in a semiconscious state for weeks. He had severe headaches, which continue to this day, and was unable to focus his vision. He reports that his pupils remained dilated for a short period after the accident, and that his right pupil continued to be larger than his left for many months. His medical records indicate that he had sustained a serious head trauma, but neither his X rays nor his EEG were evaluated by a skilled neurologist at the time. During his trial, more than ten years after the accident, Dr. Dorothy Otnow Lewis of the psychiatry department at NYU's Medical Center has reevaluated Long and found that the brain damage he sustained was serious enough to warrant a thorough neurological examination.

The injuries to Long's brain from the motorcycle accident compounded possible damage received from four previous documented head traumas he sustained before he was ten. At the age of five he fell from a swing, lost consciousness, and awoke to find that a stick had punctured his eye and was embedded in the medial portion of his left eyelid. A year later he injured his head when he was thrown from his bike, and a year after that he was knocked unconscious when hit by a car bumper. He lost several teeth and was diagnosed as having received a severe concussion. A year after that he was thrown by a pony and was dizzy and nauseous for the next several weeks. 'That was the sickest I had ever been in my entire life,' Long says about the event. 'I couldn't even stand up straight without getting dizzy.' Dr. Lewis reported to Long's defense attorney that the aggregate result of these injuries was a significant level of damage to the left temporal lobe of Long's brain, with damage to the surrounding areas of the central nervous system as well, and loss of those neurological functions generally commensurate with that type of damage. She also noted that Long had a lesion on his left temporal lobe, indicated by the results of an EEG, and irregularities in the muscular ability on his right knee and ankle. The left side of Long's face is still numb as a result of the accident, and he still walks with a limp.

The motorcycle accident, more than any other single event, transformed Long's life. 'Anybody who knew me before the accident and knows me now would say that it's like I was two different people,' Long explains. 'I knew there was something wrong with my head when I was in the hospital after the accident. I was just out of it for months and then, while still in the hospital, I started thinking about sex. That's all I could think about day and night. I thought about it with my wife, with her friends, with people I knew from before. It started driving me crazy.'

Bobby and Cindy had their first child a few months later, after his release from the hospital, but Bobby Joe's troubles were only just beginning. First there were the physical and emotional repercussions from the accident. 'I tried to tell the doctors at the hospital that there was something still wrong with me. I couldn't get these thoughts of sex out of my mind, and Cindy and I had gone from having sex two or three times a week to at least two times a day. And I was still masturbating to get relief. I thought about having sex with just about every girl I met or got to know. Then there were the headaches that wouldn't go away, and the feeling that the side of my face was dead. And there were the noises. The slightest sound would seem like an explosion. I would scream at my son to be quiet, when he wasn't really making much noise at all. It only sounded like a lot of noise to me. To this day, I can't take loud noises – they make me get mad and crazy.' Besides his insatiable appetite for sex, the most disturbing change to Long's personality was his violent reaction to anything that didn't go his way. 'Before the accident, I was pretty much laid back. I would get mad, but I never really got crazy even when I was pushed. After the accident, though – and I noticed this as soon as I got home – the least little thing would make me furious. I mean, I really got so violent that I couldn't control myself sometimes, and that made me worried. I was never like that before.'

Often violence would come over him like a thunderstorm, with little or no provocation, and leave just as suddenly. When a violent outburst of temper had passed, Long would have no memory of it whatsoever. His mother remembers one such incident when she had borrowed his car to go shopping. When she passed by where he was sitting to pick up the keys, he reached out and grabbed her, put her over his knees, and spanked her very hard on the buttocks for several minutes. He had raised several painful bruises. He then stormed out of the house. When he returned, he could not remember the incident. Even today, Long claims not to remember spanking his mother, and she has never confronted him directly about it since it happened.

Over the next few months severe character disorders emerged in Bobby Long's personality. He was contentious, overreacted to any negative situation, and suffered from constant headaches and dizziness. After two years of difficult recovery from his motorcycle accident, his career in the Army came to an end when he claimed the Army violated his enlistment contract by not providing complete medical diagnosis of his injuries. He worked sporadically as an X-ray technician but was fired from job after job for making advances toward the female patients and, in one instance, for showing obscene material to a young girl. He served two days in jail on that charge and lost his job as well. After returning to West Virginia to work at a hospital there, he lost his job because he made the female patients undress before taking their X rays. Long was never hostile or overtly threatening, but there was something menacing about him nevertheless.

From 1980 to 1983, Long committed more than fifty rapes in Florida as the Classified Ad Rapist and terrorized the communities around Fort Lauderdale, Ocala, Miami, and Dade County. He called the numbers listed in classified ads for the sale of furniture and other household articles and made appointments to meet the sellers during the day when he was most likely to encounter housewives. Once inside the house, he would pull out his knife, tie up the victim, rape her, and rob the house. He never committed any murders and was rarely violent. 'I felt sorry for them, and I told them that I didn't want to hurt anybody. I didn't even like tying them up. I think they knew that I wasn't violent because many of them victims talked to me not like I was a criminal but like I was a person. They were pretty sad too because of the lives they had. If conditions had been different, we might have had a relationship.'

The classified ad rapes continued for more than two years despite the fact that the local police had assembled task forces to catch the rapist and had brought in the FBI. During this time Long was trying to lead as normal a life as possible: coping with a divorce and his ex-wife's remarriage, changing jobs, communicating with his parents, who had since got back together and were planning to remarry, and carrying on an active social life. It was also during this period that Long was falsely charged with rape by a former girl friend. The entire incident involved changing relationships in a love triangle from which Long had tried consistently to extricate himself. He admits that the woman was able to manipulate him because he wanted and needed to have sex. However, out of jealousy of her former boyfriend's new relationship and anger at Bobby Joe Long's intervention, a woman charged Long with raping her after she had invited him back to her apartment. 'This showed me what a real bitch could do when she didn't get her way,' Long explained. 'I've committed rapes and I've murdered women. I know what happens inside of me when I get violent. I know how I feel. I can tell you that I did not rape that girl. We had sex, but she was drunk, she invited me back to her place, and she announced in front of my friends that she wanted to have sex. Then, the next day, she told the police that I raped her.'

Long was formally charged in November 1981 with rape, and the case went to trial. However, even after having been convicted, he wrote a letter to the court asking for a new trial, and the judge granted it. 'The judge took it as a motion,' Long said, 'and he granted it. The charges were later dropped because I had witnesses who told the police that the woman had asked me to take her back home and had come over in the first place looking for sex. She was a whore anyway, and once that came out, the whole charge was thrown out of court.'

Ironically, it was at this time that Long was still committing rapes and robberies through the classified ads. He claims, however, that he tried to stop. 'I was dating a nurse, and I explained my problems to her – I didn't tell her that I was a rapist – but I explained part of what was wrong. She told me that I had a medical problem, and I came very close to seeing a doctor about it. I walked out of the doctor's office, though, because I knew that once I told him what I was doing he would tell the police. If I had any idea then that my behavior might have been neurological, I would have gone to a neurologist, but I didn't know.'

For all the years after the accident and during the period of the two series of rapes, Long was fully aware of the moral implications of what he was feeling and doing. Indeed, the psychological evaluation of Long in February 1985 found him to be competent to stand trial and to be punished for what he did despite evidence of psychomotor dysfunction, impaired cerebral function, and lesions on the left and right hemispheres of his brain. The EEG evaluations that the court-appointed doctors performed were superficial because they did not cover the full thirty-six-hour period necessary to document a deep brain dysfunction, and the neurological reflex tests were compromised because Long was bound in shackles at the time. The clinical experts made no mention of the hormonal imbalance that had caused Long to grow breasts, experience a form of menstrual cycle, and had resulted in serious impairments to socialization, gender confusion, behavior alterations, and physiological deformities. The state's experts did not see the significance of Long's reported hypersexuality, nor did they relate it to the motorcycle accident. Relying on the medical reports written in 1974, the state's witnesses, like the Army doctors years earlier, determined that Long had recovered from the accident sufficiently that there was no permanent cerebral impairment. Dorothy Lewis, however, noted that Long's hypersexuality and hair-trigger violence conformed to a pattern of behavior disorders associated with neurological damage to the limbic region of the brain.

The implicit tragedy in the deaths of the women and the more than fifty rapes committed two years earlier was that, had Long known at the time that he was suffering from a medical problem, he would have had it treated. 'If there was a place I could have gone for treatment, I would have gone. I knew I was sick, but there was nothing I could do about it. I was afraid that the first thing a doctor would do would be to call the police, and they would stick me in jail. Finally I got so sick of what I was doing, I got myself turned in.'

Long recalls feeling an escalating sense of revulsion with each ensuring rape murder. He had no feelings of remorse for the victims at first because he thought they were women who used men. 'I know what I did. I raped them and murdered them. But they were the ones who offered the invitation.' He remembers that the first murder began when the victim picked him up in one of the strip bars on Nebraska Avenue in Tampa. 'She picked me up really, I didn't go after her. She was a whore. She manipulated men, and she wanted to manipulate me. Once I had her in the car, I tied her up and raped her. Then I strangled her and dumped her body alongside the highway. I knew what I was doing, but I just couldn't stop myself. I hated her. I hated her from the time she picked me up, but I didn't plan to murder her. I don't even think that I planned to rape her either. She was just sitting there in the front seat of the car, and I grabbed her, covered her mouth, and tied her up. I couldn't believe what I'd done the next morning. I was sick, and I knew I was in real trouble. Then a few days later I met the Simms girl, and it was the same thing all over again. She was a barfly. She really picked me up, and I just turned on her in the car.'

In a regular procession, the next six victims invited themselves into Long's presence and unknowingly placed their lives in jeopardy. Even after the third rape in only two months, the girls along Nebraska Avenue continued to be attracted to Bobby Long. 'I knew when the police task force was announced that I was running out of time. I should have gotten out of the area, but I wanted to get caught. I could have gone anywhere in Florida, kept on raping and murdering, and the police would never have found me. I could have gone back to California and done the same thing. Then, right before I was caught, the cops stopped me just to check on some report of a robbery in the area. But they took my license and looked over the car and then let me go. I knew they were following me then. I'm not completely stupid not to know what the cops were doing. It was just a matter of days, so I made myself visible and gave them all the time they needed to arrest me. Even Cindy called me and asked me if I'd heard about all the rapes in my area. As if she wasn't giving me a clue that the cops were on to me and that they'd already called her. But I wanted to be stopped because I couldn't stop myself.'

Then he met his seventeen-year-old rape victim. 'When I started talking to her I knew it was all over. Her own stepfather had raped her and she had to work to support him. She was the first girl that I stopped who didn't come over to me first. I knocked her off her bike. That was a first. I tied her up and blindfolded her and brought her back to my apartment, and I knew that if I let her go she would tell the police. I talked to her and asked her not to, but she hates me. When they tried me, she was among the people who wanted to see me fried the most.'

Long and his attorney, Ellis Rubin, believe that he will

get a new trial because his first confession was forced by the police. 'Once they had me in custody, I couldn't stop talking. Then I realized that I could be fried for what I was saying, so I asked for a lawyer. But they wouldn't let me see a lawyer until I finished what I was saying because they said that I already knew my rights. I know now that they had to let me see a lawyer when I asked for one.' Long's behavior when he was taken into custody fits the pattern of other serial killers who feel the immediate need to confess when they are arrested.

It was after he was put on trial, however, that he realized that his case had become a political issue. 'What kills me the most is that the girls I raped were all dope addicts and whores. Not that anybody really deserves to get killed, but they weren't saints. I'm sick. I know there's something wrong with my brain. I knew it from the first times in the hospital when I felt what I felt. I told doctor after doctor what I felt, but it made no difference. I'm no killer, not like the other guys here on the row. But it made no difference to the court or to the governor. Bloody Bob Graham needs me to die because he has to get reelected, just like he needed Ted Bundy to die to get reelected. He kept on signing death warrants for Bundy and putting him on death watch even though he knew that the court was going to step in. Everybody knew it. But it made no difference because we're here just to die so that people can get elected back into office. As far as I'm concerned, they're the real killers because they're not sick and are using the state to kill so that they can get ahead in their careers. I'm sick and I'm going to be fried alive. After I'm dead, they're going to open up my head and find that just like we've been saying a part of my brain is black and dry and dead. But they're not going to give a fuck.'

10

Leonard Lake

1. Also known as: Charles Gunnar, Paul Cosner, Scott Stapley
2. Date of birth: 7/20/46
3. Place of birth: San Francisco, California
4. Place of arrest: San Francisco, California
5. Date of arrest: 6/2/85
6. Charge: Illegal weapons, fugitive warrant
7. Convictions: None
8. Sentence: None
9. Current status: Committed suicide while in the custody of the San Francisco police department

Sergeant Ronald L. McFall, a detective in the San Francisco police department, is reviewing a videotape labeled 'M Ladies Kathy/Brenda' that was found by a squad of police and Calaveras County Sheriff's Department officers at an abandoned cabin off Blue Mountain Road in Wisleyville, a rural, densely wooded section of northern California. The scratchy video depicts a young white woman with her hands cuffed behind her sitting in a chair in the living room of the mountain cabin. A voice off camera tells her: 'Mike owes us and unfortunately he can't pay. We're going to give you a choice, Kathy. It's probably the last choice we're going to give you. You can go along with us. You're going to cooperate and in approximately thirty days – if you want a date, you can write in your calendar the fifteenth of May. We will either drug you, blindfold you, or in some way or other make sure you don't know where you are and where you're going, and take you back to the city and let you go. And what you say at that time, I don't care. My name you don't know. His name is Charlie, but screw it. By then, hopefully, Mike will have disappeared gracefully. If you don't cooperate with us, we'll probably put a round through your head and take you out and bury you someplace. No witnesses. You will give us information on Mike. Basically Mike will move off in the horizon.

'While you're here you'll wash for us, you'll clean for us, you'll fuck for us. That's your choice in a nutshell. It's not much of a choice unless you have a death wish. You'll probably think worse things in the next few weeks.'

A balding, powerful-looking man with a black beard enters the frame. His name is Leonard Lake. He puts leg irons on the woman's feet and then takes her handcuffs off. He has her undress. She is very reluctant to take her pants off. An Asian male enters the frame and says: 'The piece is on the table.'

'Don't make it hard for her, Charlie,' the bearded man says.

The woman named Kathy Allen undresses and goes to shower with the Asian male. The tape cuts to a bedroom and shows the black-haired man on a bed with a woman sitting on his back. There is another cut in the tape and the black-bearded man appears, again in the bedroom with Kathy Allen, indicating that it is four days later and that he is upset with her for bending the hasps on a lock in her cell. She is strapped to the bed while he threatens her and takes still photos of her naked body. He tells her that they killed Mike and buried him. It will soon be her turn to join him.

Now the tape cuts to a second female named Brenda O'Connor. She, like Kathy Allen, is sitting fully clothed in a chair with her hands cuffed behind her back. Standing beside her, holding a knife in his hand, is an Asian male named Charles Ng. He uses the knife point to cut Brenda's shirt off and then slowly cuts her brassiere in two. In a voice-over, the sergeant hears Leonard Lake giving her the same instructions he gave to Kathy Allen. 'If you don't do what we tell you, we will tie you to the bed, rape you, shoot you in the head, and take you out and bury you.' Lake informs Brenda that he has taken her baby and placed it with a family in Fresno, and even though Brenda becomes hysterical and pleads with Lake and Ng for the return of her baby, the two of them only repeat their original instructions. The tape ends.

Sergeant McFall is horrified at what he sees: snuff videos that combine violent sex with vivid scenes of actual murders committed on camera, photo portraits of women in chains, snapshots of dead victims moments before their burial, and bags of human bones that had been boiled down into soup. The police found the scattered teeth of Lonnie Bond, Jr., the two-year-old child Brenda O'Connor pleaded with her captives to spare, and the remains of Kathy Allen and at least nineteen other people in shallow graves off Blue Mountain Road. The task force of San Francisco detectives and Calaveras County sheriff's officers also discovered a concrete bunker that served as a torture chamber and film studio for Lake's and Ng's videos. Police also found a 100-page personal journal entitled 'The Diary of Leonard Lake – 1984.'

'Leonard Lake,' the book begins, 'a name not seen or used much these days in my second year as a fugitive.

Mostly dull day-to-day routine – still with death in my pocket and fantasy my goal.' Among the fantasies and visions described in the 1984 journal and other diaries that were found in the Wisleyville cabin is Lake's plan for Operation Miranda. Hatched in the isolated hamlet of Miranda in the hills of northern California's Humboldt County, Operation Miranda was a plan for stockpiling bunkers with food and guns to survive a nuclear holocaust. Among the provisions Lake had planned for was a cadre of 'sex slaves' who would act out the fantasies of the survivalists and be kept locked in isolated chambers.

Lake viewed other people, particularly women, as if they were property. Human beings and inanimate objects were treated as one and the same. They existed to be placed at his disposal, his for the taking, used and then discarded. He was described by the police as a man who was without morality, who preyed primarily upon transient victims without a purpose to their own lives who were drawn into his vision by the promise of a better life. Some of his other victims responded to classified ads for the sale of video equipment, and still others came to his cabin to deliver cars that he had offered to buy. He would build a shelter, he promised himself in his diary, that would 'provide a facility for my sexual fantasies. It will provide physical security for myself and my passions. It will protect me from nuclear fallout. Tapes, photographs, and weapons will be hidden away.'

Lake's existence was a stringing together of private fantasies of earlier violent times when killing was a reflection of one's personal code of justice. 'He was interested in paganism and the Vikings,' said Cricket Balazs, his former wife. 'He could quote the Bible upside down, but he didn't believe in God. He was into Odin and Valhalla.' His interest in medieval legends and fascination with the folklore of early civilization and his own study of genetics led him to become a 'co-creator of the unicorns' at the Renaissance Pleasure Faire. He worked for the people who grafted the single horn onto the head of a goat that in 1984 became a part of the Barnum & Bailey circus, and he was the barker for the attraction at the West Coast Renaissance Faire. However, another employer of his at the Philo Motel remembers entering Lake's room and seeing a large pot boiling on the stove. When Lake lifted the pot, the employer saw the head of a single-horned goat cooking into a soup.

Leonard Lake died in a San Francisco hospital in 1985 after taking a cyanide capsule while in police custody. He was arrested on a weapons charge after interceding for Charles Ng, who was caught shoplifting a vise at South City Lumber in San Francsico. While the police were questioning Lake, who offered to pay for the vise, Ng disappeared. After a search of Lake's car revealed a handgun with a silencer, the police arrested him and began a search of the car's registration and the driver's license Lake was carrying. In the police station Lake asked for a glass of water and for paper and pencil so that he could write out a statement. While left alone, he took the cyanide, swallowed it with the water that the police brought him, and scribbled a note to Cricket Balazs, his ex-wife, that read, 'I love you. Please forgive me. I forgive you. Please tell Mama, Fern, and Patty I'm sorry.' Then he blurted out his true name to the police and slumped forward. He died four days later without ever regaining consciousness; during those four days the police had traced the car Lake was driving to missing car salesman Paul Cosner. Following leads found in the car and information from a records check on Lake's background, the police uncovered a warrant for his arrest on bail jumping and information about a rural cabin in Calaveras County. A search of that property on the day Lake died revealed the remains of eight people in unmarked graves, an underground bunker with prison cells, videotapes of torture and murder, and Leonard Lake's journals.

Who was Leonard Lake? the San Francisco newspapers asked. How did he manage to lure his victims into his power at his survivalist retreat in the mountains? And what drove him to butcher not only men and women but tiny children as well, leaving bags of their remains in a long trench just beyond the bunker? Lake's grandmother, the strict disciplinarian who raised him when he was younger, refused to provide any answers to the police or for this study. To this day she maintains that Lake was a good boy misled by his friends. Lake's mother, Gloria Ebeling, revealed that the Lake family was frightened that mental illness ran in every generation. Hers was a family of alcoholics, and she had married into Lake's father's family, also plagued by alcoholism in every generation.

When he was six, Lake's parents discovered they could no longer raise him. Out of money and with mounting debts, Lake's father sent the oldest boy to live with his grandparents. The old man, also an alcoholic, subjected the boy to a militaristic upbringing, teaching him unquestioning discipline and a fear of punishment. However, Lake still maintained contact with his parents, who were raising a younger son, Donald. Lake's father was extremely cold toward the children and disciplined Leonard whenever he could. Yet Donald, who became sickly and accident prone, was taken under his mother's wing. With every accident, every fall from a swing, and every concussion he received while a child, Donald was protected more and more. He himself became a type of victim and from the age of twelve, after experiencing a serious head trauma, he became an epileptic and suffered from severe seizures and body tremors. At the same time he developed an unusual cruelty to animals, began setting fires, and sexually assaulted both his sisters. Had he not eventually become one of Leonard Lake's murder victims, he might have developed into a serial murderer like his older brother.

Although Leonard Lake displayed early signs of compulsivity and obsession, his most violent tendencies didn't emerge until after his tours of duty as a Marine in Vietnam. As a child and later as an adolescent, he protected his grandmother and mother from his father's and grandfather's violence even though his mother showed a greater fondness for her younger child, Donald. Leonard also showed early signs of hypergraphia and obsessive attention to minute detail in his experiments as a youth with rats and mice. He traced the life cycle of mice from conception to death and kept detailed notes on the various stages of their development. He kept records of which pairs of mice bred from which litters, and was able to track genetic features through many successive generations of offspring. From these early experiments as a child, he became a self-taught geneticist.

Lake was also a compulsively clean person as a child. Perhaps because this commitment to inspection status was inculcated by his grandparents or perhaps, as in most obsessively clean people, cleaning and bathing are immediately self-gratifying, he took several showers a day, often washing his hands before beginning any new activity. The tapes found in his Wisleyville cabin also show that, before beginning the sex torture ritual with any of his victims, Lake forced them to take a shower.

Lake's fascination with photographs of nude women began while he was still a child. His mother explained that their family had always encouraged Lake to be proud of the nude body and to take pictures of girls, even his sisters and cousins. 'He took pictures of pretty young girls all of his life and kept them in picture albums like a hunter keeps a trophy.' His mother was not surprised that Lake made underground porno films and kept video records of his torture rituals. Even his wife, Cricket Balazs, served as a model for some of the custom sadomasochistic tapes he shot for clients. Balazs would use the customer's first name in the tapes as she acted out his sexual fantasies. Lake scripted, directed, and filmed these while, his ex-wife explains, he was probably making even weirder violence and pornography videos on the side.

Lake believed that he was the ultimate victim of women, and in his vision of a post-nuclear-holocaust civilization, women would live to serve him. In his survivalist compound he had elaborate shackling devices that he forced his female victims to wear while they submitted to his fantasies. He made them perform slave rituals just before having sex with them, and tortured them to increase the urgency of their submission. In his videos he portrays his victims as chained prisoners, struggling against their bonds and tortured by sadomasochistic devices that force them to scream out in pain, even when there is no pain at all.

His younger half sisters explained that Lake's delusions regarding the submission of women began while he was still an adolescent, even before he joined the Marines. His younger sister looked to Leonard to protect her from the violence and aggressiveness of Donald, Lake's younger brother, who by this time was periodically losing control of his behavior. Leonard solicited and received sexual favors. Lake began to equate success with domination over women and asserting himself against a world he believed to be hostile toward him. His expectations were high, but his accomplishments never measured up to those expectations. Finally, at age thirty-nine, after having been discharged from the Marines for emotional difficulties, he told his brother-in-law that he had only one final chance for financial success.

In his final years Lake drifted from community to community, always keeping in touch with his ex-wife, who acted as a sometime fence for the goods and credit cards he stole. Police believe that even before he settled in Wisley-ville he had committed a series of murders in a similar survivalist compound at a place called the Mother Lode in Humboldt County, California. He had been arrested on weapons charges there, jumped bail, and fled to Calaveras County, where he was caught. At the Mother Lode, Lake had murdered his best friend from his Vietnam years, Charles Gunnar, and assumed his identity. It was also in Humboldt County that Leonard murdered his younger brother, Donald, who had visited him there in quest of money.

Lake lived in the Blue Mountain Road cabin under the identity of Charles Gunnar but frequently assumed the identities of his victims. His cache of documentation, found by the police in their search of the cabin and bunker, revealed stolen credit cards, drivers' licenses, and vehicle registrations for the cars Lake had taken from his victims. Even when he was arrested in the lumber store parking lot after Ng had tried to shoplift a bench vise, he maintained that he was Paul Cosner until just before he swallowed the cyanide capsule. He had also assumed the identities of victims Scott Stapley, who had tried to help Brenda O'Connor and her child, Lonnie Bond, Jr., flee Calaveras County, and Michael Carrol, whom Ng had befriended in a federal penitentiary, as he sold drugs and pornographic videos in the last months of his life.

In his final journal he described the unraveling of his life after he moved to the Blue Mountain road. His dreams of success had eluded him, he admitted to himself that his boasts about heroic deeds in Vietnam were all delusions, and the increasing number of victims he was burying in the trench behind his bunker only added to his unhappiness. By the time he was arrested in San Francisco, Lake had reached the final stage of the serial murderer syndrome: he realized that he had come to a dead end with nothing but his own misery to show for it. And he performed his final act of execution upon himself. He had prepared for it in advance by carrying the cyanide pill with him, and his final confession revealed to the police his true identity and his status as a fugitive on a weapons charge.

What Sergeant Ronald McFall couldn't see after he switched off Lake's final videotape was the support systems that had helped Lake survive during his last years. Even though he had espoused a survivalist creed and fantasized himself as an ancient warrior alone in a hostile world, he had been living off stolen property, money sent to him by his ex-wife and his mother, and money he made from pushing drugs, selling stolen goods, and producing porno films. Never had Lake been confronted with his own shortcomings, even though he was painfully aware of them. His mother, a licensed nurse who worked in a mental ward, had simply looked the other way, believing that her son was incapable of violence. His ex-wife participated in his pornographic movie business and delayed in revealing that Lake had been systematically murdering the people he was doing business with. And his grandmother to this day refuses to release any documents that will incriminate Lake in any way. His sister Fern, a registered nurse and the family member who was closest to Leonard, grieves because she too failed to intervene. Lake's life, therefore, was a series of missed opportunities for intervention, any one of which might have short-circuited the career of a killer who claimed people from all walks of everyday life as his victims of chance. Paul Cosner and the Dubs family were unfortunate enough to have done business with him. Brenda O'Connor, Lonnie Bond, and Scott Stapley were unfortunate enough to have been his neighbors in rural Wisleyville. And Kathy Allen was unfortunate enough to have been Mike Carrol's girlfriend. Each of these victims, and numerous others who had crossed Lake's path years earlier, was a sacrifice to the refusal of those who knew of Lake's propensity toward violence to intervene in his life.

As is consistently the case with the overwhelming majority of serial murderers, the people who knew Lake simply turned away and refused to acknowledge that he was a sick person preying on other people. He was allowed to go underground, to delude himself into living a survivalist's creed of independence in a hostile society, and to kill his own brother and later his best friend. To the police, who were amazed at the extent of Lake's destruction, the cases were closed when the victims were identified and evidence was collected against Charles Ng for extradition from Canada on a charge of murder in the first degree. However, what the videotapes retrieved from Calaveras County also showed was the dark side of a man who had taught grade school children in a local California 4-H Club, who donated his time as a volunteer firefighter in nearby Philo, and who worked for a company that provided free insulation to elderly people who couldn't afford to maintain their homes. He wrote that he had become increasingly sullen, withdrawn, and angry during the last years of his life and that, despite any attempts to integrate with society, there was a part of him that kept him on the outside until killing was his only response mechanism.

In Leonard Lake's case, we will never completely know what organic problems upset the fragile balance of his existence because his brain was destroyed after he was cremated. We are only left to guess and to extrapolate about Lake's problems from the problems of his brother Donald and of his father. The mystery of Leonard Lake has been best expressed by one of his neighbors at a commune he lived in a few years before the murders who called him 'the most pleasant unpleasant man I have ever known.'

11

Charles Manson and Serial Killers in Groups

1. Also known as: None
2. Date of birth: 11/12/34
3. Place of birth: Ashland, Kentucky
4. Place of arrest: Los Angeles County, California
5. Date of arrest: 10/12/70
6. Charge: Murder, conspiracy to commit murder
7. Convictions: Murder
8. Sentence: Death, commuted to life
9. Current status: San Quentin, awaiting parole

Although most serial killers are solitary individuals incapable of forming normal relationships with other people, many of them bond with one another from time to time and become 'killing pairs' or 'families.' Some, like Charles Manson, can attract many other people and form killing groups or cults in which the individual members feed one another's fantasies, sharing the episodic madness, and provide the group with most victims from the outside. While the Manson family is the most infamous of the serial or spree murder cults in the United States, killing pairs such as Leonard Lake and Charles Ng, the father/son team of Joseph and Michael Kallinger, the Kenneth Bianchi/Angelo Buono team of Hillside Stranglers, and the homosexual companions Henry Lee Lucas and Ottis Toole have also emerged as subjects of study in the 1980s. In each of these cases the fantasies of one killer were fed on the fantasies of the other: Toole killed when he became jealous of Lucas' liaisons with women; Joseph Kallinger convinced his son to accompany him on a killing spree that was ordered by God Himself; and Manson ordered the members of his family to dissolve the oppressive social order into a chaos within which frightened people ran helter-skelter amid their confusion.

No one killing group has captured the imagination of contemporary society more than the Manson family. Sociologists argued that the time was right for Manson. He was the product of all that was wrong in American society. An illegitimate child, he was passed like a football from relative to relative and finally to his mother, who brought him up in bars and on street corners where she hustled. Any sense of self-worth had long been beaten out of him by adults even before his early confrontations with the juvenile justice system. By the time he was twelve jails, courtrooms, and prisons had been his entire life. And after he had reached sixteen, he brags, there was nothing that the criminal justice system could do to him that he couldn't take. He had lost all fear. In his own words, he had been 'raped and savaged by society . . . fucked by attorneys and friends . . . beaten by guards.' There was no more pain left for Manson to bear. He had entered into his own twilight zone.

Enough books have been written about Manson and the family – both by observers and by family members themselves – that the Charles Manson story has become almost mythic in America. The cult status has reached the point where fourteen- and fifteen-year-old European adolescents who weren't even born when the Tate/ LaBianca murders were committed have turned Manson into a folk hero. His original music and lyrics were smuggled out of Vaca Ville Hospital for the criminally insane and turned up in an underground album published in France, and internationally children form their own counterculture families in imitation of the way Manson and the family lived in the late sixties and early seventies.

'I'm a mechanical man,' the lyrics of one of Manson's underground songs complain. He says that he has been used by society's institutions in thousands of ways. He has become a recreation of society, an entity that only fulfills the expectations and fears of others. In prison he complains that he is constantly on exhibit but thrives on the attention. To the psychologists who have diagnosed him, he was a subject, and to the press he was the living symbol of a culture gone wild. To the district attorney who prosecuted him and later wrote about him, Manson was an example of how justice was served. For others, he was the incarnation of the Devil at a time when some in our society needed a devil to be the magnet for their sins.

To his relatives who took him from his mother, he was the physical embodiment of their charity. They were fanatical in their religious practices and fulfilled their Christian duty by taking care of him. His grandmother dominated the household: she was stern and unwavering in her interpretation of God's plan, Manson says, and demanded that those under her roof abide by her practices. Drinking and smoking were forbidden in the house; the display of emotion toward the opposite sex was sinful. Facial makeup was evil and only used by women of the streets, and cursing or using the Lord's name in vain in front of her brought instant condemnation. As a child, Manson never saw any affectionate displays between his grandparents. His grandfather, who worked on the

Baltimore & Ohio Railroad for his entire life, was rebuked as a sinner every time he tried to comfort his wife with any warmth. He maintained harmony at home by acquiescing, letting his wife rule the house, and he became psychotic and died in an asylum from kidney failure brought on by alcoholism.

This was the family that Manson's mother, Kathy Maddox, fled from when she was fifteen and became, in Manson's words, a flower child of the thirties. She lived on the streets for a year before giving birth to her son, who was listed in the Cincinnati records as 'No Name Maddox.' He was, he claims, an outlaw from birth. The name Manson came from Bill Manson, the person Kathy Maddox lived with shortly after Charles's birth. 'He was not my real father,' Manson explains, but he did give him a name.

The parent/child bond between Charles Manson and his mother was tenuous at best. He was often handed off to relatives while his mother worked, and usually his grandmother would have to rescue the baby-sitter when Kathy Maddox failed to return from work on time to pick up the child. Once – and Manson admitted to his biographer Neal Emmons that this may be an apocryphal story – he was sold to a bar waitress for a pitcher of beer. As it was told to him, Kathy Maddox was out of cash and nursing her last beer at a local bar with her infant son on her lap. The waitress told Kathy that she envied her the child because she had always wanted a baby of her own. 'A pitcher of beer and he's yours,' Kathy reportedly said to the waitress, who disappeared and returned with the next pitcher. Kathy stayed in the bar long enough to finish off the pitcher, and two days later Manson's uncle, searching for the missing child, found him at the waitress' house. Manson doesn't vilify his mother for this incident but uses it to explain why he never conformed to any rules: he always felt he was an outsider being retrieved from strangers' homes at the last minute, left to wait with relatives, or traded for beer at a local bar. Whatever benefits the normal family provided to other children growing up at the tail end of the Depression were not benefits that Manson ever received. He was an outcast who grew up in emotional isolation even though he was surrounded by people.

Like Carlton Gary and Leonard Lake, Charles Manson was taken from his mother and placed with her relatives when he was still very young. After Kathy Maddox was arrested for armed robbery, convicted, and sentenced to the women's ward at Moundsville State Prison in West Virginia, six-year-old Charles was sent to his grandmother's house to live. He recalls that this was a time of strict discipline, thanking the Lord at mealtimes, long prayer sessions each night before bedtime, and of turning the other cheek to every aggressive act from another child. After a few weeks of being taught to be meek, he was sent to his aunt and uncle in Maychem, Virginia. There his uncle rebuked him for being a sissy and for turning the other cheek instead of standing his ground. Promising him that he would either learn to be a man or be treated like a girl, his uncle punished him for crying about being removed from his grandmother's house or about missing his mother. Finally, to bring his point to a conclusion, the uncle sent him to his first day of school dressed in girl's clothing. In a situation ironically identical to that of Henry Lee Lucas, Manson was teased by the other children until he flew into a rage and fought a violent series of battles with the other boys in the schoolyard. He remembers in his biography that dressing like a girl didn't really teach him how to become a man, but it taught him to fight hard and not give up.

Two years later Manson was back with his mother again. She was released from Moundsville at age twenty-three, and the two of them were reunited in an erratic relationship that took the pair around the Southeast. Kathy, who had now become a bisexual after her experiences in prison, fell into a variety of sexual relationships with both men and women, and Manson was a firsthand witness to all of them. He explains that he was routinely jealous of her male lovers and felt he was in competition with them. He liked it better when she had other lesbians sleeping with her because it made him feel less threatened. Years later Manson's feeling of security among lesbians would be translated to his support of sexual relationships among his own female family members in California.

Kathy Maddox soon found that she could not raise a growing boy. She would place him with moonshiner uncle Jess in Kentucky from time to time, where he acquired a taste for corn whiskey and any other type of alcohol, but was too often forced to take him back again. Finally, in desperation, Kathy placed him with the Order of Catholic Brothers, a stern, tightly disciplined monastic institution known as the Gibault Home for Boys in Terre Haute. Kathy had never told her son that this was to be his new home. It was only on the second day that the eight-year-old Charlie Manson realized that his mother was not coming back and that this was his new home.

Manson claims that infractions of the rules at Gibault were punished by severe beatings with a leather strap or wooden paddle. The few privileges that the brothers allowed the children were quickly suspended if a child violated any disciplinary rule. In Manson's case, because he was a bedwetter, he was often whipped while being promised that he was being taught how to control himself. In a phrase that echoes psychiatrist Alice Miller's description of an especially cruel form of parenting, the Christian brothers explained that they beat the children 'for their own good,' to make them mindful of their responsibilities, and to turn them into men. Manson rebelled against the rules at Gibault and was consistently whipped. He claims that he escaped twice to reunite himself with his mother, but she turned him over to the police, who brought him back to Gibault. Each time he was returned, his punishments became harsher. Finally Manson escaped again, but this time he headed for the city.

By the time he was twelve, he was living alone in a single-room-occupancy boardinghouse in Indianapolis, stealing money to live on, and scraping food out of garbage cans. He hustled money wherever he could, until the police caught him and discovered he was a minor. His landlord had also reported to the police that he believed a minor was living in the rooming house, and Manson was sent to Father Flanagan's Boys' Town. Manson remembers this as an environment that brought swift punishment for any disciplinary infraction. Manson's psychosis manifested itself yet again, and he escaped to avoid the incessant punishment. He stole a car, was convicted as a juvenile, and was sentenced to a city juvenile institution. When he proved too difficult for the city to manage, he was transferred to a state institution, the Indiana School for Boys at Plainfield.

He had made it to the big time by the age of fifteen. The inmates at the Indiana School were not wards of the state but real inmates who had been convicted of violent crimes. Again Manson claims that these guards maintained a level of brutality associated with many of the snake-pit institutions that were outlawed in the 1960s. However, this was 1949, and Manson was a fourteen-year-old inmate at the mercy of guards who today would be convicted as sexual offenders and child molesters. Manson first ran foul of a guard who used to incite the older boys to beat up the younger ones. He beat Manson on a regular basis and was fond of having the older inmates hold Manson down and beat him while the guard masturbated. He forced the boys to torture Manson until he cried out in pain, and at that point the guard was able to achieve orgasm. The same guard also incited the older inmates to gang-rape Manson on a regular basis, and he routinely forced Manson to drop his pants in the reform school yard while he asked him, 'Who's fucking you today, Manson?'

Manson claimed that there was yet another guard who singled him out for particular brutality. The guard had a penchant for a gauntlet-type game in which the inmates would line up in two rows about four feet apart. The inmate being punished was forced to run the gauntlet between the rows while the inmates on both sides hit him as hard as they could. If the boy was knocked down he would have to get up and run the gauntlet again. If one of the inmates in the rows didn't swing hard enough, *he* was forced to run the gauntlet. In this way the seeds of a love/hate ambivalence were sown in Manson and he learned never to trust anyone, particularly those closest to him. Also the head traumas he received from the almost daily beatings began to be manifested in body tics and facial spasms: the outward symptoms of temporal lobe damage and epileptic behavior that typifies episodically violent individuals.

The years at the Indiana School brutalized Manson far more than he realized until years later when he recalled his days there. He explains that, while most teenage children were living with their parents and going to high school, he was cleaning human excrement out of cells. While teenagers in the 1950s were dating and learning how to be successful, he was getting whipped by the sadistic guards and made to sit in raw effluent while his wounds were still bleeding. Deep brown scars like canals cut into his back are evident almost forty years later and bear witness to the state-sanctioned violence from which one of the most infamous of modern murderers emerged.

At sixteen, Charles Manson was finally successful in an escape attempt and made it all the way to California. There he stole cars, robbed grocery stores, and terrorized victims. He was arrested again and sentenced to the National Training School for Boys in Washington, D.C. It was there that he became institutionally hardened at last. He recalls that even the worst criminals at that federal penitentiary for juveniles had at least some family who visited them on a regular basis. Manson had no one. He was totally alone in the world and now a hardened institutionally trained criminal. He was living with older, tougher inmates who themselves were fully developed sociopaths, and he learned to survive. He developed sexual relationships with the other prisoners, and he performed the sexual acts that kept them satisfied.

In his cell at San Quentin where he is currently serving out the life sentence for instigating and masterminding the Tate/LaBianca killings, Manson is reflective about his experiences at the National Training School. It was here, he believes, that he finally accepted what it meant to be a lifetime criminal. The other boys he was serving time with knew no other way of life. They depended on the institution for a sense of identity and a sense of being. Manson grew to develop that dependence also. He grew to accept the brutality of the guards and the demeaning and dehumanizing nature of the prison system in general. And he came to understand that in the eyes of the institution human life meant very little. What mattered was that institutions thrived on order, and the maintenance of that order at the expense of the individual was the force that kept institutions functioning. Replace order with chaos, Manson discovered, and the institutions would crumble.

Manson spent more than three years in federal penal institutions where he learned to emulate not Joe DiMaggio or other celebrated sports heroes of the fifties establishment, but the mobsters and criminals who were getting away with committing crimes under the same system that had kept Manson in custody since he was twelve. Manson explains that since he was first placed in reform school he has been a victim of the system. If a guard didn't like the way he looked, Manson was beaten or tortured. If a guard wanted sexual favors from one of the juvenile inmates, he would threaten him with abuse by older inmates. It was a world of brutality ruled by the whim of the reform school guards and the older inmates who had kept Manson as a victim for seven years. Now, at nineteen, Manson was about to be set free legitimately for the first time in seven years.

In the very short time that Manson tasted freedom, he married and had a child, tried to go straight but was busted again for passing a bad cheque, was sent back to prison but was released again only to become a pimp. He was finally sent back to federal prison for seven more years for running an interstate vice ring and was released from the reformatory at Terminal Island in California in 1967. Like Henry Lee Lucas, Manson begged the authorities at Terminal Island not to release him. He said that he still needed help and required the structure of the institution in order to live. He was, in fact, terrified after his release. He refused to leave the island but sat on the dock until a passing truck driver talked him into accepting his own freedom. It was March 21, 1967, and Charles Manson had thirty-five dollars release money in his pocket, his parole officer's telephone number, an ex-wife who had taken his son Charlie and run away with a truck driver, and absolutely no vocational training that would have allowed him to survive on the outside for any appreciable period of time. He was thirty-two years old and had been in and out of prison or reform school continually for the past twenty years. The only skills he had developed were the survival skills of the functionally institutionalized, mechanisms that enabled him to navigate through the violence and capricious brutality that characterized the reform schools and juvenile institutions in the 1940s and '50s. But now it was the late 1960s, and for a newly emerged Charles Manson it was truly a brave new world.

Twenty-four hours after his release from Terminal Island, Manson found himself in the Haight-Ashbury section of San Francisco observing the free sex scene for the first time and taking a variety of drugs, including the powerful hallucinogen LSD. At a Grateful Dead concert at the Avalon Ballroom where Manson used the drug for the first time, he experienced what he later called a catharsis. In fact, the wildly colored strobe lights, the driving hard rock beat, the hallucinogen's effect on his central nervous system, and the press of hundreds of teenagers and young adults engaging in what had been for Manson a forbidden fruit sent him into a frenzy. Before he realized what was happening to him he had run out onto the dance floor and begun 'innovating' to the music of the Dead. He became the centre of attention, drawing applause from the other dancers as he spun out of control and with a complete loss of inhibition. He described it as a rebirth, as a complete transformation of his spirit, after which he collapsed and blacked out.

Whether this incident was a direct seizure or just a 'rumbling neurology,' as some neurologists call it, it was a reaction of Manson's central nervous system to the impact of the seizure-inducing strobes and the LSD. Several other epileptoid symptoms or indicators of limbic psychosis were also emerging at this time. They included wanderlust or incessant cruising from place to place, hypersexuality, hypervigilance, obsessive behaviour, and an extreme interest in religious or cult ceremony and quasi-religious totems. These are all symptoms of individuals who have sustained damage to the temporal lobe or suffer from a limbic brain psychosis. Ironically, these symptoms helped Manson integrate completely with the social groups he had found.

These were peripatetic individuals whom Manson had discovered: hippies, drug dealers, musicians, college students dropping in and out of courses on campuses across California, high-school-age runaways, and draft dodgers who had gone underground. There were also protesters and student activists among the groups at Haight-Ashbury who were traveling to keep one step ahead of the police or FBI. Manson quickly became a fixture in these groups. He could understand such people because many of them were social outcasts just like him. They were lawbreakers, fugitives, young people with neither homes nor families, and artists trying to live on the edge of society. Manson's need to cruise from place to place, to troll for new experiences, fitted into the wanderlust lifestyle his new friends had adopted. He was constantly on the move from the park to individual apartments to sleeping on the floor in strange rooms. He travelled among the cities of San Francisco, Reno, Los Angeles, and Sacramento, but always wound up back at Haight-Ashbury.

Manson was a paradox to many of the street people at the Haight. He was over thirty, yet he was like a child. His instincts were keenly survival oriented, and he had much to teach those he met about staying alive on the streets by hustling and stealing. He was a paranoid – his rejection by his mother and subsequent years in prison had taught him that much – who was able to function by reflecting what he thought other people wanted from him. He was skilled at interpreting the key elements of other people's personalities and determining what responses would put them at ease and make them allies, friends, or sexual partners. At the same time, many of the people he was meeting were not sophisticated, having only just run away from home or dropped out of school. Consequently,

Manson's skills found easy targets, and he was able to manipulate and control many of the people he met, especially the young girls. Psychologists have pointed out in their studies of empathy that this skill, when used by a trained therapist, can be quite useful in relating to a troubled patient. Yet in the hands of a person without integrity – and Manson was a sociopath – it can be a highly dangerous instrument. Manson was dangerous, and he used his abilities to assemble around him a family group he could control by changing his personality to reflect the needs of each individual member of the group. He was like a father figure to many of the girls who had run away from home, but he was also a sexual figure who seemed to know exactly what they wanted. Most importantly, Manson was not judgmental. He encouraged the street people to find their own meaning out of existence and not to accept the judgments of other people. This was a time of manic behavior for Manson; a time that he called 'helter-skelter.'

Yet he was pursuing a musical career and within a matter of months after his release he was making money by playing his music in San Francisco's tawdry bars, in the Tenderloin, and by playing his music on street corners for quarters. He also made some money by panhandling for loose change, hustling some of the young girls he'd met, and through dealing drugs. He was also engaged in outright burglary and in running con schemes on people who visited the Haight-Ashbury section to see the local color.

Soon his need to cruise had taken him beyond the Haight. Within six months after his release he had begun acquiring vans and school buses, trading up for larger and larger vehicles to support the increasingly larger groups that were assembling around him. In doing this, however, he was just like many other leaders of hippie groups and musical bands that were forming up in San Francisco in the late sixties. Many of the homeless had actually run away from privileged lifestyles and were able to drop back into their biological families to get money or items that could later be sold for cash on the outside. Manson was able to find these types of people and get them to finance his lifestyle.

Thus, by early 1969, he was considered a chic, strange figure among the dropout street people in San Francisco and Los Angeles. During the next year he lived with hundreds of different people and had sex with both young girls and boys: making them family members by becoming the reflection of their individual needs. He also became involved with several occult and Satanic groups, forming his own subgroups within them and seeking out new relationships and sexual partners. During this manic stage he kept pursuing his dream of a musical career and sought out those relationships that would help him achieve his dream.

His many faces and kinds of behavior quickly evolved into the chameleon-like demeanor of a traditional serial killer. Like a Bundy or a Long, he could blend into any group quickly so as not to appear the odd man out. Manson, however, raised it to a high art. He could actually become the significant other of any person he met by ferreting out those personality attributes the other person was seeking. As Susan Atkins, one of the members of his killing family, once described him, he was constantly changing from second to second, becoming anybody he wanted to be and putting on any face he had to put on at any given moment.

He was involved with at least three different occult groups during this period, which were heavily based on ritual bondage, sacrifice, and also murder. Manson moved easily from group to group. His contacts with movie personalities, rock musicians, and hangers-on at the major studios gained him entrance to a world of money, sex, power, and drugs. It was a world in which California money was able to buy any experience and pay handsomely those individuals who were able to provide it. At a time when people who were on the outside were thought to have more answers than those on the inside, Manson was clearly at his manic peak. It was as if he suddenly found himself in a position of power over all those who had been his abusers for the previous twenty years. And he used it to his advantage. He used his celebrity connections to circulate his music among movie studios; he was one of the religious consultants for a movie about Jesus Christ that was produced at Universal and he extracted a promise from the director to use his music in the motion picture's sound track; he became friends with Dennis Wilson of the Beach Boys and tried to get the group to play his music; and he became intimate with the children of the rich and famous who had fled from San Francisco to Los Angeles to drop out.

By 1969, Manson and his growing family were occupying the Spahn Movie Ranch from where the family began to act out Manson's dream of violence and helter-skelter. This former movie set with its ramshackle buildings reminiscent of a frontier town in the 1880s was owned by eighty-one-year-old George Spahn, who let the family live there. He was unaware of the murders they had committed. After the Tate/LaBianca murders, the family relocated to the Barker Ranch in Death Valley where they hid in anticipation of a police raid. The Tate/LaBianca murders and the subsequent murders and attempts on the lives of witnesses and people whom the prosecution brought forward to testify against the family were the final acts of rage that Manson inspired his family to commit. Throughout the ensuing trial of Manson, Tex Watson, Bruce Davis, Leslie Van Houten, Patricia Krenwinkle, Susan Atkins, and the rest of the family the media revealed that the pent-up rage that had been building in

Manson for twenty years was still far from having expended itself. In fact, 'the most dangerous man in America' had more rage than a lifetime could store.

Even before the final murders new evidence shows that Manson had become involved in underworld crime, murder-for-hire rings, and child pornography in his attempts to get his music published and to become a rock superstar. During the year preceding Tate/LaBianca, he was becoming more and more out of control and grandiose. He was taking drugs on a regular basis, having hallucinations, and participating in ceremonial rituals simulating human sacrifice and torture. And as these visions spilled over into his everyday life it became harder and harder for him to control his rage. As one of his acquaintances reported, one day Manson saw a father and daughter walking down a street in San Francisco. Uncontrollably, Manson lunged after them, knife in hand, and threatened to cut their throats. He later told a friend that he had a homicidal rage caused by an inflamed tooth that had secreted poison into his brain. This is only one example of the explosiveness of his behavior. California jurisdictions cite many more instances in which Manson and his family might be responsible for more than thirty-five murders throughout the northern part of the state.

In prison now and still applying for parole at every chance he gets, Manson exhibits much of the paranoia and frenetic behavior that characterized him twenty years ago. He paces like a trapped animal and constantly shifts his personality according to what he believes the interviewer wants to see. He maintains that he has been the ultimate victim of society and that his helter-skelter vision of Armageddon was an almost natural response to the life that was forced upon him. Even though most of his medical records are officially sealed, it is clear that he has suffered some brain damage from the repeated head traumas. His history of hallucinations and episodic delusions points to a form of limbic psychosis, and his history of drug and alcohol abuse indicates another pattern of brain dysfunction. Analysis of his hair documents a lifelong chemical imbalance. An examination of Manson's letters shows that he is dyslexic and more than likely learning disabled as well. Yet the power he derived from being at the centre of his family and his hypersexuality with partners of both sexes are evidence of his mastery of some form of socialization, even if it is only to control others. And at only fifty-two years of age, it is also clear that his story is not yet finished.

The Unifying Patterns of a Serial Killer

12

The New Criminologists

When Dr. Dorothy Otnow Lewis evaluated convicted serial killer Bobby Joe Long she was most influenced by his reports of hypersexuality immediately following his motorcycle accident in 1974. While still in his cast, Long began suffering from an overwhelming sex drive and was masturbating at least five times a day. His compulsion to have intercourse with women escalated, and within a few years after the accident he had become the notorious Classified Ads Rapist who preyed on housewives he had contacted through 'for sale' ads they placed in the local Fort Lauderdale papers. Just a few years later Long had become a rapist murderer who preyed on the barflies along the strip just outside North Tampa.

Although Long had reported significant neurological symptoms to his doctors at the time of the accident, his symptoms had gone undiagnosed until Dr. Lewis suggested that Long had probably incurred serious damage to the limbic region of the brain as a result of his motorcycle accident. That damage, in addition to damage from at least three previous head traumas, the severe hypogonadal condition in childhood when he grew breasts, and Long's deep hatred of women that had started with his mother and continued with his wife, all combined to push

Bobby Joe Long, almost like a watermelon seed, into committing murders that repelled him and that he now claims he never wanted to commit.

Was any one aspect of Long's particular syndrome the trigger that unleashed the hatred that had been building in him for thirty years? Do all people who sustain head traumas become murderers? Do all people who hate women become murderers? Do all people who sustain chronic physical abuse as children become murderers? As Long's attorney, Ellis Rubin, and the Florida state prosecutor argued the issues of culpability and mental competence, these questions bobbed to the surface of the debate. And if a biopsychosocial syndrome exists that compels individuals against their conscious will to commit series of murders, both Bobby Long's and Carlton Gary's lawyers have asked the state courts, who is competent to evaluate the medical history of the defendants?

Most traditional psychiatric evaluations only evaluate whether the defendant was competent to judge his own actions at the time of the murder and whether the defendant is competent to stand trial, knowingly participate in his own legal defense, and knowingly exercise his constitutional rights. And therefore most traditional psychiatrists and psychologists are limited in the types of evaluations they submit to the court. They determine whether the defendant knew what he was doing at the time and whether the defendant understands the nature and seriousness of the charges against him. Furthermore, they try to determine whether the defendant understands that he is being tried for a crime. Simply put, in most cases if the defendant knows where he is and what he has done, the court psychiatrists report that he is competent to stand trial and it is up to the defense to provide their own evaluation, proving that the defendant is not competent. For most defendants, who cannot afford to hire sophisticated psychiatric consultants, an insanity defense is just too expensive. For most indigent defendants, it is out of the question. It is also difficult to convince the average jury of the technical aspects required to prove an insanity defense, and as a result there is a higher probability that defendants pleading insanity will be convicted and receive the death penalty.

But traditional insanity defenses notwithstanding, because a typical psychological evaluation for the court only deals with mental competency at the time of the crime and the time of the trial, the symptoms that underlie the serial murderer syndrome usually fall outside of a traditional psychiatrist's expertise. This is why, in Dorothy Lewis' evaluation of Bobby Joe Long, she was careful to incorporate a neurological and organic as well as a psychiatric basis for her recommendation that a full workup be completed on the subject as quickly as possible.

Dorothy Lewis, a research psychiatrist at New York University, belongs to a new category of neuropsychiatric specialists who go much further in linking organic, psychiatric, and social symptoms with one another than other specialists have gone in the past. Their approach takes into account the organic, psychological, social, and environmental factors that combine to shape an individual's behavior. Ultimately, the theories they have developed through working with convicted serial murderers will become the basis for a methodology of predicting the propensity for violence in individuals. In fact, even now, according to Vernon Mark of Harvard, scientists using theories that link organic, psychological, social, and environmental factors of criminal behavior are able to predict dangerousness in individuals with an accuracy rate of ninety percent.

The type of research conducted by the new criminologists has isolated whole new areas of discovery in which seemingly insignificant symptoms and soft signs points to chemical imbalances, brain traumas, epileptoid behaviour, and other neurological dysfunctions that can result in extraordinary levels of violence. Foremost among the new researchers has been Dr. Vernon Mark, retired chief of neurosurgery at Boston General Hospital, who has demonstrated a positive relationship between episodic aggressive behavior and certain forms of psycho-motor epilepsy – a form of temporal lobe epilepsy in which sufferers can act in a confused, bewildered, and fugue state for hours or even days. Damage to the temporal lobe can cause hair-trigger violent reactions against persons perceived as threats, and people with or without temporal lobe damage resulting in repeated epileptic seizures are often suicidal. This form of epileptoid behavior, although rare in the general population, is common among serial killers and criminals who commit violence according to a definable cycle.

Most forms of epileptic attacks begin with an aura phase in which the subject experiences a form of hyper-stimulation. Among serial killers, this aura phase immediately precedes the onset of hallucinations or fantasies in which the murderer acts out the complete crime in his mind with a victim of his own creation. It is then, during the trolling phase, that he seeks to replace the victim of his own creation with a real person. Vernon Mark's investigations have revealed that the relationship between psychomotor or limbic epilepsy and severe mental disorders is profound and has a long history in the literature of psychology. In fact, during the seizure state, the limbic epileptic may have symptoms that are virtually indistinguishable from those of paranoid psychosis. Between seizures, however, the person can be completely camouflaged by a cloak of normalcy. Hence the nature of episodic fantasies, delusions, hallucinations, and violence. As in the case of Henry Lee Lucas, specifically, irritative lesions in or near the limbic cortex give rise to epileptoid discharges accompanied by emotional feelings of terror, fear, strangeness, and unreality (the aura phase), sadness, the need for emotional isolation, and feelings of a paranoid nature. As in the cases of Gary Schaefer and Carlton Gary, distortions of actual perception also occur.

Dorothy Lewis' evaluation of Bobby Joe Long focused particularly on the large number of successive head traumas he suffered as indicators of extensive damage to his temporal lobe. This portion of the brain is peculiarly vulnerable to injury despite its seemingly well-protected site low in the skull. The skull bone at this point is thinnest and puncture wounds can penetrate the brain with relatively little force. Even in the more common traumas from blunt injuries in which large areas of the brain are affected, the temporal lobe usually suffers the worst damage. Alternatively, permanent lesions on the temporal lobe can result from impact contusions to the side of the head – such as the type usually received from blows to the head – and can cause forms of amnesia and epileptic seizures. Damage can also result from internal pressure and from respiratory obstruction associated with other injuries or accidents, or from other forms of epilepsy in which the air passageway is blocked.

In Bobby Joe Long's case, physiological, behavioral, and experiential factors contributed to his extreme violence. The type of glandular disorder that produces gender misidentification puts Long in a possible high-risk group for confrontation with the criminal justice system. That risk was compounded exponentially by Long's head injuries, resulting in lesions to his temporal lobe and a loss of control over his violent impulses. His upbringing, in which he was dominated by his mother, who moved him from place to place and who shared a bed with him, made him more than distrustful of women and lit a flame of hostility that has continued to burn. His marriage to Cindy, based as it was on her manipulativeness, only fueled the fire and created a personality disorder in which manipulative women became Long's enemies. Finally, his near fatal motorcycle accident, which caused extensive brain damage, removed the last vestiges of neurological control over his behavior. Although he was aware of what he was doing and was consciously opposed to his actions, he was unable to stop himself from committing more than fifty rapes and nine murders. Fear of punishment kept him from seeking professional help during the course of his career, although he realized that he was unable to control his almost reflex impulses. In the end he finally put a stop to his career by letting one of his victims go free and simply waiting for the police to catch him.

Dr. Lewis' studies are still in their infancy and need to be replicated before any definitive predictions can be made regarding delinquent children in general. The early results do suggest, however, the existence of a critical constellation of factors that may result in an adult whose life is at risk of being marked by episodes of aggressive and violent criminal acts. Perhaps in doing so Dr. Lewis and these experts will reduce this constellation of factors to a prescription for violence. First, having a seriously psychiatrically impaired mother – as had Henry Lee Lucas – is likely to contribute to a child's violent behavior in several ways. The fact that the mother has been hospitalized for a psychiatric disorder from time to time suggests that the child has experienced a sense of loss, a pervasively inconsistent home life, and erratic nurturing. Moreover, a seriously disturbed mother is likely to have been emotionally unavailable even when physically present. And in addition to their own psychopathology, more than sixty percent of the mothers of homicidally aggressive children in Dorothy Lewis' study had married violent, physically assaultive men. Thus the households in which the children were raised were filled with violence. In Henry Lee Lucas' own biosocial history, even though his father had been incapacitated by the loss of his legs, Viola Lucas' pimp, Bernie, abused Henry and beat him regularly.

Thus, homicidally aggressive children had mothers who were either psychotic or who were hospitalized for psychotic behavior, aggressive and assaultive fathers who themselves behaved homicidally toward the child, some form of neurological dysfunction that caused at least one seizure or other neurological dysfunction and suicidal feelings brought on by their perception of the hopelessness of their own plight. The neurological dysfunction more often than not was the result of physical injury either sustained accidentally, as in the case of Bobby Joe Long, or deliberately, as in the case of Henry Lee Lucas.

There are other types of head trauma that influence behavior as well, and these result from events that can affect the developing fetus. The fetus may be malnourished, resulting in inadequate or incomplete development of the brain; it may be injured as a result of trauma to the mother; and it may suffer from oxygen deprivation as a result of a difficult birth. Any of these events may so affect the fetal brain that the child's development is compromised. Antisocial or even episodically violent behavior is certainly possible in cases such as these.

Pointers to this critical mass of symptoms are more obvious indicators that might readily come to the attention of juvenile investigators, court officers, doctors, or school guidance counselors. Among these are visual or auditory hallucinations, loose or illogical thought patterns, forms of paranoid or hypergrandiose delusions, profound feelings of isolation or withdrawal, episodic periods of deep sadness and crying, bedwetting, sleepwalking, suicidal fantasies or even attempts at jumping from windows or trying to stab oneself, series of life-threatening assaults on other children either with deadly objects or by choking, extreme cruelty to animals, deviant sexual behavior such as exposure of genitalia or molestation of younger family members, and fire starting in an attempt to inflict injury. These signs in children establish the prima facie criteria for several kinds of diagnosis of mental disorder, and if remedial measures are instituted when the behavior first becomes apparent, the development of a criminal personality in adult life may be short-circuited by intensive psychiatric and physiological treatment and by the intervention of state agencies to stabilize the child's environment.

Research suggests that these criteria are more than just a grab bag of random behavioral abnormalities: they point to an amalgamation of physiological, social, and emotional disorders that can only be diagnosed by a specialist capable of interpreting firsthand complex neurological data, conducting an in-depth psychological evaluation of the child and the child's immediate family, and interpreting the social conditions that comprise the child's environment. Most court-appointed diagnosticians, however, tend to assume that juvenile criminals are simply bad rather than sick, even though the medical, social, and psychological conditions point to other explanations. When the court-appointed diagnostician works with an adult serial killer, rarely does empathy between the accused and the diagnostician emerge because the diagnosis is tainted by the legal responsibility to declare the person either competent or incompetent to stand trial. This is a quick and dirty diagnosis that relates only to the patient's ability to remember the date, the name of the current President of the United States, his remembrance of the crime, and his ability to judge whether he committed a wrongful act. Many adult serial killers compulsively admit their guilt and admit that they have committed a wrongful act. Thus research into the paradigm of physiological, psychological, social and experiential causes of adult episodically violent behavior will have far-reaching consequences not only for the way juvenile criminals are treated by the justice system but also for the way serial killers are diagnosed by the court.

Dr. Jan Volavka of the New York University Medical Center is another researcher who is examining the importance of diagnosing psychomotor epilepsy in episodically violent criminals. Volavka has shown that the telltale vertical spike that interrupts the EEG brain-wave patterns of violent felons indicates a spontaneous and powerful uncontrollable discharge of electricity deep within the limbic brain. In many of his patients, the high-voltage spike is so great that it makes the stylus of the EEG shoot across the chart as if it were recording the impact of a bullet. These seizures originate in the most primitive area of the brain and are so deep that routine EEGs don't pick them up. The damaged limbic area where control over the primary emotions of fear and rage is exercised is repeatedly damaged by these discharges and becomes dysfunctional, unable to curtail displays of violence before they reach the surface. Volavka believes that the deep EEG spikes which indicate this type of epilepsy can be used as a litmus test for potentially violent individuals who have previously displayed extreme antisocial behavior or have regular episodes of inappropriate responses to external stimuli.

The only psychiatrist to exclusively study the serial killer, Dr. Helen Morrison of Chicago, attributes significant importance to the role played by an organic dysfunction deep within the primitive brain. In her work with serial murderers John Gacy, Ted Bundy, Richard Macik, and the 'Yorkshire Ripper' in Great Britain, Dr. Morrison has focused her attention on the activity of the hypothalamus – the emotional voltage regulator of the brain –

as an indicator of a person's inability to control primitive, violent impulses. Experiments with monkeys and lower animals over the past fifty years have shown that the hypothalamic region forms the major component of an emotional circuit that helps sustain life functions and automatically regulates the animal's defence systems through the emotions of fear and rage. Because the hypothalamus regulates the hormonal system, including the functions of the vital adrenal and thyroid glands, it is the fulcrum point of the body's basic emotional responses to all kinds of stimuli.

Damage to the hypothalamus, whether as a result of repeated head traumas or as a birth defect, can destabilize the hormonal system and short-circuit the brain's ability to measure emotional and physical responses to real or perceived threats. And because the hormonal system is largely cybernetic, requiring little direct conscious intervention on the part of the individual to monitor its emotional fluctuations, and also because critical hormonal responses to life-threatening situations are channeled through the autonomic nervous system, the higher brain has only limited control over the hypothalamic-hormonal functions. And whatever control it can exercise can be brought about only through training. An example of this emotional short-circuiting is a person's reaction when startled by the sudden or unexpected appearance of a family member or friend. Although the startled person recognizes the familiar face and has consciously turned off any emotion of fear, the unexpectedness of the appearance has sent a primary message along the neural pathways of the hypothalamus. The response – a scream or a jump – is primal and never reaches the level of conscious recognition. The startled person can be as startled by the response as he or she is by the appearance of the other person. Suddenly, the startled person screams, even after he has recognized the face of a friend.

Dr. Morrison carries this basic stimulus-response model to a much more complex level in her description of what takes place within the primitive neural circuits of the serial murderer. First, she suggests, the hypothalamus gradually asserts control over the primal emotions as the individual matures. Thus children and adolescents often have marked emotional swings resulting from their perceptions of the outside world and the presence or absence of certain hormones in the bloodstream. As the individual grows and his brain develops, the higher cerebral functions impose a fixed order over the raw perceptions based on experience and the emotional swings are not nearly so great. In homes where there is a strong family structure and both parents deal with the child in a mature and supportive environment, the maturing individual learns from his parents how to react to a variety of situations and that helps him develop the initial patterns he will build on throughout his life. In homes where one parent is particularly strong, that parent's patterns will be used as either a positive or negative model for the growing child, depending upon the sex of the parent and child and the child's relationship with the parent. In homes where both parents are weak or there is no parent support, the child can be left largely to his own devices and may or may not be able to exercise control over his primal emotions.

Similarly, if the child is beaten or chronically mal-nourished or if the fetus is injured in some way, the hypothalamus may become damaged or may never develop to maturity. In this scenario, the emotional regulator itself is flawed and never functions as properly as it should. The individual may always react as a child does to threats and strike out violently at any perceived challenge, or the hypothalamus itself may be starved

243

because of inadequate nutrition. Measuring the electrical discharges within the hypothalamus and the chemistry of the hormonal system is one indicator of organic dysfunction deep within the brain. Outward signs such as chemical imbalances or severe sleep disorders that produce confusional behavior and hallucinations are other indicators.

Many of the serial killers whom Dr. Morrison has studied have evidenced disorders of the hypothalamus that range from distorted sleep patterns to critical hormone imbalances. In our triad of the key factors of organic dysfunctions, psychopathological behavior, and social deprivation that underlie the syndrome of serial murderers, disorders of the hypothalamus, the temporal lobe, or the limbic brain have been at the crux of the symptoms. And depending upon the individual's upbringing and the way he led his adult life, the person eventually reached a level of dangerousness that translated itself into episodic crime. At the very least, individuals with damaged hypothalamuses are mortally sad to the point of suicide, and usually become their own worst enemies. Many of these people sink deeper into an irretrievable depression, even though they may never actually assault another person. These are the other victims of hypothalamic disorders whose stories never reach the front pages because they have succumbed to their own grief privately and silently.

Dr. James Prescott, a neuropsychologist, has also developed a 'deep brain dysfunction' theory to explain violent antisocial behavior in people. In comparative studies of chronically and episodically psychotic individuals, Prescott claims to have isolated the septal region of the midbrain, adjacent to the hypthalamus, as one of the controlling centres of emotion and awareness of the external world. Schizophrenics, he points out, and psychotics who suffer only from episodic hallucinations are unable to integrate feelings of pleasure and other emotions into their senses of self. He argues that, because of a dysfunction in the deep primitive brain, the individual is unable to perceive the boundaries of the self: the border between the person and the rest of the world. The person seems to meander in a semidream state, experiencing hallucinations or delusions as if he were a healthy person on the very edge of sleep. Because the psychotic has little or no self-image and is completely devoid of a sense of himself as a separate entity, his own thoughts seem to be coming from outside. As a result, feelings and sensations seem to come from outside rather than from his own mind. This leaves him deficient in emotional expression and he is characterized by a proneness to violence, rage, and excessive fear. In a healthy, integrated person, these primitive fear reactions are controlled by an ability to experience pleasurable sensations. In the psychotic person, no such balance exists, and the person is tossed about by the external pressures of fear and violence.

Prescott's experiments have shown that in psychotic individuals this syndrome is directly related to lesions in the septal region of the brain which are indicated by septal 'deep spikes' on an EEG – another litmus test for a predisposition to violent behavior. Tests on both humans and monkeys have shown that electrical stimulation of the septal region can both remedy and induce septal deep spiking and consequent violent or hallucinatory behavior. Moreover, because the episodically psychotic human subject has no basis on which to form judgments about the nature of his hallucinatory experiences, they become another level of reality, as if they were a consciousness within a consciousness. Thus, Carlton Gary's claims that another person committed the Wynnton murders might be real experiences for him and not just a story that he told to the police to exonerate himself from guilt.

Prescott and his colleagues have suggested that a

combination of early sensory deprivation in the form of tactile stimulation from the parents and maternal intimacy may be one cause of the dysfunction of the septal region. The types of visceral responses in newborns to the sound of the human voice and to human touch indicate that the infant is 'stimulus ready,' and this extreme receptivity to touch and voice is critical for the development of parts of the neurological system. Many neurological theoreticians argue that early vocal and tactile stimuli establish the border line between 'self' and 'nonself' for the infant. Without this distinction, they claim, the child never adequately makes the self and nonself distinction, which results in a severe psychosis. If Prescott is correct, a physiological correlation to this early developmental progress point is found in the brain's septal region, a portion of the emotional regulation circuitry. The psychological symptoms have physiological correlates in the midbrain which can be stimulated and measured.

Prescott's experiments on chimps have reinforced his theory that sensory deprivation retards the development in the midbrain and results in chronic or episodic psychosis-like symptoms. At first both the sensory-deprived human and the simian newborns go into states of deep, almost autistic, withdrawal. Subsequently they become violent and strike out at those around them. The violence is inappropriate in that it has no relationship to the nature of the actual stimulation. Chimps who have been living in a state of sensory isolation will begin attacking other members of their troop savagely while they are still very young. Ultimately they will turn their violence upon themselves, nip and scratch at their own flesh, beat themselves, and later they will bludgeon their heads against the walls of their cages in a final act of self-destruction. Unless sedated or restrained, they will actually commit suicide.

THE NEW CRIMINOLOGISTS

Most of the serial killers whose careers have been documented reported that they were either separated from one or both parents at an early age or otherwise deprived of the mother's direct emotional involvement. Even when the mother was in very close proximity, as in the case of Bobby Joe Long where both mother and son slept in the same bed until he was twelve years old, because she was working at night and usually never around even on her days off, Long felt deprived of maternal affection. He reported that he often felt in competition with his mother's boyfriends for her attention and often begged her to stay home with him on her nights off. Bobby Joe Long's claimed distant cousin, Henry Lee Lucas, was also deprived of his mother's attention and affection as a young child. In Lucas' case, he received negative attention from his mother, who habitually beat him with lethal weapons, inducing a coma on at least one occasion. Lucas eventually killed his mother with a knife years later. The same pattern of maternal deprivation or control was a factor in Carlton Gary's upbringing as it was for cult murderer Charles Manson and killers Richard Ramirez and Ted Bundy.

Much to the chagrin of behavioral psychologists, a growing number of researchers believe that the predisposition to criminal violence is largely congenital. Whether or not the individual in fact actually becomes a serial murderer in adult life may be a factor of his upbringing and later socialization, but the predisposition to violence and crime, some researchers believe, is already determined at conception or in utero. Among these researchers is C. Robert Cloninger, a psychiatrist at the University of Washington School of Medicine whose research on adoptees has shown that individuals whose biological parents are criminals are four times more likely to become criminals than individuals whose biological parents are not criminals. Although Cloninger has not definitively isolated the actual genes that predispose one to criminal tendencies, he believes that certain types of brain dysfunctions are congenital, as are birth defects in the neurological or hormonal systems. Scientists now know that thyroid dysfunctions tend to run in families as do heart disease, diabetes, and predispositions to cancer. Parents with congenital learning disabilities tend to have children who are predisposed to those disabilities as well.

Cloninger's research has been supported by the results of a major study on twins at the University of Minnesota in which siblings who were raised apart and had never met were found to have similar personality traits, intelligence levels, allergies, and levels of ambition. They shared these traits despite the fact that they were reared in entirely different family environments. Even traits such as reactions to stress and leadership seem to be influenced primarily by inheritance rather than by social conditioning, though conditioning can either reinforce or undermine those traits. What is emerging from the Minnesota study is an understanding that heredity and not environment plays the most important role in determining those basic traits that define an individual's personality, even among normal nonneurotic individuals. In cases where parents had criminally deviant personalities and serious psychophysiological disorders, the children manifested similar if not identical characteristics.

Dr. Sarnoff Mednick at USC also supports these findings with his own independent research on Danish male adoptees. He found that among those adoptees twenty percent of those whose parents were property criminals also became criminals. If both the biological and adoptive parents were criminals, the figure rose to twenty-four percent. Other researchers such as Philip Firestone and Susan Peters found that obvious physical and congenital defects such as webbed fingers, attached ear lobes, elongated limbs, and other abnormalities are significant in the etiology of schizophrenic behavior. It is suggested that in instances where an individual displays ten to fifteen obvious physical abnormalities there is a strong likelihood that he or she has experienced birth defects and neurological damage. When there are five or more physical abnormalities, an individual should strongly consider neuropsychiatric and neurological testing. Among the features that Mednick points to – and which are displayed by Carlton Gary – are:

1. Long second or small toe
2. Pterodactyloid fingers that are long and clawlike
3. Webbed fingers
4. Ear lobes that are connected to the side of the head
5. Bulbous or ball-like extensions on the tips of the fingers

Abnormal EEG readings are especially important indicators of genetic abnormality because they point to progressively more critical symptoms as the individual develops. Mednick discovered that boys who later became delinquents registered alpha waves on their EEGs at a lower frequency, eight or nine per second, than the higher normal frequency of from ten to twelve per second. In this case, the alpha wave deviation, although an indicator of serious organic dysfunction in the brain, only resulted in a violent personality when reinforced by events in the environment. Among serial murderers, this type of dysfunction can be triggered by the highly unstable situation that results when there is tension between the child and his difficult parents. Because many serial murderers were raised by adoptive parents or caretakers both within and outside of their biological parents' families, the stage for this type of tension was set while the individual was still a very young child. In the case of Carlton Gary, who probably was already at high risk because of the significant number of congenital defects, the inherent tension between him and his grandmother who raised him caused him to leave the home environment while still a young child to search for other relatives who could care for him. His trip to his uncle's military base is just one of the sojourns the young Carlton Gary took. Others involved trips to visit his mother in Florida and other relatives. He became self-sufficient as a child to a point well beyond criminal deviance. And as an adult his inability to form permanent relationships with people combined with his instinctive distrust of society and its institutions turned him into a sociopath long before he began his skein of serial murders in Wynnton.

Sarnoff Mednick suggests that, once the congenital predisposition toward episodic violence is established, the home environment can act as a matrix, which would explain why every person with congenital defects doesn't automatically become a violent criminal. Mednick looks for a combination of genetic and environmental factors in the individual, such as the institutionalization of one or both parents or the conviction of one or both parents for criminally violent acts. He has found that, in homes where the predisposed child had a mother who was institutionalized for alcoholism or for psychotic behavior, it was likely that the child would become withdrawn as well as violent, unable to relate to other people socially. In homes where the father was criminally violent, the child himself became a criminally violent individual, even if there had been no genetic predisposition to violent behavior. Finally, in those homes where the child had a congenital neurological defect and was raised by parents who were either criminals themselves or who committed violent acts, especially upon the child, it is logical to assume that the child could emerge as an episodically violent criminal, and possibly a serial murderer.

Environmental factors also have an impact upon the physiology of the neurological system, especially the development of the brain in growing children. The backgrounds of Henry Lee Lucas and Bobby Joe Long demonstrate that head traumas can cause severe damage to areas of the brain that control behavior and emotion. Much the same can be said for prolonged malnutrition and exposure to environmental toxins. Pioneering this research are Diane Fishbein and Robert Thatcher, both of whom are at the Unversity of Maryland School of Medicine. In their study of the environmental backgrounds of maladaptive behavior they have focused specifically on the types of factors that place the individual at high risk of eventual contact with the criminal justice system. In other words, they are evaluating those factors that disrupt behavior in such a way that the individual, most often a juvenile, commits a criminal antisocial act. They suggest that combinations of biological factors such as head traumas, exposure to environmental toxins, the abuse of alcohol or drugs, the lack of prenatal care, and the adequacy of nutrition all affect the behavior of the individual. And what is most interesting for our purposes is that the most common site for the interaction of all these variables is the brain.

Thatcher and Fishbein cite several reports that suggest that diets high in refined carbohydrates such as white flour and white sugar, cakes, candies, potato chips, and the like can create or aggravate behavioral abnormalities and learning disabilities. Among the types of antisocial behaviour that are stimulated by inadequate nutrition are mood swings from depression to euphoria, violence, irrationality, hyperactivity, inappropriate aggressiveness, and impaired cognitive function. The chronic ingestion of refined carbohydrates, in many instances, can also precipitate a condition known as hypoglycemia or low blood glucose, resulting in seriously impaired mental functions. Because glucose serves as the brain's primary source of fuel, any diet that causes wide swings in the blood glucose level affects the brain's ability to function. Therefore, the scientists suggest, aggressive or even criminally antisocial behavior in children can be treated by diet if the child is diagnosed to be chronically malnourished or hypoglycemic.

Fishbein and Thatcher also identify trace mineral elements as another aspect of the nutritional status that can influence brain functioning and behavior. These trace elements include minerals essential for the functioning of the body such as zinc, calcium, magnesium, selenium, chromium, iron, and potassium. Zinc and iron are especially important in this category because, if they are sufficiently lacking in the diet, severe behavior problems may occur and emotional stability is compromised. Iron plays a role in the ability of the blood to carry oxygen and glucose to the brain and affects the individual's overall resiliency. Zinc is directly related to the function of the hormonal system and plays a role in the stabilization of emotions and the brain's rational control over the drives of sex and rage.

The researchers from Maryland also focus their studies on other trace elements that are not nutritional but are toxic in certain concentrations and that impair brain functioning and cognitive ability and impede socially adaptive behavior. These trace substances are lead, cadmium, arsenic, aluminum, and mercury and they regularly occur in the environment. Human beings don't have a mechanism for directly excreting these substances in large amounts, and when exposure to them is significant, they can build up large concentrations in the body tissue and directly influence behavior. When they accumulate in larger concentrations, they begin to impair other neurological functions such as memory and cognition. If the individual is exposed to toxins in the foods he ingests daily, his behavior can become chronically maladaptive until the toxins are removed from his environment. His behavior will abruptly begin to shift back to a more normal state.

One significant study conducted by Thatcher revealed an important relationship between the amount of lead and cadmium concentrations in the hair of children from a school in eastern Maryland and their intelligence levels and school achievement. The higher the concentrations of lead or cadmium, the lower the performance of the individual in any cognitive exercises. What was most interesting about these studies was that, even before the loss of muscular control and the impairment of motor functions, the individual who had higher than average concentrations of lead or cadmium experienced a significant degree of cognitive impairment as the only symptom of poisoning. And what is true for the schoolchildren in the Maryland study is also true for the serial killers whom Dr. William Walsh has studied for this book.

Walsh, a chemist at the Health Research Institute near Chicago, has been doing research on chemical imbalances in violent individuals for ten years. He has developed a novel classification method for violent criminals based on distinctive patterns of certain elements in hair tissue. These patterns were first discovered during a controlled sibling experiment involving extremely delinquent, violent children and brothers who were 'all-American boys' with no history of behavioral problems. The violent siblings were found to possess abnormal trace element patterns that fell into two major categories. The Type A pattern involved an elevated copper/zinc ratio, depressed sodium, potassium, and manganese, and elevated lead, cadmium, and iron. The Type B subjects had a somewhat opposite chemical pattern, with extremely low levels of copper and sky-high values of sodium and potassium. Both groups exhibited elevated levels of lead and cadmium, previously found by other researchers to be associated with violence.

The Type A subjects exhibited episodic dyscontrol, whereas the Type B children evidenced consistent violence associated with an antisocial personality. These chemical imbalances have been the subject of three large controlled studies involving mixed violent and nonviolent subjects. In a test of 198 extremely violent children, prison residents, and ex-convicts with matched nonviolent controls, Walsh and coworkers again found the distinctive chemical patterns to be present in the majority of violent subjects and absent in most of the controls. Walsh's ability to distinguish between violent and nonviolent subjects based on chemistry alone was confirmed in two 'double-blind' experiments supervised by the University of California.

Clinical tests of 18 Type B (sociopathic) persons revealed abnormalities in blood and urine chemistry. All 18 Type B subjects were found to exhibit elevated blood histamine, depressed blood zinc and spermidine, and elevated kryptopyrroles in urine. In addition, a high incidence of hypoglycemia and toxic overload (lead and cadmium) were observed. These tests are significant not only because of the specific trace chemicals that turned up in sociopathic individuals but because they correlated a type of behavior with a distinct chemical pattern. The trace chemicals themselves may lead scientists to a 'fingerprinting' method of determining behavioral pre-disposition through chemical trace testing.

Follow-on testing of general delinquent populations revealed two additional chemical patterns (Types C and D) which are common to persons exhibiting low to intermediate violence. Type C individuals exhibit very low levels of all elements (except lead and cadmium) and are believed to suffer from malabsorption. Type D pattern is identical to Type C except for extremely elevated calcium and magnesium levels. Walsh believes that the Type D persons suffer from hypoglycemia.

Walsh and the Health Research Institute have been studying changes that occur in violent persons when their chemical imbalances are corrected. More than 80 Type A, B, C, and D subjects have been treated for chemical imbalances at the Princeton Brain Bio center in Skillman, New Jersey. The anecdotal results are very encouraging, according to Walsh. He reports that eighty percent of the treated subjects report a major improvement that lasts for more than two years. Most striking has been the improvement in antisocial-personality children following treatment. A double-blind experiment to measure the behavioral improvement associated with correcting chemical imbalances is in the planning stages.

Walsh has tested ten serial killers and found that nine exhibited the Type B chemical imbalances, usually with extraordinary elevations of toxins lead and cadmium. The Type B subjects included Henry Lee Lucas, Leonard Lake, and Charles Manson. The only exception was Bobby Joe Long, whose chemical levels were quite normal. Walsh concludes that Long's violence stems from brain damage resulting from his motorcycle accident and not from a chemical imbalance or as a result of poor fetal development. He believes that individuals possessing these imbalances are usually sensitive to their environment, especially with respect to parental influences, stress, alcohol, toxic exposures, and poor nutrition. Walsh's conclusions regarding Long coincide with the onset of Long's symptoms while still in the hospital recovering from the accident. Long did not evidence any overt hostility or violent behavior when he was younger, even though the other factors such as negative parenting and interrupted child bliss were present.

Fishbein and Thatcher argue that in the overwhelming majority of instances children receive adequate prenatal care, adequate diet, are not exposed to environmental toxins, and do not sustain repeated head traumas. The overwhelming majority of children develop adaptive behaviors that allow them to navigate through the challenges of life, learn from those mistakes they make, and become productive adults. However, when the majority of these upbringing factors are negative, when children have sustained repeated head traumas and have suffered from poor nutrition and exposure to different forms of toxins and dangerous substances, there is a much greater likelihood that as adults they will eventually adopt a criminal form of behavior as a response. The challenge to the criminologist that Fishbein and Thatcher have emphasized is to be able to isolate key predictors that indicate whether an individual will confront the criminal justice system as a result of his exposure to these factors.

One of their indicators is the presence of some kinds of learning disabilities in the child or in the biosocial history of the adult. They caution that learning disabilities in themselves do not constitute an indicator of antisocial or criminal behavior. Many people with learning disabilities and different types of dysfunction such as dyslexia overcome them and make valuable contributions to their respective professions. However, some forms of learning disabilities as a part of a pattern of physical abuse or severe head trauma, poor nutrition, and exposure to environmental toxins can frequently be traced to organic abnormalities in the brain. Environmental factors such as exposure to lead or lead fumes, for example, can have adverse effects on the development of the brain and result in learning or cognitive impairment. The same is true for the other factors we have cited. To compound the problem, the risk factors that impair brain functioning and result in a cognitive disability may also affect the brain's ability to regulate adaptive behavioral responses to life situations, thus placing the individual at an additional social disadvantage. And individuals who have such social disadvantages resulting from brain abnormalities are among the highest-risk groups with respect to confrontations with the criminal justice system. In summary, Fishbein and Thatcher have shown that learning disabilities are clear indicators of individuals who have physiological abnormalities in their neurological systems and who are at high risk of developing maladaptive and even criminal behavior.

Fishbein and Thatcher go even further and argue that, because the learning disabilities in question should have a physiological rather than a purely psychological basis in fact, they require diagnosis through an electrophysiological tool such as a computer-enhanced EEG. Non-objective analyses such as evaluations of the individual's social and psychological backgrounds can be culturally biased and open to different interpretations depending upon who is conducting the evaluation. EEGs, however, tend to minimize any subjective intervention and are a direct measure of the neuroelectrical activity in the brain. Accordingly, the researchers suggest that computer-enhanced EEG evaluations be conducted on children with known learning disabilities or abnormal reactions at an early age to determine whether the disability is the result of a neurological disorder or of a psychological disorder. Either way, the early diagnosis of the disorder could lead to therapy and remediation.

In the fields of social psychology and Jungian psychoanalysis, respectively, Marvin Wolfgang of Pennsylvania and Swiss psychoanalyst Alice Miller have developed their own sets of predictors of violence and dangerousness. Wolfgang, who studied an entire cohort of males born in Philadelphia in 1945, found that encounters with the criminal justice system were organized according to family patterns. Where a father had had criminal careers, it was overwhelmingly likely that the sons would have criminal careers as well. Where mothers were institutionalized for criminal behavior, it was equally likely that the sons would commit criminal acts during their life-times. However, where both parents had criminal back-grounds, it was a virtual certainty that their sons would have extensive criminal careers. And the more criminal violence in the family unit, the greater the likelihood that the son would become a violent criminal. As if the statistics weren't proof enough of the importance of family patterning on the development of children, Wolfgang could point to other factors that supported his findings.

He cited evidence of alcoholism and drug abuse that predominated in families and of children who were raised in foster homes or institutions where they were neglected and deprived of any parental supervision whatsoever. In these instances, the children developed in an almost feral state with no moral training or discipline. Their encounters with the juvenile justice system began very early and continued well into adolescence. In the absence of any intervention, the children became career criminals in their adult lives. In other instances, learning disabilities and other organic neurological disorders were passed on from generation to generation and often laterally through families. These organic disabilities were indicators of other neurological factors that ultimately caused maladaptive behaviors, put the individuals at a dis-advantage with respect to the rest of society, and resulted in their later encounters with the criminal justice system. In other words, the deck was stacked in one generation and every succeeding hand was dealt out according to that genetic deck. Medical intervention would have helped identify the problem and retraining or therapy might have helped remove specific individuals from their high-risk groups. However, Wolfgang learned, the institutions of society are simply not attuned to the medical and social backgrounds of violent crime. And as a result the problem that he began tracing in the male cohort of 1945 has got far worse over the intervening forty-two years despite the billions of dollars that have been spent to solve it and the ancillary problems it has created.

Alice Miller, who examined the childhood of German dictator Adolf Hitler, child murderer Jurgen Bartsch, and heroin addict 'Christiane F.,' has uncovered what seem to be two unmistakable clues that account for the vertical transmission of violence from one generation to the next and the lateral spread of that violence, including serial and mass murder, with each succeeding generation since the early part of the twentieth century. It also accounts for the epidemic rise in episodic violence in America since the 1950s. Dr. Miller explains that the roots of violent behavior in adulthood are to be found in a level of cruelty in child rearing that is invisible to the untrained eye. In her book *For Your Own Good* she explains that parents who commit implicit acts of cruelty toward their children by explaining to them that it is all for their own good are guilty of a 'poisonous pedagogy,' a perversion of the concepts of good and evil. In other words, the parents or caretakers teach the child that what is physically and emotionally painful to bear and cannot be expressed is in the child's best interests. In some cases the insanity of this reversal is evident, as in the example of Joseph Kallinger's mother and father, who forced the boy to hold his hand over an open flame until the skin blistered and charred from the intense heat. If he cried out in pain, he was brutally beaten. His mother explained that it was for his own good – he was being trained to bear pain. His most critical developmental years were spent experiencing this level of frustration. This severely damaged his own sense of his self-worth – a vital component to individual emotional development and the ability to accept a socially ordered external world – and left him permanently scarred.

In essence, poisonous pedagogy is a splitting off of feeling, sympathy, tenderness, intimacy, and pain from the individual in order to make that individual tough and hard. It is to experience brutality and not flinch – not acknowledge the terror and pain – so as to become stronger and invulnerable to weakness of feeling or remorse of conscience. These are the very emotions that serial killers first experience once they have admitted to themselves what they have done and have been placed within a stable environment. It is the force that once compelled Henry Lee Lucas to keep on confessing to crimes, not only to expurgate his own soul, but to deepen and broaden the feelings of remorse that he has, first in mourning his own lost life and then in mourning for the people he has killed. It was the emotions that Viola Lucas sought to destroy in her son when she asked him whether he loved his pet mule and then shot it, subsequently beating him for the expense it would entail to have the animal carcass removed from the property.

Miller explains that training children not to experience any feelings of love or sympathy need not be a brutal or overtly cruel or violent act. Indeed, in modern society much of this training is implicit because it is a 'right' and 'wrong' based on the parents' needs and not on the needs of the child. Parents who stress that imposing their own values on children is done for the child's own benefit commit, in Miller's words, a form of 'gentle violence,' suppressing completely the child's emerging personality and lighting a fuse of aggressiveness that will explode decades later. It is as if they are beating their children with velvet clubs that cause no overt scars, draw no public blood, inflict no visible pain, but do massive amounts of damage beneath the surface. These parents instill in their children a sense of helplessness and frustration because they are never allowed to acknowledge feelings of rage and rebellion. These naturally violent childhood emotions are, again, split off from the child's personality and never develop to a harmless stage of acceptance. By short-circuiting them, parents confine their children to reliving the frustration and rage over and over again until they can either accept it or break out in uncontrolled violence against the larger parent figure of society itself.

If Alice Miller is correct, there must be hundreds of thousands of emotional time bombs camouflaged by society who can explode at any minute. Why don't they simply explode? And isn't there a 'defusing' process that can remedy the ills brought about by Miller's poisonous pedagogy? If there is no defusing process, why has not society already consumed itself in generational violence to the point of extinction? The answer to all these questions is: yes, there are hundreds of thousands of potential aberrant violent criminals who have the critical number of symptoms. They have not yet exploded into violence because for many of them the event that is the critical trigger has not taken place. Still, the number of people who do explode into apocalyptic mass violence or serial violence increases exponentially every year.

We also know that there was once a set of natural defusing processes that kept much violence in check, but those social controls are evolving out of our social structure as the nature of the family continues to change. And unfortunately generational violence is also bringing certain aspects of our social order to a form of extinction. That is the point of the Surgeon General's warning to the American people that violence has become an issue of public health, and that is the point of most of the current research into domestic, generational, and episodic violence.

Miller's theory of generational violence – both explicit and implicit or 'gentle' – also accounts for its spreading so rapidly through post-World War II American society. She explains that in earlier social cultures, even though one parent might assume the role of authoritarian figure and suppress the child's own development, other family members, present in the same household, would support the child. In other words, the child had other adult family figures – including siblings – to whom he or she could turn for emotional relief from an overly domineering parent. The extended family structure living within the same household, the social order of the village parish, or the formally ordered structure of the family clan with its well-defined architecture of authoritarian responsibilities gave the child a multitude of support figures and outlets for rebellion and rage. The child also had cousins and siblings who shared the burden of parental abuse so that it was not heaped upon the single child of a small family. However, over the course of the twentieth century, families have been getting smaller, they have become highly unstable, with children going through serial families of pseudo fathers as a result of multiple marriages. Now, in the middle of the final quarter of the century, families are in danger of breaking down and the very concept of parental responsibilities is undergoing redefinition in the courts as a result of surrogate parenting and *ex utero* conception. Children are routinely placed in child-care enrichment programmes at age two – often under intense pressure to 'qualify' – and the parents themselves are more often than not involved in serial sexual relationships with multiple partners even while they are married. There are now more children living in homes with divorced parents than there are children living in the same home with both biological parents. In other words, the family structure is undergoing a massive restructuring, especially in the postwar period, and this has removed what Miller has called the critical family member or members who served as the parent figures who supported the child's development and counterbalanced the terrorizing parent.

In single-parent homes or 'no-parent' homes, the situation can be even more devastating for the child. An entire generation of children will shortly emerge for whom there are no normal, supportive parental relationships.

262

THE NEW CRIMINOLOGISTS

This generation, to which New York Senator Pat Moynihan has been pointing since the early 1980s, will have grown up in complete poverty, reared by the administrations of the states' welfare systems, and chronically malnourished, so that their entire adult lives will be spent requiring medical care to repair the damage done to their bodies and spirits during the development stages. They represent the largest area of population growth of our society, and they will in turn give birth to a succeeding generation of children out of control, who will carry the disease of generational violence well into the next century and well beyond the borders of the United States.

What Alice Miller and the other experts in the rapidly growing field of new criminology have shown, however, is that the individual symptoms of this disease and certain types of its carriers can be identified and diagnosed. However, the challenge is far greater than that. Scientists and doctors must understand that they are themselves impaired by a 'linkage blindness,' an inability to relate causalities in disparate professional disciplines to one another. Consequently, sociologists look for social causalities and find them; psychologists look for psychological and developmental causalities and find them; and neurologists look for organic causalities and identify them as well. The police and prosecutors simply brand criminals as 'bad,' track them down, and bring the few they find before the courts. However, each of the different professions is merely groping like a blindfolded person around the body of an elephant. Nobody can see the elephant and nobody recognizes that anybody else is there. As a result, the problem is not solved and its magnitude isn't even comprehended. It is this battle against linkage blindness that must be won first before fundamental solutions to the problems of episodic violence and serial murder can be attempted.

13

Inside the Brain
of a Serial Killer

'Around fifteen years of age, God came to me with both a voice and visual presence and ordered me to undertake orthopedic experiments to heal myself and save mankind. This was the time when I was having the strange movements, and my parents had put a lock on their bedroom door and a bat behind their door, so I felt hopeless,' Joseph Kallinger explained in an interview a few years ago.

'I kept hearing her talking to me,' Henry Lee Lucas said about the mother he had killed only a few years earlier. 'And telling me to do things. And I couldn't do it. Had one voice that was tryin' to make me commit suicide, and I wouldn't do it. I had one tell me not to do anything they told me to do. And that's what got me in the hospital, was not doing what they told me to do,' Lucas explained about the decision of the Michigan prison officials to send him to the Ionia State Hospital for the criminally insane.

'There is something the matter with me,' Ted Bundy told his former girl friend, Liz Kendall, after his arrest in Florida. He admitted to a force within him that had begun sucking in his living personality just as the supergravitational pull of a black hole sucks in all light and then the matter from the neighboring stars. He tried to suppress this force that was building in him, but it was too strong. The more energy he applied against it to keep normal, the more the force grew in him. It destroyed his ability to function in school, it continued to warp his relationship with Liz Kendall, and finally it consumed him. He was unable to lead a normal life, although he presented the appearance of someone who could exert complete control over any situation. Bundy knew when the dark feelings were upon him. He tried to stay off the streets when he felt the urgings start, so that he wouldn't encounter any women who might cross his path. However, as it became increasingly difficult, Bundy felt himself slipping under its control again and again. And the feelings escalated to the point where, if he were on the street and a pretty young woman crossed his path, he would follow her. He tried to fight to remain in control many times by just following down the street until she disappeared into a dormitory or sorority house, but many times he couldn't. Weeks later the girl would be discovered in a shallow grave.

It wasn't as though he had a split personality, he explained to Kendall, because he knew what he was doing and where he was. He didn't have real blackouts. However, he also knew that what was inside him wasn't a figment of his imagination, it was real. It was a part of him that he couldn't understand but that exercised a control so powerful that he found himself committing murder for the sheer sexual thrill of it. He also knew that whatever was inside of him prevented him from truly loving a woman. He professed love to Kendall, and to other girls he had known, but he couldn't experience love. And when he had been cold toward Kendall or what she had called cruelly selfish, he begged forgiveness with tears. But they were the tears of someone too frightened of being abandoned and not tears of remorse. Years later Kendall found out that when Bundy was acting his most withdrawn from her, as if he were protecting a part of him that she could never know, it was out of self-protection and fear. To know him, Bundy finally said about himself, was to know something despicable and inhuman. In the end he asked Kendall not even to ask about it because even he couldn't face the truth within him even though he knew he was very, very sick.

While he was still a schoolboy, just a few years after he had fallen on the back of his head from a jungle gym and had begun to have epileptic seizures, Kenneth Bianchi molded a sculpture of a head that had two faces: one in front, and one in back. The one in front is the face of a sensitive, delicate human being. The one in back is the face of a killer ape. Kenneth had been diagnosed as having temporal lobe epilepsy by a psychologist. Another psychologist wrote about him that he expended a great amount of energy keeping his hostility under control and under cover.

After his accidental fall young Bianchi routinely wet his pants. His adoptive mother used to spank him before he went into the bathroom to punish him in advance for not emptying his bladder completely at the toilet. And when he stole money from her room, she would burn his hand over a gas flame, telling him that it was for his own good and making him profess that he loved her despite the pain of the torture.

Bianchi's mother had violent tantrums, and one day when he was nine he hid under a table to escape her temper. It was there that he claims he saw, beside him under the table, another little boy whose name was Steve. Steven hated Kenneth's mother and urged him to run away from her. But Kenneth was afraid, and for the next four years, despite the fact that they were inseparable friends, Steve told Kenneth that he hated him also. When Kenneth Bianchi's father died, Steve disappeared as well.

However, for the next fifteen years the psychologically damaged Bianchi led a double life. As Kenneth, he was a handsome man who was able to form relationships with women, fall in love with a young girl named Laura, survive the pain when she left him, and fall in love with another woman named Kelli. He had a son named Sean, and he worked as a security guard at Washington State. As Steve, a person Kenneth hadn't seen for years, he collected magazines and films that featured violent pornography, and he masturbated compulsively into a piece of rabbit's fur.

While he lived in Los Angeles, Bianchi as 'Steve' and his uncle Angelo Buono became a killing pair. They trolled the streets for women whom they captured, raped, strangled, and dumped along the hillsides surrounding Los Angeles. Steve flourished as Buono's partner and took delight in the slaughter of scores of young women. However, after Kenneth moved to Washington with Kelli, Steve disappeared: but still there, still hating Kenneth for his dependence on women, and still looking for the opportunity to strike. The pent-up frustration and rage became so strong that one night Steve emerged, killed two young girls, and deliberately left enough evidence in the area to incriminate Kenneth Bianchi.

It wasn't until Bianchi was evaluated by the court to establish his mental capacity to stand trial that a psychiatrist examined him again. And under hypnosis Steve came out and told the grizzly stories about Bianchi's mother, his uncle Angelo Buono, and the women they had buried outside of Los Angeles. The story was too far-fetched for the jury, who convicted him and his uncle of murder. Steve has disappeared again while Bianchi serves out his life sentence, but a panel of five other psychiatrists believed that Steve's appearance was a real occurrence of a multiple criminal personality.

Whether a form of multiple personality or not, Lucas, Bundy, Kallinger, Bianchi, and many of the other serial murderers have all reported feelings they could not control, voices whose urgings forced them into criminal acts, or sensations from deep within their minds that seemed to take over their bodies and hold them hostage. Some killers report that what began in childhood as strange voices or sexual urgings that were different from what other children talked about escalated into rituals within which these individuals would assault other people, rape women, achieve orgasm only when the victim lay helpless before them, and even commit murder and mutilation to hide the evidence and prevent their being caught. The more violent the crime, the more the feelings of violence escalated until the crimes themselves were no longer enough to blot out the disgust and revulsion the killers felt about themselves. Never able to show remorse, never able to experience the feelings of empathy and love other people seemed to experience, these killers lived in their own dark universes until a part of them gave up, attempted suicide, or left a telltale set of clues that led the police to make the arrest.

Where did those voices and feelings originate? Were the head traumas or birth defects ultimately responsible for the obvious neurological disorders or was there a critical mass of organic, psychological, and social causes that pushed each killer into his dark world? Did the killer-to-be while still a child recognize that there was something fundamentally different about him or was this a revelation that sprang upon him at puberty or only before each murder? Where is the point at which the damaged psyche can no longer exercise control over itself and looses a primal force of destruction upon the rest of society?

To answer these questions, psychiatrists Dorothy Lewis and Jonathan Pincus examined all fifteen inmates on Florida's death row and found that they all had a remarkable similarity of neurological impairments. One of those inmates, Bobby Joe Long, also commented that there were people on death row 'so far gone that it's like they're not even there when you talk to 'em.' He admits that he thinks a part of his brain, damaged in the motorcycle accident, 'has already dried up and died. . . . But there are people here who are just plain crazy and don't even know what's goin' on around 'em.'

To understand how someone can be neurologically impaired and still function or how someone like Bundy can lead an apparently normal life, live with a woman and her young daughter, and still have episodes during which he will rape and kill other young women, one has to understand the complex of symptoms that serial killers seem to have. And to understand how that damage controls their behavior, we have to look at how what we call consciousness or sentience is the product of a biological mechanism.

There is nothing magic or mystical about how the brain operates, although it is at the center of the miracle of life. What we call consciousness or awareness is actually the high-speed overlap of millions of electrochemically communicated messages between the senses, areas of recognition, memory banks, and nerves that control muscular movement. The brain is both a parallel processor, accomplishing many things at the same time along the same pathways, and a subordinating processor that prioritizes tasks and loads them into different job queues for completion as necessary. Based on the physical state of the body at any given moment, on the nature of the external world that the brain perceives, the urgency of messages that are stored in different memory stacks, and the emotional level of the organism, the brain allocates an importance factor to each job that it must process and organizes them accordingly. In the unconflicted person, this allocation process is as routine as setting up a 'things to do' list and ticking them off as they are accomplished, only on a vastly more complicated scale. In the conflicted person, and this describes ninety-nine percent of all of us, the brain makes millions of compromises. Do we have the next cup of coffee or make the difficult phone call; do we avoid the task or jump on it; do we face a fear or run away from it? The brain makes these types of decisions every nano-second in response to the millions of messages it receives from the external world and from its own memory banks.

But this machine model of the human brain still oversimplifies the complexity of the organ and the neurological system it manages. Because the system is driven electrochemically instead of only electrically, different types of communication can take place at the same time and actually alter the mind's interpretation of the messages. If a person is tired and hungry, his body is overworked, and his mind is overstressed with concerns about the day's problems and fears not only about tomorrow but about his family and financial situations as well, he will react to the same types of stimuli differently than someone who is unstressed, not hungry or tired, and more confident. On more specific levels, a person who has not eaten all morning will tend to snap at others and be extremely more irritable than the person who has had a nutritious breakfast. The former may not actually feel hungry, but his brain feels the need for chemical nourishment. It wants to be fed, and the chemical messages it receives inhibit its ability to respond logically to negative stimuli. We may not know this is happening, as in the case when someone drinks too much and his judgment and reflexes are compromised, but it is a measurable physiological phenomenon. Sexual arousal, fear, anger, and pain elicit similar chemical messages through the hormonal system that override the dominant logic that most brains exercise over their visceral emotions. And among serial killers whose body chemistry is drastically impaired, the brain can scarcely function normally at all.

Most people have seen diagrams that indicate what area of the brain controls what body function. Carl Broca in the nineteenth century isolated one of the areas that controls speech, the scientists mapped the areas that control muscular functions, receive messages from the optic nerve, intercept auditory signals, and discriminate among tastes or smells. The early twentieth-century perception of the brain assumed it to be a set of pigeonholes or compartments, each one controlling a specific part of the body. This has been largely shown to be false. It has been supplanted by the realization that the brain is a signal-switching device whose main function is to relay messages back and forth among different areas and in so doing establish what we commonly call 'awareness.' In this, human beings are just like any lower animals who see, hear, smell, touch, feel pain, experience hunger, feel the need to eliminate wastes, fear, have sexual arousals, and experience a form of vicious rage. However, because human beings have higher brain functions, use language, and exist in a metaphysical world in which they can make judgments about the nature of reality, their brains have an awareness of their own activity. We can understand statements such as: 'I'm trying to think' or 'My mind just isn't working today,' or 'It's on the tip of my tongue.'

Thus the human brain is a complicated but elegant communication device wherein the instantaneous nature of the signal switching within the different areas of the brain between what is reported by the senses and what is stored in the memory banks provides a base level of consciousness. Deprive a person completely of his sensory input and his entire sense of consciousness will be painfully distorted. Depriving a newborn baby of fundamental sensory input — especially tactile stimulation — some think is tantamount to condemning that newborn to a life of psychological pain and violence. Experiments on monkeys and other primates show that in the absence of sensory stimulation the animals become destructive and violent, and they eventually attempt forms of suicide by banging their heads against the sides of their cages.

In the normal brain sensory information from the outside world is relayed electrically to specific centres along pathways of nerve cells. What the nerves transmit to the brain is compared with similar information the brain has stored and the information is recognized and identified. Part of this information process is used to keep the individual oriented spatially and temporally. In other words, to establish what we sense as a continuum from one moment to the next, the brain constantly 'flashes' pictures of the outside world. These hundreds of billions of flash cards comprise a conscious reality. Change a major aspect of the outside world in between the flash cards so that it no longer conforms to what the brain expects and the individual can lose the ability to orient himself. In other words, if it is twelve noon, we don't expect it to be as dark as night in the next moment. And until the ancients understood and predicted solar eclipses, they had no basis for orienting themselves to what was happening. Change an aspect of gravity, as in a rapidly descending elevator, alter sound or suddenly thrust a new person into a place where he is not expected to be, and primal brain circuits override moment-to-moment cognitive activity, throwing the person into a form of defensive reaction. We call that reaction momentary panic, and we most commonly experience it when someone unexpectedly jumps out at us into our plane of vision. Children frighten one another like this all the time.

What really happens neurologically when we are frightened in this way is that the suddenness of the appearance is transmitted along a different neural pathway to the autonomic nervous system. This is controlled in the primal area of the brain: the temporal lobe, the limbic region, and the hypothalamus. These areas control the body's prime emotions and hormonal systems. They

272

can and do override any cognitive functions because they maintain the body's metabolic balance. It is in these regions that the biological algorithm is translated from a cellular level to the level of the organism. These areas control fear and rage, the sexual drive, the sense of pleasure or well-being, and the basic sense of self that differentiates one individual from the rest of reality. The autonomic message that someone has appeared unexpectedly triggers a reaction in the hypothalamus of fear and the need for flight. We may scream and jump, the heart will pound, and we will break out into a sweat. Our first reactions – and the untrained person has absolutely no control over them – are to run or fight back. We may recognize the person with our cognitive minds as he registers in memory, but the threat presented by the sudden instrusion has gone down a different pathway and, from somewhere within the brain, we react. We are aware of this reaction. We are aware of it at almost the exact same time that we recognize the person who caused us to jump in terror, and we are embarrassed by it. But we know that something inside of us has this reaction. It is as if there is another person within us who forces us to react even though we consciously do not want to. This type of sensation – magnified hundreds of times – is much like what the serial killer feels when a part of his brain takes over from its 'normal' activity.   .

Under routine circumstances, the brain quickly identifies abnormal sensory experiences and signals a type of alert status until the abnormality is resolved. The logical control exercised by the usually dominant left hemisphere provides a matrix of order and consistency and imposes a structure upon the raw sensory data the brain receives. It serves as a filter, establishing a continuum from one reality flash card to the next, and it judges the validity and content of the information it receives through the sensory receptors. Our ability to discriminate between real and nonreal or true and false is governed to a large extent by the judgmental, logical controls resident in the left hemisphere. This is what keeps even the most emotional person functioning within the social order and behaving according to a consistent set of rules. In dreams, however, the dominance of the governing cerebral hemisphere recedes and along with it the judgmental functions that we rely upon in a waking state. When that happens the logical structure of everyday existence is no longer present and the results are illogical, fanciful dreams that we accept at face value without dismissing them.

In dreams the continuum of reality is often shattered by abrupt changes of scene from one split second to the next. Loved ones or relatives who have died can populate our dreams and interact with people alive and well in the present. In dreams we can see ourselves as children acting within the present and even acting in the present with our adult selves. Dreams can come upon us instantly, it seems, especially when we are very tired, and the dream-stimulating chemicals begin to flow, carrying us off to sleep. At these half-dream/half-waking moments, there is a complete intermix between dream reality and symbology and waking reality. The waking brain exercises some control, but we feel an irresistible force pulling us into the dream state. If nothing jars us out of it, like oncoming headlights or the sound of a horn, we might drift into sleep without even realizing it until we've awakened moments or hours later.

Dreams also have their own symbology, which protects the waking mind from the terror of some of the deepest memories and fears that are stored there. For example, people who appear in our dreams often stand for other people who elicit similar emotional reactions. Siblings sometimes replace one's children, and upon waking the dreamer has a brief moment of insight regarding his or her relationship with the child of today. Parents, relatives, and friends may be interchangeable in one's dreams, and this, too, can be a source of revelation to the dreamer or to a therapist about the person's assumptions and deeper emotions. However, these moments of insight about dreams are made not by the dreaming mind but by the waking mind or with the help of the therapist. The subordinate hemisphere has no such judgmental capability in the typical adult brain and must be analyzed by some logical entity. During the killing sprees, in the mind of the serial murderer, no such logical entity exists for any extended period of time.

The half-dream/half-waking state that mixes memories and terrors with reality is a true episodic state for the serial killer with a limbic dysfunction or with other symptoms. The aspects of dreams intrude themselves upon waking reality without warning, and the killer finds himself in a world of his own terror-filled fantasies with no basis for determining whether he is dreaming or waking. It is all the same to him. And as in dreams in which people replace people and identities become confused, the delusional or hallucinatory state of the serial killer confuses individuals from the killer's past, such as parents or siblings, with the victim who has just crossed his path or entered his car. As the killer's frenzy silently builds before he springs the trap, he has locked himself firmly into a dream world and the victim before him has no identity whatsoever, except for the identity his mind has already imposed.

The physiological reaction that trips the dream/delusion mechanism can be triggered by an event in the real world just as in Gary Schaefer's case when his mind was already troubled over his stepdaughter just as he drove by Caty Richards and her friend. Or it can be purely episodic, like the emotional menstrual-like cycle that Bobby Long experiences. His severely damaged brain, which has been battered by successive head traumas, no longer has a functioning regulator to control the flow of emotions that are stimulated by hormones. As a result, Long found himself acting out of a waking dream, unable to suppress the rage and violence that had become associated with sex during the years with his mother and his domineering wife.

For Ted Bundy, it was the sight of a pretty coed who aroused a frenzy of sexual feelings. However, Bundy had been rejected by just such a woman. Her confidence in her good looks, and her demeanor, which exuded a belief in her own self-worth, terrified Bundy at the very moment it aroused him. He hated her and lusted after her at the same time, and the two feelings intertwined and became one. He needed to dominate such a woman and destroy the power that had rejected him. To do so excited him sexually and stimulated his entire body. That became the trip wire for the part of Ted Bundy's brain that was out of control. Already trolling for victims, his arm in a cast in a feigned demonstration of weakness, he played upon the very aspects of the woman's self-confidence to entrap her. And as a dialogue between Bundy and his victim was established and he felt the woman being lured into his web, he became more and more aroused. The emotional force that was surging in his brain became more powerful and spiralled him to the next phase of the crime. And at the moment of triumph, when she was beside him in the car, he had her. A quick succession of blows to render her helpless, and Bundy was at the penultimate stage of the crime. Now that she was unconscious and near death, he would rape her – sex and his hatred of this woman had become one and the same – and then he killed her. Now, at the post-mortem of the crime, he was filled with self-loathing. His acts of violence had proved nothing, and he had a body to dispose of. He buried her and placed a late phone call to Liz Kendall in a desperate effort to lurch back to reality and to establish himself as a living being. And this pattern continued through the lives of more than thirty victims in Seattle, more in Colorado, another set of victims in Utah, and a final set of murders in Florida.

For John Gacy the impetus was that he had to destroy something he felt was active and cancerous inside himself. The ritual of slaughtering the young men he encountered was a reenactment of a terrible dream in which his father was slaughtering the boy John Gacy that he had grown to despise for his own weakness and perceived lack of masculinity. Gacy assumed both his father's role and his own role at one and the same time. And, as in a waking dream, his damaged brain allowed the physical playing out of the self-torture and hatred that had been stored in memory since Gacy was a young child. The feelings of helplessness and rage and the childhood need to destroy what was most painful came to the surface when Gacy brought his victims back to his house. But in his own despondence after the failure to achieve a true release from the pain, he buried his victims in the soft mud under his house.

Although Gacy, Bundy, Manson, Lucas, Kallinger, Bianchi, Long and the others all evidence at least one trip mechanism in each of their particular behaviors, the truth is that there is usually more than one set of causes at work in the individual. If that were not the case, anyone with damage to his limbic brain or to his hypothalamus would automatically become a serial murderer. We know that the brain is a far more resilient organ than that and has a compensating mechanism that tries to correct for deficiencies. If a person has gone for many hours without eating and begins to react with inappropriate violence toward those around him, his normal sense of social order, though diminished, will respond to a direct query such as 'Don't you know what you're doing?' or 'Why did you do that?' The fear of disturbing the equilibrium of one's family or of losing one's job also serves to counterbalance temper tantrums or violent outbursts. Even alcoholics who are pushed to the brink, if their upbringing has been supportive, can still rebound and benefit from treatment or therapy.

The brain can also sustain repeated damage and continue to function because it is still a 'plastic' organ that reforms neural pathways to compensate for those that have been damaged. People who have experienced strokes on the left side of the brain and have lost muscular control on the right side, as well as the power of speech, can be retrained to function. Neurologists know that there is an *ur* speech area on the right side of the brain that to a large extent mirrors Broca's area on the left side. That area can be taught to take over from the left hemisphere in many cases of stroke and resulting speech impairment. We also know that neural pathways that control other motor functions can likewise be compensated for in a physical therapy programme after a stroke. And brain tissue can also rejuvenate itself after the destructive effects of alcohol abuse. Once the source of the toxin is removed and the tissue is allowed to recover, many cerebral functions that had been lost during the period of greatest abuse gradually return. A person may never recover one hundred percent of his previous cognitive abilities or long-term memory capacity, but he will recover enough to allow him to function without obvious impairment.

Paradoxically, it is the brain's gyroscopic capacity to right itself and compensate for damage and error that constructs the matrix out of which serial killers are produced. It is a form of defense mechanism which is so complex that when fully operational has turned the individual into a violent predator of other living creatures. To appreciate how a defense mechanism can evolve into a destructively aggressive behavior, one has to appreciate that the prime directive of any living organism is to survive. This is a type of biological algorithm, a biochemical reaction that is basic to the distinction between

living and nonliving matter. Reproduction is a manifestation of the biological need to survive: the reproduction of
genetic material mirror-like fashion to guarantee the
development of another living host for it. Thus, sexual
arousal is a primal chemical reaction.

Self-defense in all of its forms is also a manifestation of
the need to survive. Therefore fear, violence, rage, flight,
terror, and panic are all chemically induced reactions that
exist in almost all living creatures in one form or another.
They are a part of the compensation process that keeps
living entities from simply blundering into death. In
human beings, the primal self-defense reactions were
socialized very early in the evolution of the species – at
about the same time verbal language was developed – so
that humans could function in groups and survive the
elements and their natural predators in nature. This
social evolution of the species is mirrored in the psychological and social development of each individual. In
other words: ontogeny, the development of the individual,
follows philogeny, the evolution of the species. If that
development process in the individual is impaired in any
way so that the brain or neurological system has to
compensate in order to regain an internal balance, the
individual no longer mirrors the rest of society. He
becomes a psychophysiological mutation. This is what
happens in the development of a serial murderer.

The behaviors that serial killers display, although they
are ultimately self-destructive, are the behaviors that their
brains have developed to compensate for the levels of
physiological and emotional damage they have incurred.
If the child has not received the sensory stimulation he
requires and therefore has not established a boundary
between himself and the outside world, the brain will
compensate, but a vital component will be missing. A
portion of the infant's brain never develops to the point
where it can exercise regulatory control over primal

emotions. The individual may become all-encompassing and see only himself and nothing else. He recognizes no physical limitations to himself and seems literally to 'walk over everyone around him.' He has no sense of hurting anyone else, feels no remorse, and shows no sympathy. When the behavior is at its most extreme, the individual exists in his own universe, isolated from the rest of humanity. He may perform violent acts upon small animals at first and ultimately upon people. His own rage is an extension of himself, not capable of being held in check by the part of his brain that never developed properly. To a lesser extent, the individual displays sociopathic tendencies. He may be selfish and demanding and simply unresponsive to the needs of other people. He still exists in his own universe, but perhaps because his brain functions are not seriously impaired, or because of a more cohesive upbringing, or by having learned how to function in a socially ordered environment with great difficulty, he has trained himself to control violence.

In the cases of a Kenneth Bianchi, a Charles Manson, or a Henry Lee Lucas, in which the levels of childhood physical abuse were so extreme that each day was a challenge to survive, the developing psyche was simply crushed. It was taught that it was unloved and adrift within a hostile universe where it could find no solace except in self-gratification. To survive, it became a predator of others and, like a wild animal, it took what it could while avoiding contact with creatures that would destroy it. The physical damage impaired these killers' brain functions while the emotional damage resulted in elaborate defence mechanisms to enable them to withstand the constant torture. Paradoxically, in order to survive, the child had to be dead. Thus, figuratively speaking, the psyche died so that the physical entity could live on. Had there not been physical damage to the brain, perhaps the psychotic individual who emerged would not have lacked control over primal brain functions. But, given the physical damage, there was no control. Consequently, all of Lucas' and Bianchi's primal urgings were given free rein by an impaired brain, they lost control, and they became serial killers.

A close examination of the histories of each of the serial killers researched shows that what society called criminal behavior was in reality a type of defense mechanism against what was confronting him. And this amalgamation of psychological devastation, physiological brain damage, and a history of either substance abuse or crippling chemical imbalances, resulted in each case in an individual who is beyond our normal definition of insanity. The biological algorithm that was at work in this person kept him in a form of equilibrium. However, the forces that were at work both without and within him so skewed that equilibrium away from the mainstream that the individual is no longer recognizable in human terms. We perceive him to be a monster, and of course he perceives himself to be almost nonhuman when measured against the normal people he sees around him. Yet, tragically, what he has developed into was not entirely of his own choosing. In order to survive, as Charles Manson has described himself, he had to make a virtue of a necessity and embrace the creature he had become. Thus, in Manson's violent world of chaos, where bad was good and good was bad, his psyche's response was 'helter-skelter,' the absolute devastation of the external world in a mirror image of the devastation of his own internal universe.

If there is any hope in the description of how serial killers develop and what internal and external forces cause this particular form of mutation, it still lies in the resiliency of the human mind. Bundy, Long, Lucas, Kallinger all realize that they are sick. Even Manson recognizes that his behavior is well beyond the bounds of normalcy. He blames society and his upbringing for the pain that was inflicted upon him, but within the structured environment of prison he recognizes what he did. Susan Atkins, Tex Watson, Henry Lee Lucas, and other serial killers have embraced the revelation of fundamentalist Christianity as their structure for recreating their personalities. With the institutional structure of prison imposed upon their lives, having been detoxified from the residual effects of drug and alcohol abuse, and receiving a relatively stable diet of institutional food, the bodies of incarcerated serial killers begin to restabilize. Most of them realize that they might kill were they to be summarily released, but all of them now know that proper intervention would have kept them from killing in the first place or at least helped them understand what was happening even after their killing sprees had started. And one killer, Bobby Joe Long, was at the point of turning himself over to psychiatric care, but he became afraid of the consequences of prosecution at the last minute and walked away from the therapist's office building.

Most of the serial killers knew what was happening to them and either tried to suppress it themselves, as Bundy explained, or pleaded with authorities to help them. Lucas, Long, Gary, and Ed Kemper all told prison or medical authorities that they were sick and needed help. Lucas frankly told the prison doctors that, if released, he would go on killing sprees. The officials released him anyway. Bobby Joe Long tried for years to tell his Army doctors that he was severely injured and was experiencing symptoms that worried him, but the doctors rejected his claims as an attempt to increase his veteran's benefits. And when Carlton Gary explained to doctors and parole officers in New York's Ossining penitentiary that he was experiencing homicidal feelings and needed treatment, they claimed that he was looking to do easier time.

Clearly more research is needed, not only in the area of

episodic violence specifically, but also in the area of brain development and operation. Recent studies that have linked the organic growth of new neurons and neural pathways in response to the stimuli of learning new items promises new fields of research. The work of Drs. Lewis, Mark, Mednick, Walsh, Fishbein, and Thatcher will indicate new directions that criminology will take. And in the area of public policy, now that even the Surgeon General himself has recognized that violent crime is an issue of public health, the only course of action is to develop programmes that will identify victims of abuse and family violence before they retreat into their twilight worlds. Otherwise some of them will only emerge ten to fifteen years later as grisly headlines in local newspapers.

14

The Serial Killer Profile

On the basis of substantive interviews with more than a dozen serial killers and their immediate families and extensive casework interviews with neurologists, surgeons, psychiatrists, social workers, medical examiners, and research chemists, we have developed biological and social profiles of the potential serial killer. With the help of attorneys who have defended serial murderers, homicide detectives who have pursued them, and members of the Behavioral Science Unit of the FBI, we have been able to refine these profiles to include relevant details about the serial killer's habits and predilections. As our understanding of the serial killer syndrome deepened, we realized that these profiles could lead to the development of a diagnostic or prediction instrument that would identify individuals who might be at risk or whose backgrounds might require an extensive investigation or a biopsychosocial evaluation.

Unlike the phrenologists of the late nineteenth century, who examined the shapes of people's heads and bumps on their skulls, or even some of the behaviorists of the early 1940s, we are not looking specifically for 'criminal types.' Most police investigators will argue that anybody can become a criminal type simply by committing a crime and being processed through the justice system. We are hypothesizing, however, that serial murdering is a form of disease rather than simply a lifestyle, a syndrome that has specific hard and soft signs that are symptoms and identifiable long before the potential murderer commits his first homicide. The disease is the most ultimate form of episodic aggression. This we have learned from interviews with killers who revealed that they had experienced violent fantasies for many years before they stalked their first victims. And the subsequent murders they committed were, in most cases, reenactments of those fantasies and a response to the mounting dyscontrol.

We have learned that the disease has some of its origins in diagnosable organic disorders within the subject's neurological and central nervous systems. Injuries to the brain, prolonged and chronic biochemical imbalances, genetic disorders, and severe cases of epilepsy of the limbic brain all leave traces of the tissue damage and soft signs. These organic disorders are directly related to behavioral disorders, schizophrenic-like reactions, learning disorders, aggressive behavior and sometimes criminally antisocial activities. The afflicted person seems to have epileptic-like seizures that take the form of hallucinations, intruding themselves upon his consciousness, distorting time and reality and leaving only vague afterimages in their wake like the phantom traces of nightmares against the morning. The only signs that doctors may have as indicators are the long spikes on a deep-probe EEG or a series of soft neurological signs such as dyslexia, obsession with fires, memory gaps, and so on.

What indicators prompt diagnosticians and neurologists to order such an extensive test as a deep-probe EEG? How does a doctor determine when to send a hair sample to a toxicologist for chemical analysis? Do all children with learning disabilities have the types of dysfunctions that could eventually lead them to careers as

murderers of women and children? And what of the killer
who has committed his first homicide? Is there a way to
intervene before he paralyzes an entire community like
the Atlanta Child Murderer or the Son of Sam? And how
many future Charles Mansons are developing in the
darkness of our institutions and in their own miseries? Are
their fears and desperations the catalysts translating them
into nosferati? What are the signs that will alert those with
whom they come into contact? What will it take to
stimulate urgently needed research?

The behavioral and biological patterns and psychological profiles set forth in this chapter are the signs that
indicate a probability that an individual may be predisposed to episodic violence and criminal activity. A
critical number of signs point to the potential of
dangerousness without actually labelling anyone a
criminal. They can only be considered red flags. This is an
important distinction. It may be that many individuals
are able to navigate through life on the border between
incipient violence and normal behavior and without ever
treading over the line. They may live in fear of their own
potential for destruction and in terror of what they know
lies beneath the surface of their own social demeanor, but
they have not been pushed into violence by some critical
combination of forces. Their upbringing may have given
them a structure of behavior that allows them to look upon
themselves critically. They may be so aware of nutritional
deficiencies that they use diet as a means of behavioral
self-control. And most likely they will have found a spouse
or a significant other who provides them with an objective
sense of reality. Although these people may demonstrate
some of the biological and psychological symptoms of the
serial killer syndrome, they will spend their lives as
carriers of the disease and may never emerge as violent
criminals. The patterns developed in this chapter will

apply to these people only incidentally, but can be used as directional guides for research.

The purpose of defining a set of patterns and predictors is to help identify afflicted people at an early stage in their careers or lives. Children who inflict extraordinary violence upon their peers or upon animals, who repeatedly start fires and become entranced by the sight of flames, who have themselves been the victims of family violence or abuse and have suffered contusions or head injuries, and who exhibit chronic learning disabilities or other forms of organic neurological dysfunction are among the likeliest candidates for further evaluation. Similarly, juvenile offenders in institutions who seem incorrigible for reasons other than simply their home environments or those whose home environments are so tragically violent that they have become scared are also candidates for further evaluation. In any case, the patterns that follow are not intended to be a primary tool in predicting or labeling individuals as serial murderers or potential serial murderers but only as a guide or model for gathering further information about such people who are suspected of suffering from those or similar symptoms.

Essentially, the profile should serve as a diagnostic tool, for both medical professionals and officers of criminal and juvenile courts, indicating that the offender is actually himself a victim and requires intervention and not only punishment. It is not meant to exonerate individuals of the crimes they have committed but to suggest that the crime may have its origins in the serial killer syndrome, identified by some as dyscontrol syndrome or limbic brain psychosis, and that certain forms of medical help, therapy, and positive correction may prevent him from embarking on a life of chronic homicidal violence. In other words, skilled use of these patterns may save the lives of many thousands of potential victims by short-circuiting the careers of their murderers-to-be. The profile can be of significant benefit to people belonging to the following groups:

1.   Individuals who are afraid they are experiencing symptoms and are losing control of their violent tendencies. This is not meant to scare anyone into thinking he is a potential serial killer but to alert people who are truly suffering from delusions of violence, hallucinatory fantasies of ritualistic violence, and violent hypersexuality to the presence of a real disease. Ideally people, such as other episodically violent people like rapists, wife beaters, and repeated assaulters, so alerted will seek some form of medical help before they succumb to their increasingly perverted and more violent fantasies.

2.   People or groups who act as advocates for individuals they suspect of being at risk. Friends, relatives, children, or spouses who fear abuse from an individual yet realize that he may be acting out a behavior pattern not entirely of his own making. Especially important in this group are people who live with individuals who experience episodic behavioral disorders. The more regular these episodes become and the more bizarre the behavior aberrations associated with these episodes, the more important it is that the spouse or relative seek intervention. Potential victims can protect themselves first by recognizing the likelihood of violence and then obtaining intervention to help the potential offender, even if that person is a spouse, parent, or intimate friend. In all the killers researched, a relative or a significant other missed opportunities to intervene prior to or during a killing spree.

3.   Judges, prosecutors, defense attorneys, police investigators, and other law enforcement personnel who confront potential serial murderers often through the criminal justice system. By approaching the phenomenon as an illness and recognizing the behavioral symptoms,

criminal justice professionals will be better equipped to investigate the crimes, protect potential victims, and apprehend the killer before he has a chance to elude detection and leave the area.

4.   Members of parole boards, pardon committees, and professionals in the corrections professions who must understand the complexity of the disease that drives serial murderers. Often episodically violent persons are released prematurely or, like Henry Lee Lucas, Charles Manson, and Carlton Gary, they are released despite their own threats that they might act out asocially or violently again or that they will not be able to function outside of the institution. If members of parole boards understood more about the dynamics of the serial murderer's personality they would know better what symptoms to look for and would better recognize the danger signs in the people whose cases they must evaluate and the critical signs therein.

5.   Doctors, nurses, hospital emergency room personnel, neurologists, psychiatrists and other therapists, social workers, and teachers who may frequently come in contact with individuals who display symptoms of this syndrome. These professionals, victims notwithstanding, are the primary contact groups because the early and subsequent confrontations between serial murderers and society's institutions take place in elementary schools, hospital emergency rooms, and psychiatric wards as well as in juvenile courts and police stations. These institutions are society's early warning system, and the records they keep often unknowingly track the developments of potential serial murderers as they make their first passes at society. An emergency room doctor who treats the same child for repeated head injuries or homicidally aggressive behavior on many subsequent occasions might be in a unique position to call that child's case to the attention of

a social worker or a juvenile officer at a local police department. At least by being brought to the attention of the emergency room's supervising physician, the case might make its way into the official records. A school nurse who sees the same child on numerous occasions for headaches, blurred vision, aberrant social behavior, unexplained bouts of crying, temper tantrums, unexplained but chronic bruises, symptoms of malnutrition, or just because the child is always at the centre of trouble might be watching the child's first clashes with social authority. Is the child secretly emotionally or learning-disabled? Does the child have an undetected neurological dysfunction that makes him incapable of following instructions in the same way as the other children? Does the child's antisocial behavior result in fights with the other children every day after school? Does the child look as though he has been abused physically, emotionally, or sexually in his home environment? Does the child exhibit other nonresilient qualities? These are the types of questions that should prompt school officials to consider the predictors developed in this chapter, always being careful not to label someone as a potential murderer but to suggest diagnosis and follow-up.

6. Researchers in medicine, education, law enforcement, and the social sciences who are in a position to pursue definitive studies into serial murder and other forms of episodic aggression as a form of public health issue can use these patterns to establish early parameters for their models. These patterns are meant to stimulate research by defining areas of need that require further investigation.

The following list of behavior patterns is a result of all the data that has been compiled on the very nature of a person suffering from the symptoms of episodic aggressive behavior.

THE SERIAL KILLER PROFILE

Twenty-one Patterns of Episodic Aggressive Behavior

1. Ritualistic behavior
2. Masks of sanity
3. Compulsivity
4. Search for help
5. Severe memory disorders and a chronic inability to tell the truth
6. Suicidal tendencies
7. History of serious assault
8. Deviate sexual behavior and hypersexuality
9. Head injuries or injuries incurred at birth
10. History of chronic drug or alcohol abuse
11. Alcohol- or drug-abusing parents
12. Victim of physical or emotional abuse or of cruel parenting
13. Result of an unwanted pregnancy
14. Products of a difficult gestation period for the mother
15. Interrupted bliss or no bliss of childhood
16. Extraordinary cruelty to animals
17. Arsonal tendencies without obvious homicidal interest
18. Symptoms of neurological impairment
19. Evidence of genetic disorders
20. Biochemical symptoms
21. Feelings of powerlessness or inadequacy

Pattern 1 – Ritualistic Behavior

The ritual that is always a part of the serial murderer's modus operandi is either explicit at the scene of the crime or made explicit by the murderer when he confesses to the police. This ritual is a repeated observable pattern, so that there is a fundamental sameness from crime to crime that even the killer can't alter. It forms the basis of the serial killer's personality and is evident, perhaps even in outline form, long before the first crime is ever committed. Serial killers use ritual as a kind of behavioral skeleton – much like an insect – to provide an architecture for their fantasies and a structure to the violence that informs their conscious existence.

Many times the first investigators to arrive at the crime site become aware that the victims were treated in a ritualistic way, either by decapitation, forms of mutilation or sexual molestation, or burial after the crime. Many times the killings seem random until the killer makes a confession and the police see the edges of ritual that tied the crimes together. Killers may take photographs or shoot videotapes of their victim's suffering, they may make audio tapes of their cries of pain or pleas for mercy, or they may incarcerate their victims for days before killing them. The ritual may be present in the way the victims are caught or in the poses the killer uses. Ted Bundy usually feigned weakness or injury, for example, preying on an innocent girl's desire to help out an obviously charming, good-looking, and ingratiating man. Leonard Lake, who committed suicide in a police interrogation room in San Francisco, made videos of the ritualistic torture of his victims. Bobby Joe Long would ride with his victims sitting next to him in his car for hours, as if he were on a date with them, before killing them and dumping their bodies. And Gary Schaefer reenacted the same ritual of killing his older sister with a rock with each of his victims.

What investigators discover is that the ritual is primal; it is the behavior of a human being that lacks civilized humanness and now acts as though a deeply primitive neuropsychological circuit were continally firing and stimulating itself over and over again. This is the behavioral model of psychomotor epilepsy or the episodic cycles of electrochemical turbulence within the limbic brain and hypothalamus regions. There is a primal identity that the serial killer seems to adopt during these episodes that is part of his normal social personality but is mostly fixated on the desperate need to satisfy an almost feral instinct. Unfortunately, that instinct manifests itself in forms of violence toward other people.

In essence, ritual killings are a part of a developing downward spiral, a metastasizing loss of control which may have started when the individual was only eight, nine, or ten. When the complete ritual is analyzed and traced, which can only happen after many hours spent in gaining the trust of the killer and dealing with his inconsistencies and memory gaps, the ritual appears to be a sum total of the perceived childhood horrors and his chronic damaged physical condition. It turns out to be the survival pattern of a person who has never developed the channels for emotions such as fear, lust, and rage and is driven by them as if he lives within a primordial neurological soup, an unstructured conscious dream world in which there is no logic and no social order. These are the interictal episodes of behavior during which the crimes are committed and the ritual of the crimes is an outward depiction of the fears and rage that are exploding deep within the most primitive parts of the killer's badly damaged brain, psyche, and spirit.

To the killer during the act of the crime, the rituals are a form of morality play. They have an internal purpose and methodology that can be interpreted after society's external structure has been imposed upon the killer. They have a theme and the victims are archetypal symbols to the killer. Henry Lee Lucas killed his mother over and over again. Each time a woman confronted him, or baited or challenged him, she became a victim. Charles Manson was convinced that society needed to hear his paranoid message, and in a recent interview disclosed that most of the killers on death row in San Quentin believe that they are incarnations of Jesus Christ or the Antichrist. They claim to be carrying out divinely inspired instructions to

wage war on society. Charles Manson's primary concession today is that he has not killed enough people. He has
not made his message plain enough. He dogmatically
reminds anyone who will listen that he is a reflection of
society and that his crimes are the crimes society has
created. He instructed Tex Watson, the surrogate leader
of the Manson family, to make the Tate and LaBianca
killings as 'messy' as possible so as to bring home to
society the message that 'helter-skelter,' the apocalypse of
Manson's obsession, had already begun.

The structure of ritual with its reliance on totemic
objects, can be observed in most normal, healthy children.
Toddlers have their special 'thumb-sucking' blankets or
even pieces of cloth without which they cannot go to sleep.
Gradually they lose their interest in these objects and
replace them with others. As adults, normal people have
favorite articles of clothing, robes, pajamas, or other items
of comfort, but the pleasure derived from them has been
intellectualized. There is nothing inherently magic about
them, and they have no abnormal powers as objects.
Although people may have 'lucky' pens without which
they will not sign a contract or an agreement, these, too,
have become intellectualized.

The serial killer, however, is a different animal. For
him, the objects involved in his ritual do have a power
over him. They are the tangible embodiments of forces
that drive and sustain him, objective forms of the
hallucinatory metaphors that structure his ritual. And the
reliance on this ritual and its associated totems is evident
in his penultimate killer state, and persist long after the
normal adult has lost the need for personal ritual and
private totems.

The presence of these ritualistic fantasies and the
preservation of totemic objects taken from would-be
victims or potential crime scenes indicates that even a
person who has not committed a murder is involved in a

ritual that could someday be acted out. Inherent in his dark scenarios are always themes of perverted meaning known only to himself. There are interwoven patterns of lust, rage, judgment enacted upon the enemy, punishment of the demons who haunt them, dominance over friend and foe, submission by the innocent, perversion of good into evil, a damaged creative spirit, androgyny, and a final concession of the powerlessness of the individual. Then there is a lapse into a postvision depression in which the morbid fears of the serial killer dominate him and force him into conformity with the rest of society. In a symbolic and kinesthetic way, the killer is acting out a montage of primal impulses, perceived racial memories, the hormonal messages of a damaged or perverted libido, and in so doing is using the immediate victim helpless before him as a way to hold the entire community at bay.

Pattern 2 – Masks of Sanity

As if he had a split personality, the very dark behavior of the serial killer is often masked by a veneer of very good and socially rewarded behavior. This is his mask of sanity and it is manifested through grandiosity or a belief in his own superhuman importance, hypervigilance or an extraordinary concern about acting morally and properly, and social adeptness to the point of extreme manipulative ability. Serial killers, like most mass murderers, have extremely well-honed manipulative skills. Charles Manson, Ted Bundy, John Gacy, Carlton Gary, Ed Kemper, and even Henry Lee Lucas all demonstrated one of the basic attributes of the effective manager: the ability to get other people to do what you want them to do. Manson, like a bomb-sniffing police dog, was able to sense the inferiority in others, the need to be dominated and told what to do, and the desperate need for approval. Although Susan Atkins and Leslie Van Houton might have seemed like normal, upstanding young people, albeit with free spirits, they were actually deeply scarred people who actively sought domination as a missing component in their own personalities. They derived strength from Manson as did Tex Watson, who offered his life to Manson as proof of his fidelity.

By having a keen sense of what is required to conform to the outward trappings of society, serial killers are able to exhibit acceptable, indeed often exemplary behavior in their communities. Their need for approval and their ability to second-guess confrontation is so great that they go undetected by the public at large and until they are confronted by family members, spouses, friends, or primary sexual partners as their conditions worsen. The qualities that compel serial killers to behave as they do are eerily like the qualities of achievement that American society expects from successful individuals. Manson, Leonard Lake, Carlton Gary, and Bundy were all involved with their communities during their murder sprees and 'doing good' in their own eyes, having penetrated the very society they hated so much.

There is a part of the personality of the serial killer, as there is in all of us, that needs acceptance and requires achievement. However, the more acceptance and achievement that come their way, the greater the need itself becomes. There is no satisfying or satiating it, whereas normally developed people can decide when to be 'selfish' and preserve quality time for themselves. The compulsive needs of serial killers are such that they have no self-esteem – psychobiologically, many of them can't even determine the boundaries of their own selves and thus can't conceive of themselves as having separate identities – and this factor is critical to their later explosions of violence. They have spent a lifetime repressing the cancerous rage at the core of their personalities. They have been experiencing a progressive and escalating loss of control and sense of madness from the time they first became aware of their own dark primal urgings. They have learned to fear and hate the dark sides of themselves yet succumb to them in moments of pure reactive violence. But they have developed a chameleon-like mask of sanity or normalcy whose purpose is to protect them from the turbulent and hostile violent central element of their psyches. This mask of sanity also camouflages them from the society they have learned to fear and hate.

During this period of development a unique set of defense mechanisms emerges, composed of the same elements that make for sociopathy or sociopathic and multiple personalities, and these interact with the neurological impairments that cause significant but convenient losses of memory and gaps in reality: the episodes during which the serial murders are committed. The drive to live within society, the ability to hope and dream about the possibilities the future holds for them, and the sense of self that allows them to benefit from personal and vocational achievements have all been physically or emotionally beaten away from them in their earlier years. Many have success, but they cannot feel successful. Manson, although quite capable as a classical guitarist and composer, failed at being a songwriter. And recent evidence shows that he killed for a music contract that had been based on a verbal promise that was not fulfilled. Leonard Lake was making his one last try at success when he ran afoul of the law after his companion Charles Ng was caught shoplifting. He told his brother-in-law that he would rather die than not be financially successful. And Carlton Gary was selling cocaine, robbing homes, even while dating a variety of women, including a policewoman and psychiatric nurse, while he was raping and murdering the matrons of Wynnton. Simultaneously he was providing emotional support for his beloved aunt Alma, who was in a nursing home. He would regularly visit her and walk the grounds with her, she on her walker and he holding steady, until she died. He was also a male fashion model and appeared on local television at the same time that he was robbing, raping, and killing his victims.

The killer who best personified the mask of sanity was the homophobic murderer John Wayne Gacy. At eighteen, Gacy began his involvement with Chicago politics by working as an assistant precinct captain on behalf of the Democratic candidate Philip Elderman. At long last he felt pride in himself of the same type that he'd felt when he ran the Chi Rho social club in high school. Although his father had constantly abused him by verbally castrating him as a child, and berated him for his involvement in community activities, as an adult he remained active in local Democratic politics. He would also become a member of the JCs and would be known to many as the hardest-working community volunteer in town. He was the grand marshal of the Polish Day Parade in Chicago for several years during which he directed the efforts of more than seven hundred people. During the same period that he ritualistically killed at least thirty-three young boys and buried their bodies in a muddy crawl space beneath his house, he began a construction business, tried to keep his marriage alive, and had many legitimate and illegitimate business deals all going on the side with a variety of young men who were working for him in his construction business. The deals ranged from getting better prices for lumber to arranging for robberies and the sales of drugs. And all the while Gacy was fighting a compulsive battle within himself to keep his composure and maintain his ability to navigate within a social reality. It was a battle that he eventually lost.

Dressed in sad-faced clown makeup and known as Pogo the Clown, Gacy would go with other JCs on a legitimate mission of mercy, namely, the entertainment of young children at hospitals in the Chicago metropolitan area. One of his favorite methods to lure laughter out of bedridden children was to trick them into handcuffing themselves. The surprise at being handcuffed was quickly mitigated by the clown's laughter and the release of the magician's young assistant. It was a favourite trick for the children who saw his act. He later used this same paraphernalia as part of his seduction ritual of the young males he killed. He would lure them into the handcuff trick at his moment of springing the trap. They would later be tortured and killed. During this period he was named the best JC chaplain for the state of Iowa. When the police searched his house they found pictures of Gacy shaking hands with Mayor Richard Daly and with Rosalyn Carter, the wife of President Jimmy Carter.

It was not enough that Gacy earned more than two hundred thousand dollars a year from his new business, nor was it enough that he was named the best JC of Waterloo, Iowa, or that he perceived that the mayor of Chicago depended upon him to deliver his precinct's votes. The more he accomplished, the more he needed to achieve and the more his grip upon normalcy was challenged by the drive to commit more murders. He would wash old ladies' windows, funnel complaints by people in his political precinct to the Democratic district leaders, and he was even assigned to escort Rosalyn Carter through Chicago on one of her campaign visits in 1976. And all the while he was a killer of young boys, lapsing into episodes of violence, the disclosure of which would rock an entire community and outrage a nation.

The other star performer who led a double life was Ted Bundy, who is still awaiting execution on Florida's death row. During the time he was killing more than thirty-five college coeds in Seattle he was doing course work for a prelaw degree, volunteering on a suicide prevention hotline, and working in local politics. Although a rapist, he wrote a rape prevention guidebook for the state of Washington and even obtained a mail-order Ph.D. in psychology from a degree mill in Washington which enabled him to open a private practice as a psycho-therapist. What was most astounding about Bundy's double existence was that Bob Keppel of the Seattle police was investigating Bundy at the time. Bundy managed to elude him, flee the state, and finally get arrested in Florida after murdering young women in a college sorority house.

Bundy had been courted by local politicians and administrators at the university who sought his help in ministering to the needs of the large student community in the campus area. Bundy was chivalrous and handsome, and although his fiancée was aware of the dark side of his personality that would make him withdrawn, sullen, and smoldering on the precipice of a violent explosion of temper, she never spoke to the police until close to the very end. She confided her suspicions to a friend, but it was only when a girl referred to the guy who tried to pick her up as Ted that Bundy's fiancée called homicide detective Bob Keppel. By that time Bundy had made plans to flee the state, and his friends still couldn't believe that he was really implicated in a series of unsolved rape-murder cases stretching back for several years.

And finally even Henry Lee Lucas, although of a significantly lower socioeconomic level, managed to fit into the societies he tried to enter. 'He is one of the gentlest and most loving Christian persons I have ever known,' says Clementine Schroeder, confidante, jail minister, and Lucas' lover. Sister Clemmie, as she is known, is a naive country woman from rural Texas who became acquainted with Lucas and his case during her frequent visits to the Georgetown jail where he was held and where she was the ad hoc minister and religious counselor to the inmates. Since converting Lucas to Christianity – he had already claimed a religious vision in his cell after being arrested for the murder of Granny Rich – and becoming convinced that God sent Lucas, the most evil man in the world, into her ken for her to convert and nurture, their friendship has evolved into a lovers' relationship. Their stated dream is for Lucas to become free so that they can open a halfway house for prisoners. Lucas was also well loved by the family of Ottis Toole in Jacksonville, Florida, to the point where they allowed him to raise two of their youngest children, Becky and Frank Powell. Little did they know at the time that Lucas would train them both in the ways of murder, teach them the religious ministrations of Satanism, and become the common-law husband of Becky, whom he would ultimately stab to death, dismember, and bury. Frank Powell is confined to a mental institution in Florida to this day.

Lucas was able to ingratiate himself with the Powells and with the Riches because he was self-effacing, humble, and bore all the marks of a victim himself. Because he never had to work himself into a fury to kill those people he knew – it was a split-second, hair-trigger reaction – he never posed a threat. Granny Rich's children in Texas recognized that something was wrong with Lucas and pressured their mother to ask Lucas and Powell to move out, but to the members of the House of Prayer community, Lucas was just another drifter who signed on to do day work for the roofing company. He was able to camouflage himself amid the group until the very end when he no longer cared about evading the sheriff.

Pattern 3 – Compulsivity

Serial killers and potential serial killers have deeply compulsive personalities, and the compulsivity is manifested in more than one or two ways at a time. Several of the killers researched for this book had compulsivity concerning their physical appearance. Bobby Joe Long took several showers a day, sometimes as many as six, during most of his adult life even before the motorcycle accident. Carlton Gary was also a compulsive showerer.

He interrupted the court proceedings on several occasions because of self-criticism he had about the way he was dressed or the way he thought his physical appearance seemed to onlookers in the courtroom. Leonard Lake also had a compulsivity about being neat and clean around the home, according to his ex-wife Cricket Balazs, who reported that the two often argued about her cleanliness. As part of his murder ritual, he forced his victims to take showers prior to their rape and eventual murder.

Many serial killers are also compulsive record keepers. They maintain scrapbooks and organized memorabilia concerning the killings as well as preserving parts of their victims' bodies or clothing. This pattern is so common among the killers that some homicide detectives feel that the discovery of souvenirs is a high-priority piece of evidence during the investigation. Among the items of memorabilia catalogued by the serial killers in our study were scrapbooks with press clippings of the murders, press clippings of other or similar serial killings, books on psychology and deviant behavior, books on people who suffered from multiple personalities and manifested violent criminal behavior, biographies of Hitler and other mass murderers, personal items or body parts of the victims. These are especially indicative of the serial murderer syndrome because the taking of a victim's body part is associated with the ritualistic fantasy and it becomes a totem. Among the items catalogued were teeth, fingers, toes, nipples, breasts, and penises. Clothing and underwear were also collected as were snippets of hair, barrettes, and articles of decoration that the victims wore.

In some cases, killers have preserved whole sections of their victims' bodies, such as legs, trunks, and torsos. Edmund Kemper, for example, murdered his mother and kept her head in his possession for weeks after the killing. He also preserved the heads of some of his other victims. He would use the decaying heads as masturbatory objects as well as dart boards. He went so far after killing his verbally manipulative and cruel mother as to remove her vocal cords and run them through the garbage disposal unit.

Ed Gein kept his mother's cadaver, which he had amateurishly embalmed, on the property for many years. Gein masturbated with his mother's cadaver on frequent occasions during his killing sprees. He also made lamp-shades out of the skins of his victims and wove bracelets out of their hair.

A third pattern of compulsivity is the taking and cataloguing of photographs of victims by many of the killers. Leonard Lake kept an elaborate set of photo-graphic records of his crimes. He attracted victims to his rural northern California encampment with classified ads in the San Francisco papers offering different types of equipment for sale. Records now in police custody include home videotapes of the torture of his victims, photographs of nude young girls, and photo scrapbooks of his victims. In some cases Lake murdered entire families whose only legacies are the photographs of their final agonies.

As a child, Lake was also a compulsive record keeper and maintained active studies about the life cycles of rats. From these recorded observations, the gifted child became a self-taught geneticist. His record keeping and neurotically compulsive attention to repeating the same patterns of behavior formed one of the basic patterns of his life.

Obsessive attention to detail and compulsivity regard-ing the performance of ritualistic daily activities are two behavioral symptoms that might indicate a violently unstable personality. These forms of personal emotional rigidity appear very early in afflicted persons and do not disappear as the persons grow older. And while it is natural for some children to develop rigid personalities in response to a difficult home environment or to social difficulties, this rigidity subsides after adolescence. Shades of it may linger into adult life, where it forms a cushion against an uncertain world, but the compulsive person tends to be neurotic and shrinks from violence. In the sociopath, interference with one's compulsivity can be punished by violence, especially when the compulsivity points to a deeper ritualistic behavior. This becomes the psychological no man's land for the emerging serial killer and often forms the trigger that launches his career. The more persistently compulsive the adult becomes, and the more habits are involved in the compulsion, the greater the probability that there is a severe underlying instability that could be a time bomb waiting for a skein of victims.

Compulsion and obsession manifest themselves further in the trolling or cruising activity associated with a search for a victim. Like the relentless animal hunt for food, the killers patrol their areas with little attention to the time of day or season of the year. If they sense the nearby presence of potential victims – the lounges and sorority houses of college campuses for Ted Bundy, the strip bars just north of Tampa for Bobby Joe Long, or the Chicago bus station for John Gacy – the killers weave through an area for a vulnerable victim as a fisherman trolls with his net for the catch.

Many killers have extraordinarily high mileage on their cars, and this can lead to their identification and arrest. Pierce Brooks and other FBI theorists have developed a component of the VICAP that can trace killers during their compulsive driving patterns from state to state. The best known and most successful of these FBI manhunts was the search for Christopher Wilder, a serial murderer who preyed on beauty contestants at pageants.

The serial killer's trolling pattern seems to have a biological correlative in the aura state preceding a seizure-like episode in the limbic brain. The trolling pattern, a relentless and obsessive weaving from place to place as if laying out a net, possibly being enacted out of a rhythm of electrical activity. It mirrors the activation of a primal self-stimulation circuit just below the conscious awareness of the killer. Possibly the killer is becoming hyperstimulated in the aura phase as neurons deep in the primitive brain begin to fire and cause a turbulence of early memories and primal emotions to mingle with live sensory data. The delusions and fantasies take over the killer's consciousness and the compulsion to kill drives him in search of his next victim.

Pattern 4 – Search for Help

Each killing or set of killings has a gestation period in that a killer reaches an unconscious point of no return. At this point he loses the conscious ability to control his actions. Prior to this, the serial murderer reaches out in various ways to ask for help. He can sense the primal rumblings of the violence fomenting in a part of his brain. He may, especially if he suffers from psychomotor epilepsy, experience an aura immediately preceding the seizure. Or the first images of his delusions may intrude upon his sleep and fill his dreams with his most primal fears from early childhood. It is at these moments, when he feels reality slipping away again, that he is most vulnerable and apt to cry out for help. Unfortunately, these moments can be fleeting, and once he becomes trapped in his own fantasies he is out of control.

However, long before the serial killer fully emerges, sometimes even in late childhood, the conscious brain tries to seek help to prevent the damaged primitive brain from exercising control. Edmund Kemper's career was marked by this reaching out as were the careers of Henry Lee Lucas and Bobby Joe Long. Kemper, who was in the hospital as a teenager after killing his grandparents, had been receiving psychotherapy with fair results. He asked for help and revealed the hatred that he had for his mother and the fear of manipulation and control that she aroused in him. The staff psychologist agreed with the patient and recommended to the parole board that he should not be released into her custody. 'This young man's mother has had her pound of flesh from Kemper,' the psychologist reported. He suggested that the boy be 'set free from the mother.' Kemper felt the same way, but the parole board intervened and rejected the recommendation of the psychologist and of Kemper's own testimony. They appointed the mother custodian of the vulnerable boy and returned him directly to the environment that had helped nurture his feelings of hatred and violence. This deadly pairing at the time that Kemper had pleaded for intervention and help culminated in Kemper's finally killing his mother and decapitating her.

Carlton Gary also revealed his violent tendencies when he was serving time in Ossining, New York, for the robberies of welfare recipients in Albany almost five years before he began his killing spree in Columbus, Georgia. He reported that he told the prison psychiatrists that he was a killer and was compelled to commit crimes at regular intervals by forces inside him that he could not control. The prison psychiatrists rejected his sensational claim and returned him to the cell block.

Similarly, Bobby Joe Long spent years after his motor-cycle accident and resulting severe head injury trying to convince Army and civilian doctors that he was suffering from an injury-induced behavioral disorder. He reported to doctors that after he awoke in the hospital he felt that his sexual needs and his whole life were out of control. This frightened him because he had never felt that way before and because he realized that there was something seriously wrong with the way he was feeling. The Army doctors argued that he was simply trying to get more medical benefits or a medical discharge from the service and did not conduct further examinations. Other neurologists in Florida also failed to pursue the issue. Even in prison today the examinations he received were cursory until Dorothy Lewis began her neuropsychiatric evaluation.

Long also felt the need to seek medical attention even while he was committing the classified ad rapes. He was dating a nurse who suggested that he visit a psychiatrist and explain the strange forces that seemed to be driving him. While standing outside the doctor's office building, Long became afraid that he would be summarily turned over to the police and that his problems would remain unsolved. Hence he did not keep the appointment, and the rape/burglaries escalated into rape/murders within a few short years.

And finally Long's probable cousin, Henry Lee Lucas, reported that when he was about to be paroled after serving six years for the murder of his mother he tried to warn the personnel at the hospital that he was not ready to leave and still needed help in learning to cope with life. 'I tried marriage, and that didn't work. I tried religion, and that didn't work. And I tried to make friends, and I tried to reunite myself with my sisters, and none of that worked.' All his attempts to find an anchor in life that would keep him from drifting into the control of the destructive forces within him failed. No other people bonded with him to help him exert control over those forces. It was only in the prison environment that Lucas could find the necessary structure that would keep the forces in check and in which he could maintain a homeostasis concerning his most violent tendencies. He warned the prison officials in Ionia that he would kill again if released. However, they had severe overcrowding at the prison and released him on parole. Lucas reports that he raped and killed a woman near the prison and deposited her body just outside the gate. The body of another Jane Doe turned up five miles away from the prison just a few days later, and Lucas confessed to that murder as well.

Pattern 5 – Severe Memory Disorders and a Chronic Inability to Tell the Truth

Often individuals predisposed to episodic violence become pathological liars. On the one hand, lying is simply an extension of their chameleon-like ability to blend in with their background. They sense the information that people around them want to hear and provide it. Truth is not an issue for them, survival is. On the other hand, the concept of living according to a standard of honor and truth is a higher, intellectual virtue that can only be maintained by a person who is not a sociopath and does not have fundamental character disorders. The types of physiological damage to the hypothalamus and to the limbic region of the brain or the temporal lobe that helps the developing infant individuate himself from the rest of the world so distort the person's behavior that the concepts of truth and honesty are meaningless. Truth demands that the person perceive a modicum of self-worth. Because most episodically violent individuals perceive themselves as having no worth and no meaning for life, they are honest neither with themselves nor with others.

On a practical level, lying is a form of manipulaton. If one can lie successfully one can get others to believe what one wants them to. It can also be argued that, in politics and business, people lie as a rule and are not serial killers. Institutions routinely lie to protect themselves and their officers, and different cultural groups routinely lie to one another out of self-protection and the need to manipulate. Therefore, lying is also a practiced skill that the serial killer practices better than most.

When lying becomes chronic in the schoolchild or in the person whose recapitulation of basic facts may change from day to day, it is an indicator of other serious behavioral disorders. However, the clinical distinction must be made between lying out of practice and lying out of the brain's need to survive. Most serial killers sincerely believe the stories they are telling when they are telling them. Henry Lee Lucas, for example, confessed to more than three hundred murders. Some of those confessions were true, others were deliberate lies, and others were lies because police presented him with facts and he confessed to them because he thought it would please the authorities. Lucas might have truly believed he committed many of the crimes he confessed to. He might have felt that, if the police had evidence against him and his memory of the events was obscure, he would confess and save them the trouble of keeping the case open on the books. Besides, there was a behavioral pattern at work. When Lucas confessed to a crime he was rewarded and praised. It was easy to obtain rewards and praise from the police by confessing to all the crimes they asked him about.

Soon after some of his confessions proved to be inaccurate, Lucas recanted. Ultimately he recanted all of his murder confessions, including the killings of Becky Powell and Granny Rich. He changed his story because other prison authorities suggested that Lucas had done a bad thing by confessing to crimes he really hadn't committed. Now he had a new set of authorities to please, and he promptly changed his story to earn praise and rewards from them. His strategy has succeeded, and he changed the details of his past to conform to the wishes of the person who was conducting the interrogation.

Some experts feel that the memory disorders that afflict episodically violent people result from the periods of epileptic-like seizures, loss of conscious awareness during hallucinatory periods, and the dreamlike states that could even result from organically induced delusions from within the limbic brain. Similarly, killers who are chronic drug or alcohol abusers have lapses of memory during stupors and walking coma-like states. This loss of memory is counterbalanced by a pattern of hyperamnesia, or an extraordinary ability to remember the tiniest details of an event, that is also manifested in serial killers. The two patterns can coexist because the brain is unable to impose a structural management upon the neurological memory banks. Hence there are severe lapses of memory punctuated by reminiscences of small events like islands in the middle of an ocean of darkness.

Pattern 6 – Suicidal Tendencies

Often serial killers who are not caught eventually kill themselves. This is the final act in a life of utter despair and hopelessness. The suicide of such a serial killer is an active thought that has probably been with him since childhood. He learns to live with it as a daily option, choosing to act upon it only when his revulsion at what he is doing is too great to bear any longer. Most serial killers find ways to turn themselves in before they choose to commit suicide. They accomplish this by becoming too despondent to take the care to conceal their latest crime. In Bobby Joe Long's case he simply let a young woman, his next to last victim, free without killing her. She alerted the police within hours and provided a description of Long, his apartment, and his car. Unfortunately, the police were unable to place him under surveillance until after he had committed his next murder, and he committed that murder in the open. He also drove around Tampa with the body still in his car, hoping to get caught.

Long didn't flee the city after he let her go even though he realized that the police would soon catch up with him. When his wife called him to ask him about the sequence of rapes taking place in his area, he realized that the police had been in contact with her as well, and still he didn't leave the area. He began his confession the moment he was placed in police custody.

Lucas' story is similar. After he killed Becky Powell he grieved over the body. Then he promised her that he would find a way to end his career. He later revealed that after Becky's death all the energy seemed to flow out of him and he no longer had the need to protect himself. He wanted his career to end and made himself available to the police until they had the evidence to arrest him. He, too, began confessing his crimes shortly after he was arrested.

Pattern 7 – History of Serious Assault

Serial killers do not emerge in a vacuum. All of the killers in our study had a history of serious assault long before they committed their first murders. Often these assaults began in elementary school and took the form of attacks upon peers with lethal weapons or heavy objects. This indicator, readily apparent to teachers, school nurses, and guidance officers, is an early sign that the individual has a severe behavior disorder which can only be expressed through an inappropriate level of violence. The histories of Lucas, Kemper, and Carlton Gary serve as examples of the early background of criminal assault which occurred long before they committed their first homicides.

Pattern 8 – Deviate Sexual Behavior and Hypersexuality

Most of the serial killers on our list had long histories of deviate sexual behavior in their childhoods. Many, like Henry Lee Lucas, frequently exposed their genitalia to their peers when they were very young and escalated very quickly to forms of sexual assault upon their peers and younger siblings. In Lucas' case, he claimed he committed sex with relatives while still very young, and later testified to bestiality with animals he had killed. Lucas committed his first rape and murder when he was fifteen and then had sex with the dead body before he buried it.

Although his sister denies this, Gary Schaefer claimed in his confession to the Caty Richards murder that he was forced to have sex with his sister, who beat him afterwards to frighten him into keeping silent about the event. Joseph Kallinger and Charles Manson also reported histories of deviant sexual behavior in their early lives.

Pattern 9 – Head Injuries or Injuries Incurred at Birth

A history of head trauma or head injuries from birth is one of the common patterns uniting most of the serial murderers. When Dorothy Lewis begins her evaluations of convicted killers, she looks for a history of head injury first, because the damage that can be sustained to the temporal lobe, limbic region, or hypothalamus can severely alter behavior to the point where the individual is no longer responsible for his actions during episodic electrical discharges. The electrobiological pattern of aura-seizure activity-postactivity stupor mirrors the actual behavior pattern of delusions or hallucinations that precede a trolling period, discrete periods of criminal violence, depression and sleep, and memory loss or memory confusion of the entire sequence of events. When this pattern is present in the criminal behavior of the individual, it is likely that it is the result of damage to the areas of the primitive brain.

Henry Lee Lucas, Bobby Joe Long, Carlton Gary, Ted Bundy, Charles Manson, Leonard Lake, and John Gacy have all had either severe head injuries, repeated head traumas, or damage that occurred during birth. Almost all of them suffered signs which resemble some form of psychomotor epilepsy or severe hormonal imbalance which can be the result of a disorder in the hypothalamus. Because the primitive brain is the most vulnerable to injuries occurring on the side of the head – because of the thinness of the skull at that point and the lack of internal fluid protection – individuals who have received sustained blows to the side of the head are often at risk. Therefore it is incumbent upon medical personnel, especially school medical personnel, who are aware of children who have a history of head injuries, even if those injuries seem minor at the time, to identify those cases for possible follow-up. One of the similarities in all serial murder histories is that the individuals seem particularly vulnerable to repeated head traumas after they have received the first one. Lucas, for example, sustained so many head traumas and invasive eye injuries during his childhood that he lost his eye and experienced a coma on more than one occasion. Bobby Joe Long also had at least three severe head injuries before the massive concussion in the motorcycle accident that sent him into a coma. Repeated head injuries are one of the most important patterns for identification of individuals who are at risk of becoming episodically violent, even if there is no diagnosed brain malfunction.

Pattern 10 – History of Chronic Drug or Alcohol Abuse

Most multiple killers whom we have studied, serial killers as well as mass murderers, are consistently addicted to or dependent upon drugs or alcohol or both. These drugs include both prescription medications, such as psychotropics and barbiturates, and recreational drugs, such as amphetamines, psychedelics, cocaine, and heavy narcotics. Henry Lee Lucas reported that he was drunk every time he killed someone. John Gacy reported that he would start drinking before he went out cruising for a new encounter in the gay hustler bars and bus stations. Bob Long was, for a long time, a very heavy user of LSD and marijuana in the 1970s and routinely consumed large amounts of alcohol in the strip bars where he was searching for new victims. Nightstalker (Richard Ramirez) was addicted to cocaine during the year that he committed his murders in Los Angeles, and Carlton Gary was a cocaine addict as well as a pusher during the period in which he committed the murders in Wynnton.

Both narcotics and alcohol have similar effects on the brain and neurological system: they depress general body function while they suppress the normal social controls that keep aberrant behavior impulses in check. If the individual already has a damaged social control mechanism, the narcotic effects of alcohol or drugs, especially during periods of episodic delusions or hallucinations, can unleash a Hyde-like character capable of extraordinary violence. All human beings have this type of neurological entity within them. However, the overlying structures of the higher brain, the hormonal control mechanisms in the normally functioning hypothalamus, and the learned behavior to which people adapt within the typical family and social structure teach them how to subordinate their most primitive feelings and keep them in check.

Even with normal adults, if those social controls fail, the individual may find himself losing the ability to temper his anger or restrain his violent impulses. If a person has had even a little alcohol, he may find that his judgmental abilities have become impaired; recreational drugs such as marijuana in small amounts also allow people's more primitive feelings to come out; and during periods of dieting and reduced nutritional intake people are normally short-tempered and unable to cope with minor adversities. The episodically violent individual must live with these feelings of rage, fear, hopelessness, and incipient violence on a daily basis, even when he is not hallucinating or in the throes of a deep brain seizure. The critical combination of brain damage, child abuse, inability to secrete toxins, and the use of alcohol or drugs is already considered by some experts as a predictor of dangerousness.

Pattern 11 – Alcohol- or Drug-abusing Parents

A large segment of the criminal population in American prisons come from families in which one or both parents were chronic substance abusers. Some of these criminals were born with congenital drug dependencies and have lived the lives of junkies or alcoholics without ever having the ability to detoxify their systems. Other criminals were introduced to alcohol or drugs before adolescence and indulged in the substances as a matter of course. Henry Lee Lucas' mother was an alcoholic and his father was a bootlegger. Lucas was drinking regularly before the age of ten and by his teenage years had himself become an abuser.

The presence of alcohol or drugs in the family situation also influences the family life to a large degree and is symptomatic of other types of disorders. Therefore children who grow up in homes where a chronic substance abuse is present are at risk because the substance abuser cannot make an effective parent and will introduce the child, either passively or actively, to either alcohol or drugs, and if the substance abuse problem is congenital it is possible that the child may have inherited it.

Pattern 12 – Victim of Physical or Emotional Abuse or of Cruel Parenting

Marvin Wolfgang and others have shown conclusively that child abuse begets abuse. In his study of males born in the Philadelphia area in 1945, those individuals who were abused as children were very likely to become abusive adults. This finding is borne out by the serial killers in our study. Every one of them was abused in some way as a child, either physically or emotionally. Henry Lee Lucas is the extreme example. He was beaten, knocked unconscious, and repeatedly injured by his mother and her pimp. He grew up with absolutely no sense of self-worth and routinely inflicted abuse on animate and inanimate objects alike. In his confessions he described human beings as pieces of flesh to be cut up, burned, and used as masturbatory articles. He referred to his victims not as people but as 'strangles' or 'stabbings,' nameless entities that had the misfortune to encounter him during his periods of episodic violence. It was only after he had actually nurtured Becky Powell and felt love for her that he was able to feel remorse and guilt at having stabbed her. That broke his skein of murders.

Alice Miller has written that parents need not necessarily be physically abusive to the child. The passively cruel parent who imposes a rigid set of conflicting beliefs upon the child can create a monster. Bobby Joe Long describes his mother as cruel in her disregard for his needs. After he had reached adolescence he claims he was manipulated into conflict with one of her boyfriends on at least one occasion during which he had to beat the man up just to protect himself. On another occasion he was so angry at the attention his mother showered upon her little dog, in contrast to the neglect that he received, that he shoved a .22-caliber bullet into the dog's vagina.

Pattern 13 – Result of an Unwanted Pregnancy

Although many children are not actually planned, and a significant number might not be wanted at first, most parents accept the fact that they are going to have a child and do not deliberately inflict the inconvenience of the child's existence upon him. When that does occur, the child will grow up to be a scarred adult, but, again, most healthy people can live with those scars and not become emotionally disabled. Serial killers, however, belong to the extreme category of children who were not only unwanted but were punished for having been born. Children in this category are invariably at a high risk of confrontation with the criminal justice system at some point before they reach adulthood. Their socioeconomic status, the quality of their home life, the amount of physical or emotional abuse they receive, and the violence present in their environment will, in large measure, determine the extent of that risk. Senator Patrick Moynihan has suggested that the lack of sex education among young people today, especially children who have grown up in families on welfare or below the poverty level, is creating an entire generation of unwanted children who will become almost permanent wards of society. They will tax the ability of the social services system to provide for them and will ultimately enter the criminal justice system, where they will create an additional burden. These are unwanted children, children whose very existence is perceived by their parents as a form of retribution. As they reach childbearing age, they will also spawn another generation of children who are unplanned and unwanted. Unless this public health issue is addressed, society will simply be creating more generations of potentially violent offenders.

Pattern 14 – Products of a Difficult Gestation Period for the Mother

Almost all of the serial killers studied were born to mothers who had a difficult time during the pregnancy. In some cases the difficulties were self-inflicted because of alcohol or drug addiction. In other cases the extreme poverty of the family made the pregnancy difficult to sustain, and medical attention was almost nonexistent. And, in still other situations, because the mother did not want to be pregnant in the first place she was emotionally conflicted throughout the term and the child suffered accordingly.

Just what role a happy pregnancy plays in the development of the child has not been adequately documented. Researchers know, for example, that anxiety and tension in the mother are translated into the secretion of hormones that can affect the developing fetus. If the anxiety occurs immediately after the first quarter of the pregnancy, when the fetus' brain and autonomic nervous systems are developing, some form of brain malformation can result. At the very least, the brain may be dysfunctional in one or more ways. The area of the dysfunction and the seriousness of the damage determine how likely the child will be to have severe developmental problems and become a violence-prone individual. Even if the child is not damaged at birth, the mother's anxieties may result in a colicky, unhappy baby who becomes the object of mistreatment and abuse by a mother who was unhappy about being pregnant. Such mistreatment is also a factor in the development of a violence-prone individual.

Pattern 15 – Interrupted Bliss or No Bliss of Childhood

Serial killers are deeply sad people who can take no joy whatsoever in anything they derive from life. A major component of their sadness is that they never learned how to be happy, they were incapable of allowing themselves any pleasure as children. For most normal people, childhood is a pleasurable experience in which the developing individual learns how to be happy and how to derive happiness from as many situations as possible. We learn how to be optimists or pessimists as children and where to find happiness and pleasure. Because serial killers were deprived of this bliss of childhood, they do not have the emotional mechanism that allows them to feel pleasure as adults. As simple neurotics, they are condemned to look at the underside of life, seeing only the unhappiness that reflects their own unhappy state. As psychotics and sociopaths, they completely lack the ability to understand happiness or joy. These are foreign emotions. As brain-damaged or dysfunctional individuals, their organic pleasure centers in the primitive brain do not operate, and they are physically incapable of sensing pleasure.

Pattern 16 – Extraordinary Cruelty to Animals

It is not abnormal for a child to become fascinated with how ants can still walk after they've lost two or three of their legs or with the dance of a dying fly or spider. It is, however, quite abnormal for a child to torture household pets and larger animals for the pure delight of watching them suffer. Children who beat dogs and inflict injuries on cats out of a sheer lust for watching the animal suffer are children in crisis, and most of the serial killers in our study have taken just such delight in the pain of other creatures.

Henry Lee Lucas used to torture animals until they died, and then have sex with their remains. Bob Long, as we mention above, was so jealous of the attention and love that his mother showered upon her little dog that he shoved a .22-caliber bullet into the dog's vagina. He still remembers the incident and recalls that his frustration at not being able to receive any attention from his mother drove him into a fury. 'She wouldn't even bother to feed me,' he explains. 'But she would cook steaks and stews for that dog to eat. I had to make my own dinner.'

Pattern 17 – Arsonal Tendencies Without Obvious Homicidal Interest

Fire-starting is one early warning sign of psychotic or sociopathic dangerousness. The interest in fires is more than the passing fascination with the movement of the flames, it is the delight in the destruction that fire itself can cause and it is the interest in the indirect damage that one can inflict by igniting a fire. Carlton Gary was a fire-starter before adolescence as was Henry Lucas. But both individuals set fires as means of destruction without seeking the death of another person. The interest in setting fires usually disappears shortly after the individual reaches adolescence and begins committing violence with his own hands.

Pattern 18 – Symptoms of Neurological Impairment

Almost all serial killers display symptoms of neurological impairment, both soft and hard signs. These can be as straightforward as a consistent confusion between right and left, a reversal of letters of numbers, or more profound reading and learning disabilities with associated behavioral disorders. Depending upon the degree of damage to the underlying neurological structure, the individual may experience a complete distortion of sensory experience even during periods of nonviolence. During seizure-like violent episodes, the delusions or hallucinations might involve significantly greater distortions. The following impairments should be considered high-risk factors if they still appear in individuals after adolescence:

1. Dyslexia
2. Reading, mathematics, or directional problems
3. Hypergraphia
4. Grandiosity
5. Hypervigilance
6. Hypersexuality
7. Hyposexuality
8. Hyperreligiosity
9. Visual or auditory hallucinations
10. Loose, rambling, or illogical thought processes
11. Paranoid feelings or chronic feelings of persecution
12. Chronic feelings of isolation, alienation, or withdrawal
13. Prolonged and profound chronic depression and crying
14. Incontinence
15. Sleep disorders
16. Difficulty with spatial coordination and perception
17. Poor muscular coordination
18. History of seizures or seizurelike episodes

19. Reading or mathematical disabilities that resist remediation
20. Chronic headaches or migraine headaches
21. Lability of moods
22. Choreaform body movements or animallike body movements

Pattern 19 – Evidence of Genetic Disorders

Researchers have suggested that if an individual has at least three to five physical anomalies, such as webbed skin between his fingers or earlobes that are connected to the sides of his head, it is likely that he also has a genetic disorder of the primal brain. Because the development of the fetal brain takes place at the same time that the skin develops, any skin or cartilage abnormalities are usually indicators that the brain, too, has not completely developed. When such abnormalities prevail in families – for instance, the similarity of long toes in the Long and Lucas families – then it is likely that a congenital defect is causing the damage. The following abnormalities are representative indicators of genetic damage:

1. Bulbous fingertips
2. Fine or electric wire hair that will not comb down
3. Very fine hair that is soon awry after combing
4. Hair whorls
5. Head circumference outside a normal range of 1.5 cm or less than 1.5 cm
6. Epicanthus – upper and lower eyelids join the nose (the point of union is either deeply covered or partially covered)
7. Hyperteliorism – larger than normal distance between tear ducts or lower than normal distance between tear ducts
8. Low-seated ears – the point where the ear joins the head is not in line with the corner of the eye and the

nose bridge; it is either lower by .5 cm or greater than
.5 cm

9. Adherent earlobes – lower edge of ear is extended
   upward and backward toward the crown of the head
10. Malformed ears
11. Asymmetrical ears
12. Very soft or very pliable ears
13. High-steepled palate
14. Roof of mouth is definitely steepled or flat and narrow
15. Forward tongue with deep ridges
16. Speckled tongue with either smooth or rough spots
17. Curved fifth finger – marked curve toward the other
    fingers or slightly curved inward toward other fingers
18. Singular transverse palmar crease
19. Third toe is longer than second toe or equal in length
    to second toe
20. Partial syndactyly of two middle toes
21. Larger than normal gap between first and second toes
22. Abnormalities in teeth
23. Abnormalities in dermatoglyphics

Pattern 20 – Biochemical Symptoms

Episodically violent individuals are often victims of toxic
poisoning either through the inability of their systems to
throw off toxins or because their environments have high
levels of toxins. William Walsh's experiments on Lucas
and other serial murderers have shown that episodically
violent people have extraordinarily high levels of lead and
cadmium present in strands of their hair. Other trace
minerals appear in large concentrations in the chronically
violent individual.

Pattern 21 – Feelings of Powerlessness or Inadequacy

Part of the tragedy of the serial killer's predatory behavior
is that each killing only proves to him that he is powerless.
The ritualistic murder that is an enactment of his power

turns out to be only further proof that he is powerless to deal with the living and can only assume life-size proportions over the dead. The serial killer thrives among the dead; they rather than living people are his companions. And because of this he is truly dead inside.

This sense of powerlessness is an important indicator of future behavior because representations of it will appear in young people, particularly adolescents. One of the early signs that a child is reaching emotional adolescence is that he begins to exercise power. Sometimes that power takes the form of a direct confrontation or challenge to adult authority, but this challenge is normal. When the authority responds to the challenge in a supportive fashion and does not seek to crush the adolescent, the adolescent grows to accept an adult interpretation of authority and the social order and can deal with it. The powerless adolescent, however, will not seek to challenge authority directly. Nor will he seek confrontations. His behavior will be abnormal, even criminal, and will avoid direct confrontation whenever possible. The powerless adolescent will adopt a demeanor of camouflage but will cross swords with authorities in oblique ways. Eventually he will seek invisibility and will finally express himself in bizarre or abnormal behavior.

The sense of powerlessness will soon begin to express itself in the form of deviant sexual behavior, attacks on physically weaker members of the same or opposite sex, petty crimes, extreme cruelty to animals, and even attempted suicide. A large proportion of teenage rapes are actually committed by boys who have a sense of powerlessness so overwhelming that they are actually afraid of young girls. These individuals may also prey on pre-adolescent girls or young children. If these attacks seem episodic rather than strictly random, the person has a high probability of emerging as a serial killer within ten to fifteen years.

It would be easy to misinterpret these patterns as absolute predictors of future criminal behavior or to measure individuals against these patterns in order to label them as criminal types. This is not the intent of the patterns. The patterns are simply the synthesis of the combined symptomatology of hundreds of serial killers. The overwhelming similarities between them and the identical patterns of injuries that they have suffered; the similarities in their EEG charts and in their lack of physical and emotional resiliency; and the common bond of cruel or bizarre parenting that unites them – all are obvious indications that certain forces shape potential serial murderers. When these forces can be detected individually, especially in children who have not yet confronted the juvenile justice system, it is likely that any potential criminal or antisocial behavior can be short-circuited at the start. In any event, the patterns provide the direction and structure for future research by criminologists, neurologists, and chemists into the organic or physiological basis of criminal behavior.

15

Conclusion

What can society do about the growing menace of serial killers? Simply putting more police on the street and building more jails won't end the violence because the normal forms of deterrents don't work for serial killers. Executing convicted serial killers faster and closing down their avenues of appeal won't work either because most serial killers have a death wish to begin with. In other words, society's reactive attempts to deal with the problem will always fall short. There are too many episodically violent serial murderers emerging too quickly and attacking too many victims for the criminal justice system to keep up. For every one serial killer who is apprehended and brought to trial, three more are emerging and beginning their careers.

The current knowledge of experts in the fields of neurology, internal medicine, psychology, and criminal justice shows that the disease of serial murder is generational. It is passed on through child abuse, negative parenting, and genetic damage. It is activated by the environment through injuries to the person's head, heavy drinking, heavy use of drugs, and prolonged malnutrition. Even after it is activated, it normally requires a combination of serious traumatic events to pull the trigger. In the case of Henry Lee Lucas it was the confrontation with his mother in a bar in Tecumseh, Michigan. For Bobby Joe Long it was the motorcycle accident that left him in a state of hypersexuality. For Charles Manson it was a combination of drugs and the accessibility to all the forbidden fruits of his youth. In the cases of other serial killers, we might never know.

What we do know is that, because normal methods of criminal justice and current medical psychiatric diagnosis don't work, we have to treat serial murder in a different way. If we look at it as a symptom of the type of social violence that Surgeon General C. Everett Koop has described as an issue of public health, then we can treat serial murder as an infectious disease and adopt preventive measures. There is ample evidence to support treating violence as a public health issue. First, homicide is among the ten leading causes of death for all Americans. However, for black males between the ages of fifteen and twenty-four, homicide is currently the leading cause of death, according to the United States Department of Justice.

Second, in addition to the rise in the number of homicides since 1980, the number of aggravated assaults and occurrences of domestic violence have risen sharply as well. The National Crime Survey reports that almost twenty percent of the entire population is involved in spousal abuse, that more than fifty percent of the incidents of abuse against wives occurs on a regular basis at least three or four times a year, and that domestic violence is the foremost cause of injury to women.

Finally, almost two million children and adolescents are the victims of physical violence each year, much of it in the form of sexual abuse committed by a relative or family member. This physical abuse directed against children is called multigenerational domestic violence, and it is one of the core causes of the epidemic of serial murder. It is logical to suppose that as child abuse and domestic violence grow, so does the aggregate number of serial murder victims. The 260 serial killers researched for this book claimed a total of 10,360 victims during the course of their respective careers. This averages out to just under 40 victims per serial killer, a highly disproportionate number of homicides.

Many experts are just beginning to realize that within the next ten years most forms of episodic aggression – including serial murder – could be prevented through an organized programme of testing and diagnosis and intervention. Many of the new testing techniques rely on recent developments in the fields of psychopharmacology, psychosurgery, and nutritional therapies as well as on new diagnostic procedures and 'dangerousness' predictor scales. However, just because the techniques are available, it doesn't mean that the public will be able to set aside its perceptions of some of the most violent criminals in society and see them as truly diseased people.

In order to change political and public opinion about serial murder, the public health service must develop an information campaign about violence and the underlying causes of violent crime. Information about the causes of violence will itself help prevent its spread. Public health labeling that has been so successful with regard to cigarette packaging should be extended to alcohol and violent pornographic and sadistic and demonic materials as well. Warnings that state, 'The chronic consumption of alcoholic beverages can produce violence in some individuals,' or 'The chronic exposure to violent pornography can produce violence in some individuals,' are necessary so that high-risk people will become aware of the dangerous nature of the products they are using.

Rapists, child abusers, sex offenders and individuals convicted of having committed acts of domestic violence against spouses and children should be assigned to rehabilitative therapy groups as a part of their sentences or requirements for parole. These high-risk groups are one of the primal seedbeds out of which serial killers emerge because they usually begin their careers with chronic abuse and sexual assault crimes. While the vast majority of sexual offenders do not go on to become serial murderers, the vast majority of serial murderers were sexual offenders or were fantasizing heavily before they committed their first murders.

Hospitals, emergency trauma centers, clinics, medical offices, schools, and the juvenile departments of local police forces should be expected to investigate the background of any suspected child abuse victim. If the child seems to be a chronic victim, the backgrounds of the child's parents or guardians should be investigated as well. If the child is a victim of abuse, then the court must intervene to protect the individual within the limits of the law. This type of vigorous action might serve as a firebreak by preventing the routine spread of this kind of violence from one generation to the next.

Much research needs to be done on the development of a scale to predict dangerousness in high-risk individuals. The basis for such a scale already exists, but the implementation of a workable set of predictors on a broad basis is still years away and requires the financial support of government and private agencies. It is to everyone's advantage to see this research carried out because state and local governments are already spending hundreds of millions of dollars on apprehending and trying serial murderers and are not even making a dent in preventing new serial murderers from emerging. The private sector is ultimately paying the bill, both in tax dollars and in human lives. And because the number of serial killers and serial murder cases keeps increasing every year, it is clear that present methods of apprehension and adjudication just aren't working. Society needs to aim toward preventing the crimes from happening in the first place, and the only way to accomplish that is to stop the disease in individuals before it claims any victims. This is the reason for the predictor scale and for the financial commitment to developing one that can be used by doctors, school officials, and juvenile justice officials within their respective offices.

The predictor scale should be the result of inter-disciplinary projects, especially in the fields of bio-chemistry, neurology, genetics, social psychology, and criminal justice. And researchers should share knowledge among their respective disciplines, thus avoiding the problem of linkage blindness. The research should also include first-hand and verified information gleaned from stabilized serial killers, rapists, sexual offenders, and other episodically violent individuals. Their observations about their own behavior are invaluable because they offer scientists insight into the workings of the darkest side of the human psyche. Too often, research into the causes and motivations of criminals is conducted by individuals who have never seen the inside of a prison or spoken to convicted felons. More experts simply need hands-on experience.

The public health and criminal justice institutions that come into direct contact with potentially dangerous individuals are already in a position to prevent these people from becoming threats to themselves and to others in the future. First, prisoners who ask for psychological counseling should receive it. Sex offenders who claim that they are subject to hallucinatory experiences or delusions of violence should be taken seriously and given some form of treatment. Had prison psychologists listened to Lucas or to Gary, for example, they might have short-circuited their careers before they began their serial murder sprees. Had Army doctors listened to Bobby Joe Long's com-plaints about his neurological symptoms, he might have received the treatment he needed. There are convicted rapists in jail at this moment who are asking for medical attention, but they are not receiving it. Some of these people, all of whom will sooner or later be released from prison, are human time bombs who will eventually become tomorrow's lurid newspaper headlines. Even Gary Heidnick, a suspect in a recent torture and serial murder case in Philadelphia, repeatedly asked for but was denied psychological treatment while in prison.

Similarly, schools, which routinely encounter cases of child abuse and extraordinary violence in children, should follow up when the person seems to be potentially dangerous to himself or to others. Had Lucas' school-teacher, Annie Hall, been able to help Henry without fear of reprisal, he might have become a different person. However, current school procedures prevent most school-teachers, administrators, and medical personnel from even raising suspicions about child abuse.

The many state laws requiring suppression of police and court records of juveniles further impair the abilities of justice authorities to intervene when a child is at risk. Because so many of the children who appear before the courts are themselves victims of chronic abuse or have already become abusers, they are in dire need of some form of crisis intervention. By the time many of them have reached the adult courts their juvenile criminal records, which are indicative of a life of violent crime, have been suppressed and the criminal courts are forced to start from scratch. If police were allowed to view juvenile records in cases of extraordinary violent crime or when chronic child abuse was noted, they would be better able to prevent this individual's becoming a potential killer.

The entire concept of criminal insanity must be updated and redefined so as to bring it out of the nineteenth century. What scientists now know about the chemical and biological causality of behaviorality has long since overturned traditional concepts of sane and insane behavior. From what we have learned about Henry Lucas, Bobby Joe Long, Albert DeSalvo, and other killers we know that it is possible for a person with severe damage to areas of his primitive brain to act within the guidelines of normalcy during periods between his violent episodes. During their episodes, however, they are acting as if under a different set of programming instructions. They lose touch with reality, experience blackouts, and feel as if something inside of them is directing their actions. Most serial killers can name the President of the United States and can tell their interrogators what year it is and where they are at the moment of their interrogation. However, they cannot account for the forces that compelled them to commit their crimes. These people need medical attention. By redefining insanity to account for episodically violent behavior, a whole new class of criminals will be admitted to state-administered therapy programs. In so doing, states will routinely be preventing potential serial killers from committing their first homicides.

The fear among defense lawyers, some doctors, schools, and civil liberties organizations is that any attempt to identify people, especially children, as potentially violent individuals would inevitably lead to a Draconian system of cataloguing people and identifying them as criminals in the making. The resulting tracking and identification procedures would leave individuals so catalogued with invisible tags that would be attached to them for the rest of their lives. These fears are justified. Without question, if an irresponsible society began tagging individuals as predisposed to criminal behavior, the potential for abuse of civil rights would be enormous. That is one of the reasons why, when Richard Nixon's personal physician, Arnold Hutsnecker, suggested a similar program eighteen years ago, he was widely criticized by civil rights groups.

The programme that we're suggesting is not a labeling

mechanism for identifying a potentially violent murderer but a crisis intervention plan designed to protect all children from abuse or from an illness. If a pediatrician recognizes that a child's tendencies go well beyond normal aggressiveness into the realm of extraordinary violence or homicidal aggression, he or she should have a method of reporting it to the parents or to the local juvenile authorities without fear of reprisal. Similarly, an emergency room physician or a school nurse who treats a child for what he or she believes to be physical abuse should be able to forward information to the police without fear of being sued by the parents, even if the suspicions prove to be untrue. If the report is made in good faith, neither the nurse, the doctor, the school, nor the hospital should be held liable, and the utmost integrity is required.

Such a program for identifying educational under-achievers or children with chronic learning disabilities already exists as an entitlement program of the federal government. Procedures that provide for diagnosing these children, establishing independent educational plans for them, while at the same time safeguarding their rights as they progress through school can easily serve as the basis for establishing a program for identifying the abused or extraordinarily violent child. In other words, if a school nurse or physician recognizes a 'homicidally aggressive' child, the child should not be labeled as a potentially violent murderer but should be seen as an individual suffering from an illness akin to chronic depression or a childhood psychosis. The focus should be on finding out what is causing the extraordinary aggressiveness in the child's environment and then channeling the feelings of aggression positively.

We must ask ourselves what the proper limits of intervention are. At what point may a health professional, educator, or officer of the court legally enter a domestic setting to make a decision regarding the environment of the child? When might such an entry constitute an unlawful intrusion and a violation of rights that outweighs a clear and present danger to the child? These are the questions that society has to answer if its institutions are not to be overwhelmed by an epidemic of serial murder and other forms of episodic violence. But decisions have to be made soon because time is quickly running out. If the present generation is allowed to spawn another generation of serial killers and mass murderers, the legal and social institutions won't be able to handle them. At that point the society we know can be consumed in its own violence and repressiveness.